Global Governance of Space Cyber Security

The book explores the regulatory and institutional aspects of global governance of space cybersecurity.

Focusing on the regulatory aspects, this book argues that the current international law cannot handle the threats posed by malicious cyber and space activities, as regulatory gaps exist owing to terminological ambiguities and legal loopholes. A law-making process in the space field is proposed with a focus on developing soft law instruments through multistakeholder platforms. To enhance the implementation and enforcement of laws concerning space cybersecurity, it is crucial to emphasise the roles of international organisations and industries. Furthermore, empowering existing international institutions with supervisory powers and promoting national legislation and domestic judicial systems are feasible approaches to enhance compliance with the law.

The book will attract international law scholars, especially those studying space law and cyber law.

Du Li obtained her PhD from the University of Paris-Sud in 2011, with her thesis on space law and national space legislation. She is an associate professor at the Law School of Hainan University. She has published extensively in Chinese, English, and French.

Global Governance of Space Cyber Security

Regulatory and Institutional Aspects

Du Li

Routledge
Taylor & Francis Group
LONDON AND NEW YORK

First published 2025
by Routledge
4 Park Square, Milton Park, Abingdon, Oxon OX14 4RN

and by Routledge
605 Third Avenue, New York, NY 10158

Routledge is an imprint of the Taylor & Francis Group, an informa business

British Library Cataloguing-in-Publication Data
A catalogue record for this book is available from the British Library

Library of Congress Cataloging-in-Publication Data
Names: Li, Du, 1984– author.
Title: Global governance of space cyber security : regulatory and institutional aspects / Du Li. Other titles: Global governance of space cybersecurity
Description: Abingdon, Oxon [UK] ; New York, NY : Routledge, 2024. | Includes bibliographical references and index.
Identifiers: LCCN 2024032291 (print) | LCCN 2024032292 (ebook) | ISBN 9781032671840 (hardback) | ISBN 9781032915463 (paperback) | ISBN 9781003561996 (ebook)
Subjects: LCSH: Computer networks—Law and legislation. | Cyberspace—Security measures—Government policy. | Computer security—Law and legislation. | Space warfare. | Outer space—Government policy.
Classification: LCC K564.C6 L495 2024 (print) | LCC K564.C6 (ebook) | DDC 343.09/995—dc23/eng/20240716
LC record available at https://lccn.loc.gov/2024032291
LC ebook record available at https://lccn.loc.gov/2024032292

ISBN: 978-1-032-67184-0 (hbk)
ISBN: 978-1-032-91546-3 (pbk)
ISBN: 978-1-003-56199-6 (ebk)

DOI: 10.4324/9781003561996

Typeset in Times New Roman
by Apex CoVantage, LLC

Contents

Acknowledgements

I would first like to thank each and every person who has dedicated their time to comment on the whole or parts of the draft manuscript, to suggest, and to provide valuable information. I must, therefore, particularly thank Yun Zhao, Wen Duan, Ming Qu, and Jinyuan Su. However, all opinions and errors are mine.

I must also thank Zixu Fan, Wenqian Wang, and the team at Taylor & Francis Group for helping to put together this study for publication.

Lastly, I would like to express my deep gratitude to my parents, who have unconditionally supported and encouraged me throughout my life. Gratitude also goes to my friends, who have accompanied and encouraged me while drafting the manuscript.

Abbreviations

AAs:	Artemis Accords
APEC:	Asia-Pacific Economic Cooperation
APSCO:	Asia-Pacific Space Cooperation Organization
ARSIWA:	Articles on Responsibility of States for Internationally Wrongful Acts
ASEAN:	Association of Southeast Asian Nations
AU:	African Union
AUC:	African Union Convention on Cyber Security and Personal Data Protection
BBs:	Building Blocks for the Development of an International Framework on Space Resources Activities
CCDCoE:	Cooperative Cyber Defense Centre of Excellence
CCPCJ:	Commission on Crime Prevention and Criminal Justice
CD:	Conference on Disarmament
CDR:	Common but Differentiated Responsibility
CGG:	Commission on Global Governance
CoC:	Code of Conduct for Outer Space Activities
COPUOS:	Committee on the Peaceful Uses of Outer Space
COSPAR:	Committee on Space Research
DCG:	Diplomatic Conference of Geneva
ECHR:	European Convention for the Protection of Human Rights and Fundamental Freedoms
ECSL:	European Centre for Space Law
ESA:	European Space Agency
EU:	European Union
GCA:	Global Cybersecurity Agenda
GEGSLA:	Global Expert Group on Sustainable Lunar Activities
GGE:	Group of Governmental Experts
GIC:	Global Cybersecurity Index
GNSS:	Global Navigation Satellite System
HLEG:	High-Level Experts Group
IADC:	Inter-Agency Space Debris Coordination Committee
IAEA:	International Atomic Energy Agency
ICANN:	Internet Corporation for Assigned Names and Numbers

ICC: International Criminal Court
ICJ: International Court of Justice
ICoC: Internatinal Code of Conduct for Outer Space
ICRC: International Committee of the Red Cross
ICTs: Information and Communications Technologies
ICTY: International Criminal Tribunal for the former Yugoslavia
IETF: Internet Engineering Task Force
IGF: Internet Governance Forum
IHFFC: International Humanitarian Fact-finding Commission
ILC: International Law Commission
IMO: International Maritime Organization
IO: International Organisation
ISO: International Organization for Standardization
ITU: International Telecommunications Union
LTS: Long-Term Sustainability
MCAs: Malicious Cyber Activities
MCASAs: Malicious Cyber Activities Against Space Activities
MVA: Moon Village Association
NASA: National Aeronautics and Space Administration of the United States
NATO: North Atlantic Treaty Organisation
NGO: Non-Governmental Organisation
NPS: Nuclear Power Sources
NSA: Non-State Actor
ODCWG: Orbital Debris Coordination Working Group
OECD: Organisation for Economic Cooperation and Development
OEWG: Open-Ended Working Group
OST: Treaty on Principles Governing the Activities of States in the Exploration and Use of Outer Space, including the Moon and the Other Celestial Bodies
PAROS: Prevention of an Arms Race in Outer Space
PCA: Permanent Court of Arbitration
PCIJ: Permanent Court of International Justice
POA: Programme of Action to Advance Responsible State Behaviour in the Use of Information and Communications Technologies in the Context of International Security
PPP: Planetary Protection Policy
PPWT: Draft Treaty on the Prevention of the Placement of Weapons in Outer Space, the Threat or Use of Force against Outer Space Objects
SCO: Shanghai Cooperation Organization
STSC: Scientific and Technical Subcommittee
TCBMs: Transparency and Confidence-Building Measures
TEL WG: Telecommunications and Information Working Group
UDHR: Universal Declaration of Human Right
UK: United Kingdom
UN: United Nations

UNESCO:	United Nations Educational, Scientific and Cultural Organization
UNFCCC:	United Nations Framework Convention on Climate Change
UNGA:	United Nations General Assembly
UNIDIR:	United Nations Institute for Disarmament Research
UNODA:	United Nations Office for Disarmament Affairs
UNODC:	United Nations Office on Drugs and Crime
UNOOSA:	United Nations Office for Outer Space Affairs
US:	United States
VCLT:	Vienna Convention on the Law of Treaties
WMDs:	Weapons of Mass Destruction
WSIS:	World Summit on Information Society
WTO:	World Trade Organization
W3C:	World Wide Web Consortium

Part I

General Introduction

1 Introduction

Defining the Research

Cybersecurity with respect to space activities has been acquiring significance with the increasing reliance of space activities on cyber technologies. The development of space activities has dramatically improved human life, rendering the space sector vital to States and individuals. However, malicious cyber activities against space activities (MCASAs) could easily invade and destroy a space system from anywhere, at almost no cost, with devastating aftermaths, constituting a major threat to space cybersecurity. The general vulnerabilities of space assets and activities towards cyber threats lead to the situation. Several factors lead to the vulnerabilities (Livingstone & Lewis, 2016; Sgobbi et al., 2015). First, enhancing the cybersecurity standards of space activities may be expensive. This contradicts the fundamental interests of private capital invested in the space sector to pursue economic return. Second, not every State can master core cybersecurity technologies. Moreover, spacefaring States differ significantly in terms of cyber technologies. Consequently, some States are unable to guarantee cybersecurity in their space systems. Third, a significant part of space assets in service were launched into outer space years or even decades ago when cybersecurity was not at stake. In addition, as space systems are becoming more interconnected than ever, the risks of MCASAs are increasing.

The reported cases of MCASAs are not abundant; however, they have alerted the world regarding the actual threats of MCASAs and the necessity to tackle them. The first reported MCASA occurred in 1998 when hackers hacked into the computers at the Goddard Space Flight Center in Maryland, assumed control of the US-German ROSAT X-Ray satellite, ordered the satellite to turn its solar panels directly towards the sun, destroying its batteries and rendering it useless (Akoto, 2020). Similarly, in 2010, the Indian telecommunication satellite INSAT-4B-S suffered a severe loss of power owing to a cyberattack, leading to a reduction of more than 50 per cent of the satellite's capacity (Pasco, 2015). In 2007 and 2008, Landsat 7 experienced interference through the cyber, and in 2008, Terra (EOS AM-1) had similar unpleasant experiences (US Council on Foreign Relations, 2011a, 2011b). The most recently reported MCASA occurred in 2022 against the KA-SAT network run by Viasat, causing a partial interruption of KA-SAT's consumer-oriented satellite broadband service and severely impacting several thousand customers in Ukraine and tens of thousands of other fixed broadband customers across Europe (Viasat, 2022).

DOI: 10.4324/9781003561996-2

The imminent and widespread destructive impacts of cyber threats on space activities justify tackling the issue at the international level. Thus, two questions arise: What is the scope of cyber threats with respect to space activities? How can these threats be coped with at the international level? This chapter addressed these two questions, which also contribute to demarcating the scope of the work.

1.1 Defining Space Cybersecurity and Malicious Cyber Activities Against Space Activities

Cybersecurity is closely related to the concept of cyberspace. Cyberspace has been defined in various ways in different dictionaries (Kittichaisaree, 2018). International organisations and scholars also adopt different definitions. According to the International Committee of the Red Cross (ICRC), cyberspace is 'a virtual space that provides worldwide interconnectivity' (ICRC, 2015). In a report of the United Nations Institute for Disarmament Research (UNIDIR), cyberspace is used to indicate 'computers, computer networks and systems, and disparate information distribution or delivery technologies', enabling 'the creation, storage, modification, exchange and exploitation of information via interdependent and interconnected networks using information technologies' (Kavanagh, 2017). A more concise definition of cyberspace could be a 'globally accessible technological infrastructure of interconnected computers and networks which is used for the transmission of signals and data' (Popova, 2018). Despite the differences, critical elements of cyberspace deduced from the definitions are the basic infrastructure, networks for communication, and data. Thus, cybersecurity could be understood in a rather broad way to encompass the security of basic cyber infrastructure, the security of networks for communication, and data security.

Although no harmonised definition of cybersecurity exists, its comprehensiveness has been recognised. The first United Nations (UN) Groups of Governmental Experts (GGE) report published in 2010 has indicated that threats in the sphere of information security, emanating from various sources and manifesting themselves in disruptive activities that target individuals, businesses, national infrastructure, and governments alike, may carry significant risk for public safety, the security of nations, and the stability of the globally linked international community as a whole (UNGA, 2010). Considering this understanding, cybersecurity encompasses not only the security of information but also that of assets, persons, and so forth. Moreover, the definition of cybersecurity given by von Solms and van Niekerk,

> the protection of cyberspace itself, the electronic information, the Information and Communications Technologies (ICTs) that support cyberspace, and the users of cyberspace in their personal, society and national capacity, including any of their interests, either tangible or intangible, that are vulnerable to attacks originating in cyberspace
>
> (von Solms & van Niekerk, 2013)

has reflected the comprehensiveness of this concept.

Space cybersecurity should also be understood broadly. As indicated in the Memorandum on Cybersecurity Principles for Space Systems, space systems 'reliant on information systems and networks from design conceptualisation through launch and flight operations' and 'the transmissions of command and control and mission information between space vehicles and ground networks' reliant on 'the use of radio-frequency-dependent wireless communication channels' can be vulnerable to malicious cyber activities (MCAs) that 'deny, degrade, or disrupt space operations, or even destroy satellites' (Administration of Donald J. Trump, 2020). Thus, space cybersecurity incorporates the protection of all space activities, including the launching and recovering of space objects and the monitoring of space systems and space application activities, against malicious activities emanating from cyberspace.

The MCASA is the primary threat to space cybersecurity. It is a combination of several concepts, including cyber activities, MCAs, and space activities. Cyber activities are conducted through an infrastructure, and data are transmitted through networks. Thus, cyber activities could be defined as 'the exchange of digitised data', and they 'take place through the use of cyberspace infrastructure using the universal language of code' (Popova, 2018). Three critical elements of cyber activities should be highlighted: (1) they are in the information environment and are performed through logical functions; (2) they depend on physical domains; and (3) they perform effects either in cyberspace or in the physical domain (Kaiser, 2020). The third element is particularly significant as it reveals that cyber activities could impact both cyberspace and the physical world.

Cyber activities could be distinguished into two categories depending on their ways and purposes: unmalicious, legitimate, or authorised cyber activities and MCAs. Different terms are used to denote MCAs, such as hacking, cyberattack, unauthorised, damaging, or unlawful cyber activities (Li, 2023). The term cyberattack most commonly depicts the process of intruding into computer systems, referring to a type of computer operation seeking to disrupt, deny, degrade, or destroy information, computers, or computer networks (Maybaum, 2013). However, legal professionals avoid using the term cyberattack broadly because of the different implications of the word 'attack' in the law of armed conflict and for fear that cyber intrusion may be considered a new means of war (Kaiser, 2020). Thus, this study adopts the term MCAs, which is intuitive and legally neutral.

Scholars have defined space activities in various ways. Most definitions are rather broad and include some activities occurring on Earth. Lachs considers 'all activities directed towards outer space and within it' as space activities (Lachs, 1964). According to Cheng, space activities are those related to outer space, in outer space, or involving outer space (Cheng, 1997). Lyall and Larsen adopt a similar definition but extend the scope to further include terrestrial activities such as concluding an insurance contract concerning a particular space launch (Lyall & Larsen, 2009). However, some scholars take a limited perspective towards space activities, contending that space activities only include activities and consequential matters in outer space (Diederiks-Verschoor & Kopal, 2008). Some of these definitions focus on the purpose of space activities, typically referring to space exploration, research, use and development of space technologies, and the use of outer space, whereas others concentrate on the content of the activities with an enumerative listing, notably including the launching of space activities, operating space objects, activities in outer space, and operation or use of facilities and installations (Kaiser, 2020). This study adopts a broad interpretation of space activities to include all terrestrial activities related to the use and exploration of outer space and all activities therein.

Following the concept of MCAs, MCASAs could be described as the process of intruding into the computer systems of space systems without authorisation for malicious purposes. They are launched for different purposes in various forms, resulting in diverse consequences. The purposes of MCASAs may vary significantly from those of normal MCAs aforementioned. In most cases, MCASAs do not aim at the computer systems *per se*. Their purposes range from obtaining data collected and transferred by satellites and interrupting the functioning of space systems to destroying a space object in orbit. Typical forms of MCASAs include spoofing sensor data, corrupting sensor systems, jamming or sending unauthorised commands for guidance and control, injecting malicious code, conducting denial-of-service attacks, and so forth (Administration of Donald J. Trump, 2020). Some MCASAs are trivial and almost unnoticeable, such as invading a space system without further actions, whereas some may result in devastating consequences. For example, if the malicious cyber actor sent an unauthorised command to a satellite to deorbit and hit a spacecraft, this would not only destroy the spacecraft but also create a large constellation of space debris and even kill the persons therein. Moreover, the Viasat incident of 2022 illustrates how extensive the impact of MCASAs could be.

However, all types of MCASAs are not included in the present study. Space law applies in cases where MCASAs constitute space activities. MCASAs could be categorised into three types in terms of their relations with space activities, which can be determined by three locations: the place of conducting the MCAs, transmitting unauthorised commands, and the influenced area. Although launched against space systems, some MCASAs are purely terrestrial as all three locations are found on Earth. For instance, a malicious cyber actor intrudes into the computer system of a constellation of remote sensing satellites to acquire remote sensing data stored in terrestrial assets. These MCASAs are not fundamentally different from normal MCAs.

The second type of MCASAs, which occurs in outer space, qualifies for space activities *per se*. For instance, a space tourist staying in a spacecraft in outer space invades the controlling system of another satellite. Some scholars contended that if the effect of such MCASAs occurs on Earth, cyber activities cannot be space activities (Kaiser, 2020). However, it is the particular location where MCAs are conducted which determines their nature as space activities. Taking advantage of the location in outer space for conducting an MCA or selecting at random outer space as the originating place of an MCA does not deprive the activity's nature as the use of outer space, irrespective of where their effects occur.

The third type of MCASAs impacts activities in outer space or exploits space activities. An actual example of this type is the ROSAT incident, in which the hacking occurred on Earth, the unauthorised command was directly forwarded to ROSAT without transmission by other satellites, and the satellite failed in outer space. Whether this type of MCASAs constitutes space activities is yet to be determined. The malicious cyber actors themselves are not direct participants in space activities; however, as the malicious activity targets space objects and operations in outer space, or the purposes of the malicious cyber actors can only be realised through space systems, the MCAs are sometimes profoundly intervened with space systems or space activities such that they could be considered as 'absorbed' into space activities, rendering the application of space law possible. The role that the 'space' factor plays in MCASAs is decisive for its nature. A two-step test, which lies in appraising the weight of the 'space' factor in an MCASA, should apply to determine whether it constitutes a space activity before addressing legal issues. A detailed explanation of the two-step test is provided in Chapter 5 of this study.

As the first type of MCASAs denotes no particular legal characteristic other than normal MCAs, this study focuses on the second and third types of MCASAs aforementioned.

1.2 The Global Governance of Space Cybersecurity: Why and What?

Global governance has become ubiquitous, notably in dealing with issues of universal concern, such as global trade, climate change, global health, and so on. An abundance of literature is available on the global governance of outer space and cyberspace. Therefore, why is the global governance of space cybersecurity, a combined issue of space activities and cybersecurity, necessary? What should be the global governance system?

1.2.1 Global Governance

After several decades of debates, global governance remains an ambiguous notion and has become ubiquitous and even abused by academics and policymakers (Weiss & Wilkinson, 2014). The concept and theory of global governance were first presented in the 1990s by the Commission on Global Governance (CGG) in its report on global governance (CGG, 1995). The discussions on the concept permeated since; however, as Finkelstein highlighted decades ago, global governance is ambiguous and appears to be virtually anything (Finkelstein, 1995). The word 'global' is deemed to reflect 'the great changes that have been occurring both in the dynamics of relations in the world of States and in understanding those dynamics', such as the internationalisation of several problems that were initially national and the increasingly significant role of new actors in the world of States (Finkelstein, 1995). 'Governance' is not synonymous with 'government' (Rosenau & Czempiel, 1992). The CGG report states that governance is a continuing process participated by individuals and institutions, public and private, through which conflicting or diverse interests may be accommodated and cooperative action may be taken

(CGG, 1995), and that it entails a 'broad, dynamic, complex process of interactive decision-making that is constantly evolving and responding to the changing circumstances' (CGG, 1995). Further, governance is also defined by the UN Economic and Social Commission for Asia and the Pacific as 'the process of decision-making and the process by which decisions are implemented (or not implemented)' (UN Economic and Social Commission for Asia and the Pacific, 2007), and by other international organisations and academia in various ways (Ferreira-Snyman & Ferreira, 2006). Despite the heated discussions and multi-channel efforts, a coherent concept of global governance has not yet been reached (Pęciak, 2017). A flexible definition of global governance may be theoretically and empirically unavoidable (Dingwerth & Pattberg, 2006). It could be used to denote a phenomenon of governance arrangements encompassing the globe (Qoraboyev, 2021), as an analytical concept that provides a perspective on world politics different from the more traditional notion of 'international relations' (Dingwerth & Pattberg, 2006), as an attempt to control the pernicious aspects of accelerating economic and social change (Craig, 2008), and so forth. This study adopts the functional concept of global governance, regarding it as an approach to cope with threats to space cybersecurity.

Despite the different interpretations, some elements are common in all uses of the notion of global governance. As a product of liberal thinking, it embodies the global values, norms, standards, and rules (Makinda, 2001). To be more detailed, the critical elements of global governance include the values or goals pursued, the actors and the mechanisms of interactions among these actors, and the norms, principles, and rules framed and used by the actors to achieve the goals.

1.2.2 Why Is Global Governance Necessary for Space Cybersecurity?

As technical measures are typically considered the major means to tackle space cybersecurity issues, one may wonder regarding the necessity of global governance to cope with this seemingly technical problem. With the globalisation process, a myriad of universally impacting issues emerge. The report of the CGG lists the challenges confronting modern society as a whole and concludes that 'the effective and equitable management of these problems calls for a systemic, long-term, global approach' (CGG, 1995). Global governance, as 'a halfway house between the international anarchy underlying Realist analysis and world State' (Weiss, 2013), could be the solution. Weiss summarised three reasons for the emergence of global governance: interdependence and globalisation, the proliferation of non-State actors, and the fact that many analysts are embarrassed by the supposedly simplistic notion of supranationalism (Weiss, 2013). The third reason explains why global governance is adopted rather than a global government, whereas the first two reasons account for the inherent incentive and the factual basis supporting global governance. Moreover, this analysis reveals the reasons why the global governance of some specific fields is existent and possible. They share similarities in that the challenges in these areas are global in scale and impossible to tackle through traditional approaches. They have a solid institutional basis, that is, the proliferation of various relevant actors. Space cybersecurity has acquired global significance as it may impact the welfare of the current and future generations of human beings. Owing to the interconnectivity of space systems, space cybersecurity cannot be guaranteed only through national legislation and practices or by international rules, which are incompetent to deal with the challenges, as will be demonstrated in Part II of this study. In terms of institutions, apart from the States and the UN, other actors, including non-governmental organisations and industries, are already participating in global space governance and global cyberspace governance, as explained in Part III. They form a solid foundation for the space cybersecurity.

As the work of Weiss testifies more to global governance as a phenomenon, Acharya adopts a demand-side understanding of global governance and introduces five determinants to perceive the demand for global governance in a specific area: strategic, functional, normative, domestic politics, and regionalism (Acharya, 2016). The motivations for the global governance of space cybersecurity are more of a combination of the former three determinants. The functional demand for the global governance of space cybersecurity is self-evident, as space cybersecurity is a global concern. Space cybersecurity is a critical component of space safety and security, notably for the superpowers and the spacefaring States, as these States rely heavily on space activities and space technologies to guarantee their national security, military and defence interests, the normal functioning of the State machinery, and the welfare of nationals. Other States benefit from space applications as well. All these actors demand global governance for some strategic considerations; however, their strategic demands vary substantially. Superpowers seek to retain their hegemony and maximise their benefits in the space sector, other spacefaring States are attempting to expand their influences towards a multi-polarisation of powers, and the States without or with limited space capability strive for their right to space applications services, international technological cooperation to enhance their space capability, and so on. In addition, private space entities, whose ultimate pursuit is economic interests, play a role in the global governance of space cybersecurity. For private entities, space cybersecurity is bi-faceted: it is vital for the quality of their services, and the cybersecurity of other commercial space systems may also affect that because of interconnectivity; however, significant investment is required to guarantee the cybersecurity of space systems, which, in turn, will hamper the profitability. They demand a strategic balance to ensure their economic interests from global governance. The advent of new international norms, such as space security and safety, the sustainability of space activities, and responsible behaviours in outer space, also necessitates the global governance of space cybersecurity. Normative pressures, combined with the difficulties in resorting to the traditional way of international law-making—through concluding international treaties or forming international customs—demand new institutions and mechanisms of global governance.

1.2.3 What Should Be the Global Governance for Space Cybersecurity?

The global governance of space cybersecurity shall combine the features of global space and cyberspace governance. Global space governance is defined as 'a collection of international, regional, or national laws as well as regulatory institutions and actions/manners/processes of governing or regulating space-related affairs or activities' (Jakhu & Pelton, 2017), highlighting its three essential elements, the law, the institutions, and the mechanism of implementing the rules by these institutions. Prevailing literature on global space governance corresponds well to this definition, as most studies focus on one or several of these elements (Hertzfeld et al., 2016; Jakhu & Freeland, 2018; Stelmakh, 2015). The governance of cyberspace originates from private practices in the United States (US) and Europe and is spread to the governmental level and worldwide (Jakhu & Pelton, 2017). Cyberspace governance is complex owing to its status as a global common, the obligatory balancing between State sovereignty and the fragmentation of cyberspace, and the fierce debates between multilateralism and multistakeholderism (Liaropoulos, 2016). The multitude of actors and the rules and practices at different levels are implied. As Grewlich argues, governance of cyberspace

> may possibly assume some sort of umbrella function covering both the normative principles, agreements and arrangements pertaining to the subjects of public international law, and the principles and self-regulatory schemes that would respectively apply to business, civil society and other non-governmental entities.
>
> (Grewlich, 1999)

Four key elements should be incorporated into the global governance of space cybersecurity. The first element is the goals of the global governance of space cybersecurity. The study contends that good global governance is necessary to guarantee space cybersecurity. Therefore, what is good global governance of space cybersecurity? As the report of the CGG indicated, the quality of global governance will, to a large extent, be determined by the broad acceptance of 'a global civic ethic to guide action within the global neighbourhood', coupled with 'courageous leadership infused with that ethic at all levels of society', implying a common commitment to a set of core values by people from various backgrounds (CGG, 1995). The aims of good global governance are embedded in these shared values. The values pursued by actors of the global governance of space cybersecurity should combine the common values of global governance and the specific values of the global governance of space activities and cyberspace. Human well-being in the long term, survival, and development of humanity are common goals for global governance (Pęciak, 2017; Qoraboyev, 2021). As space activities are becoming more critical for improving human welfare, boosting economic growth, and eventually discovering new planets for human survival, space cybersecurity is relevant to all these common goals, which should also be incorporated into the goals of the global governance of space cybersecurity. The aim of global space governance, initially set to ensure peaceful uses of outer space (Trur, 2021), as enshrined in the Treaty on Principles Governing the Activities of States in the Exploration and Use of Outer Space, including the Moon and the Other Celestial Bodies (OST) of 1967 (UNGA, 1967), is expanding to include sustainability of space activities and space safety and security (Koskina & Angelopoulou, 2022; Martinez, 2020; Stelmakh, 2015; Trur, 2021). The meaning of sustainability of space activities is contentious and diversified. It has a robust environmental denotation. It encompasses mitigating harmful consequences of exploration to ease the burden of future activities (Newman, 2015). In a broad sense, space security indicates 'all aspects related to the questions of how to make space operations more safe and secure as well as protect the usage of outer space to enhance terrestrial security' (Schrogl et al., 2015). Space safety could be defined as freedom from manmade or natural harmful conditions, which can cause death, injury, or illness of human life, damage to or loss of systems, facilities, equipment or property, or damage to the environment (Jakhu & Pelton, 2017). The boundary between space safety and security is somewhat blurred, rendering their respective implications ambiguous and their occasional combined uses. Despite the overlapping and ambiguities, both space security and safety are the goals of the present global space governance. Although the goals of cyberspace governance are manifold, cybersecurity is undoubtedly among the most critical ones. To sum up, the global governance of space cybersecurity should guarantee the interests of human beings in outer space and in using space applications through protecting the cyber infrastructure of space systems and space information while considering the needs of the space economy. In accordance with these goals, considering the fact that MCASAs constitute the major threat to space cybersecurity, the global governance of space cybersecurity should have two major functions: preventive; and remedial and punitive. The preventive function comprises identifying the obligations and responsibilities of the stakeholders and guaranteeing they abide by the norms, principles, and rules. Moreover, there should be rule-making mechanisms facing possible regulatory loopholes. Legal and practical consequences shall intervene in case of non-observance of the rules, remedying the negative impacts and cautioning the violating actors through punitive measures.

The second element is the subjects to be governed. As MCASAs constitute a primary threat to space cybersecurity, the actors that may contribute to the occurrence and the dire consequences of MCASAs should undoubtedly be subject to the global governance of space cybersecurity. Two groups of subjects should be distinguished. The first group comprises the originators of the MCASAs, that is, malicious cyber actors and the State exercising jurisdiction over MCASAs. Malicious actors are essentially regulated at the national level. International law seldom applies directly to individuals, except for certain rules of international law of human rights and international criminal law. States enjoy sovereignty over any cyber infrastructure located on their territory and activities associated with that cyber infrastructure (Schmitt, 2017). Thus, a State shall exercise territorial jurisdiction over all cyber infrastructure and persons engaged in cyber activities on its territory and cyber activities originating in or completed on its territory (Schmitt, 2017). The protective principle, according to which 'States may exercise jurisdiction over aliens who have committed an act abroad which is deemed prejudicial to the security of the particular State concerned' (Shaw, 2008), implies that a State also has jurisdiction over cyber activities having a substantial effect in its territory. In addition, according to the principle of nationality, a State may exercise prescriptive jurisdiction over the cyber activities conducted by its nationals outside its territory. Thus, it is incumbent on the State to ensure that the cyber activities conducted on its territory and by its nationals conform to international law. The second group is the State responsible for the space activities involved in MCASAs. Some MCASAs qualify as space activities. Others may target space activities or objects or manipulate space activities, leading to various consequences on Earth and outer space. Considering cybersecurity issues while conducting space activities is significant for States responsible for space activities. The measures to guarantee cybersecurity during space activities may be derived from the international obligations bearing on the States, the breach of which may constitute internationally wrongful acts. As failure to comply with relevant international rules by these two groups of subjects may lead to, or at least facilitate, the occurrence of MCASAs, they constitute the major subjects to be regulated. Various studies focus on regulating the activities of the first group of actors, and more relevant research continues to emerge. Therefore, the second part of this study, dedicated to the regulatory aspects of the global governance of space cybersecurity, focuses particularly on the second group of actors.

The third element is the rules to ensure space cybersecurity. The sources of the existing rules for space cybersecurity are manifold. First, space cybersecurity issues relate to various branches of law, such as space law, cyber law, environmental law, law of armed conflicts, and general international law. Second, both international law and national law are relevant. For instance, the international space law regime has already been framed with the adoption of the five treaties: the OST; the Agreement on the Rescue of Astronauts, the Return of Astronauts and Return of Objects Launched into Outer Space of 1968 (Rescue Agreement) (UNGA, 1968); the Convention on International Liability for Damage Caused by Space Objects of 1972 (Liability Convention) (UNGA, 1972); the Convention on Registration of Objects Launched into Outer Space of 1975 (Registration Convention) (UNGA, 1975); and the Agreement Governing the Activities of States on the Moon and Other Celestial Bodies of 1979 (Moon Agreement) (UNGA, 1979). In accordance with these treaties, many States have enacted national space laws, and industrial practices are emerging. Although the international legal regime for cyberspace is yet to be formed, abundant rules and practices exist at the national and industrial levels. Third, the existing rules relevant to space cybersecurity incorporate not only binding rules but also non-binding soft law rules. The second part of this study is devoted to this element focusing on the regulations and practices at the international level. Moreover, critical legislation and practices at the national level have been considered to ensure the essentiality of this part.

The fourth is actors and mechanisms. Actors could be divided into two categories according to their functions in the global governance of space cybersecurity: those framing and clarifying regulations, including States, international, governmental and non-governmental organisations, and the industries; and those implementing and enforcing the rules, typically represented by States, industries, and judicial authorities of different levels. The effectiveness of global governance is guaranteed by effective cooperation and coordinating mechanisms among actors.

As highlighted by Finkelstein, global governance is a continuing process for pursuing specific interests through interactive decision-making (Finkelstein, 1995). Actors participating in the global governance of space cybersecurity are from different domains and rank differently in the conventional power hierarchy. To ensure the effectiveness of global governance, institutional interaction and coordination are indispensable. The third part of the study on institutional aspects examines the dynamics and the mechanisms of the two categories of actors, respectively.

1.3 Conclusion

MCASAs constitute a major threat to space cybersecurity. The nature of MCASAs determines the applicable international law rules. Three types of MCASAs could be distinguished: entirely terrestrial MCASAs, MCASAs constituting space activities, and MCASAs manipulating or impacting space activities. As abundant studies exist on terrestrial cyber activities, this study focuses on the remaining two categories of MCASAs.

As a challenge confronting modern society as a whole, space cybersecurity necessitates global governance. Global governance on space cybersecurity shall combine the features of global space governance and global cybersecurity governance, incorporating four key elements: (1) the purposes of global governance, including safeguarding the peaceful exploration of outer space, ensuring the security and sustainability of space activities, guaranteeing cybersecurity, human well-being in the long term, humanity survival, and development; (2) the subjects subject to global governance, including the malicious cyber actors and States exercising jurisdiction over the MCASAs, and the States responsible for space activities involved; (3) a set of rules, entailing preventive functions and reparatory and punitive functions; and (4) actors participating in the global governance on space cybersecurity. The third and fourth elements constitute the second and third parts of this study, which are followed by a conclusion.

References

Acharya, A. (2016). Rethinking demand, purpose and progress in global governance: An introduction. In A. Acharya (Ed.), *Why govern? Rethinking demand and progress in global governance* (pp. 1–30). Cambridge University Press. https://doi.org/10.1017/CBO9781316756829

Administration of Donald J. Trump. (2020). Space policy directive-5: Memorandum on cybersecurity principles for space systems. *Daily Compilation of Presidential Documents*, 1–4.

Akoto, W. (2020, February 12). Hackers could shut down satellites—or turn them into weapons. *The Conversation*. https://theconversation.com/hackers-could-shut-down-satellites-or-turn-them-into-weapons-130932

CGG. (1995). *Our global neighborhood: The report of the commission on global governance*. Oxford University Press.

Cheng, B. (1997). *Studies in international space law*. Clarendon Press.

Craig, C. (2008). The resurgent idea of world government. *Ethics & International Affairs*, *22*(2), 133–142.

Diederiks-Verschoor, I. H. P., & Kopal, V. (2008). *An introduction to space law*. Kluwer Law International.

Dingwerth, K., & Pattberg, P. (2006). Global governance as a perspective on world politics. *Global Governance: A Review of Multilateralism and International Organizations*, *12*(2), 185–203.
Ferreira-Snyman, M., & Ferreira, G. (2006). Global good governance and good global governance. *South African Yearbook of International Law*, *31*, 52–94.
Finkelstein, L.S. (1995). What is global governance. *Global Governance: A Review of Multilateralism and International Organizations*, *1*(3), 367–372. https://doi.org/10.1163/19426720-001-03-90000007
Grewlich, K. W. (1999). *Governance in 'cyberspace': Assess and public interest in global communications*. Kluwer Law International.
Hertzfeld, H. R., Weeden, B., & Johnson, C. D. (2016). Outer space: Ungoverned or lacking effective governance? New approaches to managing human activities in space. *SAIS Review of International Affairs*, *36*(2), 15–28. https://doi.org/10.1353/sais.2016.0017
ICRC. (2015, October 31). *International humanitarian law and the challenges of contemporary armed conflicts*. www.icrc.org/en/document/international-humanitarian-law-and-challenges-contemporary-armed-conflicts
Jakhu, R. S., & Freeland, S. (2018). Vital artery or stent needing replacement: Global space governance system without the outer space treaty. *Proceedings of the International Institute of Space Law*, *61*, 505–520.
Jakhu, R. S., & Pelton, J. N. (Eds.). (2017). *Global space governance: An international study*. Springer.
Kaiser, S. A. (2020). When cyber activities are space activities: Definitions are key. *Proceedings of the International Institute of Space Law*, *63*, 297–308.
Kavanagh, C. (2017). The United Nations, cyberspace and international peace and security: Responding to complexity in the 21st century. *UNIDIR Resources*. https://unidir.org/wp-content/uploads/2023/05/the-united-nations-cyberspace-and-international-peace-and-security-en-691.pdf
Kittichaisaree, K. (2018). *Public international law of cyberspace* (pp. 1–2). Springer. https://doi.org/10.1007/978-3-319-54657-5
Koskina, A., & Angelopoulou, K. (2022). Space sustainability in the context of global space governance Athena: Critical inquiries in law. *Philosophy and Globalization*, *2*, 29–72.
Lachs, M. (1964). The international law of outer space. *Collected Courses of the Hague Academy of International Law*, *113*. https://doi.org/10.1163/1875-8096_pplrdc_A97890286150211
Li, D. (2023). Legal dilemma for combatting malicious cyber activities against space activities. *Acta Astronautica*, *207*, 47–53. https://doi.org/10.1016/j.spacepol.2022.101522
Liaropoulos, A. (2016). Exploring the complexity of cyberspace governance: State sovereignty, multistakeholderism, and power politics. *Journal of Information Warfare*, *15*(4), 14–26.
Livingstone, D., & Lewis, P. (2016, September). *Space, the final frontier for cybersecurity?* www.chathamhouse.org/2016/09/space-final-frontier-cybersecurity
Lyall, F., & Larsen, P. B. (2009). *Space law- a treatise*. Ashgate.
Makinda, S. (2001). Recasting global governance. In R. Thakur & E. Newman. (Eds.), *New millennium, new perspectives: The United Nations, security, and governance* (pp. 163–181). United Nations University Press.
Martinez, P. (2020). The role of soft law in promoting the sustainability and security of space activities. *Journal of Space Law*, *44*(2), 522–564.
Maybaum, M. (2013). Technical methods, techniques, tools and effects of cyber operations. In K. Ziolkowski (Ed.), *Peacetime regime for state activities in cyberspace: International law, international relations and diplomacy* (pp. 103–131). NATO CCD COE Publication.
Newman, C. J. (2015). Seeking tranquillity: Embedding sustainability in lunar exploration policy. *Space Policy*, *33*, 29–37. https://doi.org/10.1016/j.spacepol.2015.05.003
Pasco, X. (2015). Various threats of space systems. In K-U. Schrogl, P. L. Hays, J. Robinson, D. Moura & C. Giannopapa (Eds.), *Handbook of space security: Policies, applications and programs* (pp. 663–678). Springer. https://doi.org/10.1007/978-1-4614-2029-3_9

Pęciak, R. (2017). Global governance in the context of global challenges. *The Macrotheme Review: A Multidisciplinary Journal of Global Macro Trend*, *6*(1), 117–128.
Popova, R. (2018). Cyber law and outer space activities: Legal and regulatory challenges. *Proceedings of the International Institute of Space Law*, *61*, 659–670.
Qoraboyev, I. (2021). Global governance. In K. de Feyter, G. E. Turkeli & S. de Moerloose (Eds.), *Encyclopedia of law and development* (pp. 99–103). Edward Elgar. https://doi.org/10.4337/9781788117975
Rosenau, J. E., & Czempiel, E.-O. (1992). *Governance without government: Order and change in world politics*. Cambridge University Press.
Schmitt, M. N. (Ed.). (2017). *Tallinn manual 2.0 on the international law applicable to cyber warfare*. Cambridge University Press. https://doi.org/10.1017/9781316822524
Schrogl, K-U., Hays, P. L., Robinson, J., Moura, D., & Giannopapa, C. (Eds.). (2015). *Handbook of space security: Policies, applications and programs*. Springer.
Sgobbi, D., Michelangelo, L., Frasca, D., Piantelli, V., & Sciascia, G. (2015). Space and cyber security. In K-U. Schrogl, P. L. Hays, J. Robinson, D. Moura & C. Giannopapa (Eds.), *Handbook of space security: Policies, applications and programs*. (pp. 157–186). Springer. https://doi.org/10.1007/978-1-4614-2029-3_49
Shaw, M. N. (2008). *International law*. Cambridge University Press.
Stelmakh, O. S. (2015). Global space governance for ensuring responsible use of outer space, its sustainability and environmental security: Legal perspective. *Proceedings of the International Institute of Space Law*, *58*, 685–698.
Trur, A. (2021). Governance aspects of space sustainability: The role of epistemic actors as enablers of progress. *Acta Astronautica*, *180*, 451–459. https://doi.org/10.1016/j.actaastro.2020.10.012
UN Economic and Social Commission for Asia and the Pacific. (2007). *What is good governance?* www.unescap.org/sites/default/files/good-governance.pdf
UNGA. (1967). *Treaty on principles governing the activities of states in the exploration and use of outer space, including the Moon and the other celestial bodies*. (UNGA Resolution 2222 (XXI)). UNTS. (610, No. 8843).
UNGA. (1968). *Agreement on the rescue of astronauts, the return of astronauts and return of objects launched into outer space*. (UNGA Resolution 2345 (XXII)). UNTS. (672, No. 9574).
UNGA. (1972). *Convention on international liability for damage caused by space objects*. (UNGA Resolution 2777 (XXVI)). UNTS. (961, No. 13810).
UNGA. (1975). *Convention on registration of objects launched into outer space*. (UNGA Resolution 3235 (XXIX)). UNTS. (1023, No. 15020).
UNGA. (1979). *Agreement governing the activities of states on the Moon and other celestial bodies*. (UNGA Resolution 34/68). UNTS. (1363, No. 23002).
UNGA. (2010, July 30). *Report of the group of governmental experts on developments in the field of information and telecommunications in the context of international security.*(UN. Doc. A/65/201). https://documents.un.org/doc/undoc/gen/n10/469/57/pdf/n1046957.pdf?token=ULDOKKys4URVerV1bX&fe=true
US Council on Foreign Relations. (2011a, November). *Interference with NASA satellite landsat 7: Recurring interference with a joint NASA-U.S.* Geological Survey satellite in 2007 and 2008. www.cfr.org/index.php/cyber-operations/interference-nasa-satellite-landsat-7
US Council on Foreign Relations. (2011b, November). *Interference with NASA satellite terra (EOS AM-1): Recurring interference with a NASA observation satellite*. www.cfr.org/cyber-operations/interference-nasa-satellite-terra-eos-am-1
Viasat, Inc. (2022, March 30). *KA-SAT network cyber attack overview*. https://news.viasat.com/blog/corporate/ka-sat-network-cyber-attack-overview
von Solms, R., & van Niekerk, J. (2013). From information security to cyber security. *Computers and Security*, *38*, 97–102. https://doi.org/10.1016/j.cose.2013.04.004
Weiss, T. G. (2013). *Global governance: Why? What? Whither?* Polity Press.
Weiss, T. G., & Wilkinson, R. (2014). Rethinking global governance? Complexity, authority, power, change. *International Studies Quarterly*, *58*(1), 207–215. https://doi.org/10.1111/isqu.12082

Part II

Regulatory Aspects of the Global Governance of Space Cybersecurity

As public international law has been transforming from the Westphalian system to a 'comprehensive blueprint for social life', its substantive norms are increasingly focusing on the realisation of community interest and the promotion of global public goods, in the context of which lies the significance of international law in the regulatory framework of global governance (Nowrot, 2004). For the global governance of space cybersecurity, international law is essential for achieving the regulatory purpose: the realisation of the shared interests of all States and human beings, that is, their interests in exploring and using outer space through protecting the cyber infrastructure of space systems and information while considering the needs of the space economy.

Without specific international rules dedicated to space cybersecurity, the legal instruments that could be applied directly to combat malicious cyber activities against space activities (MCASAs) are fragmented and diversified in forms. At the international level, undoubtedly, the two sets of legal instruments most relevant to space cybersecurity are space law and cybersecurity norms and practices. Other branches of international law may also be concerned, notably international environmental law, the law of armed conflicts, and international criminal law. Chapters 2, 3, and 4 examine and appraise the effects of space law, cybersecurity norms, and other relevant branches of international rules in combatting MCASAs and ensuring space cybersecurity. According to the *lex specialis derogat legi generali* principle, special law rules shall prevail in case of the existence of actual inconsistency between the special rules and the general rules or of a discernible intention that one provision is to exclude the other (ILC, 2001). If lacunae exist in special regimes or the application of the *lex specialis* would cause consequences incongruent with the objectives of the regimes, a fallback on general international law is expedient to serve the purposes of the special regime (Simma & Pulkowski, 2010). As demonstrated in this part of the study, the *lex specialis* could barely cope with all MCASAs, and general international law will also play a role. Chapter 5 explores the situation where general international law will apply to tackle MCASAs and evaluates whether it suffices to complement the *lex specialis*. This part of the study argues that legal gaps exist in the existing international rules relevant to combatting MCASAs, which hampers achieving the regulatory goals of global governance

DOI: 10.4324/9781003561996-3

of space cybersecurity. Bridging the gaps is indispensable, the possibilities and approaches of which are discussed in Part III of the study.

References

International Law Commission (ILC). (2001). *Commentaries to the draft articles on responsibility of states for internationally wrongful acts*. Report of the ILC. (Supplement No. 10 (A/56/10), chp.IV.E.2).

Nowrot, K. (2004, November). *Global governance and international law*. https://opendata.uni-halle.de/bitstream/1981185920/76421/1/BeitraegeTWR_33.pdf

Simma, B., & Pulkowski, D. (2010). Leges speciales and self-contained regimes. In J. Crawford, A. Pellet & S. Olleson (Eds.), *The law of international responsibility*(pp. 139–164). Oxford University Press. https://doi.org/10.1093/law/9780199296972.001.0001

2 The Status Quo of Space Law Confronting Malicious Cyber Activities Against Space Activities (MCASAs)

Space law was promptly formed during the 1960s and the1970s under the auspices of the United Nations (UN) after the successful launch of the first artificial satellite, Sputnik-1, in 1957. Five treaties have been adopted: the Treaty on Principles Governing the Activities of States in the Exploration and Use of Outer Space, including the Moon and the Other Celestial Bodies of 1967 (OST) (UNGA, 1967); the Agreement on the Rescue of Astronauts, the Return of Astronauts and Return of Objects Launched into Outer Space of 1968 (Rescue Agreement) (UNGA, 1968); the Convention on International Liability for Damage Caused by Space Objects of 1972 (Liability Convention) (UNGA, 1972); the Convention on Registration of Objects Launched into Outer Space of 1975 (Registration Convention) (UNGA, 1975); and the Agreement Governing the Activities of States on the Moon and Other Celestial Bodies of 1979 (Moon Agreement) (UNGA, 1979). These treaties establish the fundamental principles guiding space activities. Despite the fact that the effectiveness and appropriateness of these treaties to cope with emerging phenomena in the space sector, such as the commercialisation of the space sector and the proliferation of space resources activities, are often questioned (Lee, 2012; Taghdiri, 2013; Tronchetti, 2009; Ziemblicki & Oralova, 2021), the conclusion of new space treaties is challenging, and the non-binding soft law is playing a more critical role (Freeland, 2011).

The space law rules applicable to malicious cyber activities against space activities (MCASAs) could be divided into two sets from a functional perspective: preventive rules and remedial and punitive rules. The preventive rules essentially comprise principles and rules imposing international obligations on States, requiring States to adopt measures to prevent the occurrence of MCASAs and their consequences. The remedial and punitive rules help to redress the aftermaths of MCASAs. This chapter analyses these two sets of rules separately to appraise their effects on preventing MCASAs and deterring States and other actors from failing their duties.

2.1 The Preventive Rules

Except for Article VII of the OST and the Liability Convention, most rules established by space treaties are preventive as they envision international obligations imposed on States Parties to the treaties, with varying relevance to space

DOI: 10.4324/9781003561996-4

cybersecurity. However, the ambiguous terminology of the provisions enables various interpretations, causing difficulties in determining the substantive content of States' international obligations derived from space law in the context of MCASAs. Further, the current debates on the implications of the emerging soft law instruments related to issues such as space safety and security and the sustainability of space activities demonstrate the complexities in their direct application to MCASAs.

2.1.1 Binding Principles of Space Law

Not all space law principles are directly related to space cybersecurity. The most relevant ones are enshrined in Articles III, IV, VI, and IX of the OST.

2.1.1.1 Article III of the OST

Article III of the OST confirms the application of general international law, including the Charter of the UN, to space activities and that space activities shall be carried out 'in the interest of maintaining international peace and security and promoting international cooperation and understanding'. It is generally accepted that this article does not imply an automatic extension of international law to outer space, including the UN Charter *in toto* (Lachs, 2010). Difficulties may arise in determining the international rules to apply in specific circumstances. Therefore, in the context of MCASAs, the international obligations posed by general international law other than space law are yet to be determined.

The provision of maintaining international peace and security emphasises the underlying premise that the exploration and use of outer space may not jeopardise international peace and security (Hobe et al., 2009), as enshrined in Article 1 of the UN Charter (UN, 1945). The connotations of international peace and security remain debated. According to Article 39 of the UN Charter, the Security Council shall determine the existence of any threat to international peace and security. However, the answer to what constitutes threats to international peace and security is clouded by 'redundancies, contradictions, imprecisions and other ambiguities' of relevant resolutions adopted by the Security Council (Byers, 2021), resulting from combined legal and political concerns. Consequently, no uniform criteria can be applied to decide whether an MCASA violates the 'international peace and security' provision. It shall be subject to case-specific examinations, particularly considering the disparities of the impacts that different MCASAs may exert. Owing to this uncertainty, the international obligations deriving from Article III are unclear.

2.1.1.2 Article IV of the OST

Compared with Article III, which emphasises international peace and security, Article IV focuses more on peace and security in outer space. The first paragraph of the article provides for a 'partial prohibition of arms' (Hobe et al., 2009) as it forbids the placing of nuclear weapons or other types of weapons of mass destruction

(WMDs) in outer space and on celestial bodies. WMDs are defined as 'atomic explosive weapons, radioactive material weapons, lethal chemical and biological weapons, and any weapons developed in the future which might have characteristics comparable in destructive effect to those of the atomic bomb or other weapons mentioned above' (UNGA, 1977). Despite discussions on the possible expansion of the scope of WMDs (Berman, 2005; Betts, 1998; Felix, 2003), for the time being, it continues to be accepted that the weaponry qualifiable as WMDs should have the potential to

> produce in a single moment an enormously destructive effect capable of killing millions of civilians, jeopardise the natural environment, and fundamentally alter the lives of future generations through their catastrophic effects; cause death or serious injury of people through toxic or poisonous chemicals; disseminate disease-causing organisms or toxins to harm or kill humans, animals or plants; and deliver nuclear explosive devices, chemical, biological or toxin agents to use them for hostile purposes or in armed conflict.
>
> (UNODA, n.d.)

MCASAs could barely produce similar effects to conventional WMDs in a direct manner. However, they may interfere with the services of space systems, resulting in large-scale destructive consequences. For instance, supposing a malicious cyber actor intrudes into a satellite navigation system and sends false information to users on Earth, causing the crash of an aircraft carrying poisonous chemicals on board in the urban centre of a city. In this case, the satellite navigation system is manipulated for the occurrence of the catastrophic aftermath. Nonetheless, it would be inappropriate to consider normal space objects, even destined for military purposes, as WMDs. Thus, the first paragraph of Article IV does not entail special obligations for States Parties in the context of MCASAs.

In the context of MCASAs, demanding States Parties to ensure that their space activities on the Moon and other celestial bodies are carried out for peaceful purposes, as prescribed by Article IV(2), implies that at least two sets of technical measures should be adopted: measures to supervise the cyber system of space activities so that the unauthorised access could be perceived, and measures to curb the invasion to prevent manipulation of the space systems for non-peaceful purposes. However, the specific technical measures to be adopted are challenging to determine. First, this is owing to the fierce debates over the meaning of 'peaceful purposes'. The term 'peaceful purposes' is conceived as non-military by some scholars (Cheng, 2000) and States, and non-aggressive by others (Hobe, 2015; Mosteshar, 2004). Both interpretations are purpose-oriented; however, their divergence would result in uncertainties regarding States Parties' obligations. Non-militarisation of outer space refers to 'the prohibition of using space-based facilities for any military purpose' (Su, 2010). Owing to the dual-use feature of most space technologies and objects, identifying their purposes is difficult in practice. The non-aggression principle, established by national law theory, 'prohibits the initiation of force against persons or property' (Chartier, 2010). According to this principle, deploying weapons on the Moon and other celestial bodies is lawful as long as they are not used to incite conflicts, let alone placing civil or dual-use space objects. The controversial provision on peaceful purposes renders identifying specific international obligations of a State Party uncertain when confronted with MCASAs. Malicious cyber actors may invade the controlling system of a lunar rover to spy over another State's lunar activity for military purposes (Scenario 1) or manipulate a lunar rover to destroy the lunar installation of another State (Scenario 2). According to the two-step test, which helps to determine whether an MCASA constitutes a space activity (see Chapter 5 for more details), in both scenarios, the malicious cyber activities (MCAs) are deeply embedded in space activities, without which the malicious cyber actors' purposes cannot be achieved. Thus, space law shall apply to the States Parties operating the space system or object. However, the obligations arising from Article IV(2) may differ according to the two interpretations of 'peaceful purposes'. According to the non-military understanding, States Parties should ensure that the space objects are not for military purposes. Suppose the States conducting space activities in both scenarios are all States Parties to the OST, then all these States failed their duties. If the non-aggressive understanding were adopted, the State conducting space activities in Scenario 1 would not be held responsible, whereas the State in Scenario 2 would be held responsible. Thus, States Parties cannot determine their substantive obligations under Article IV(2) in the context of MCASAs, which would be further complicated by the fact that malicious cyber actors' final intentions are difficult or even impossible to predict. Second, requiring States Parties to strictly guarantee that their space systems are used exclusively for peaceful purposes on the Moon and other celestial bodies is technically demanding during MCASAs. Not all States have the technical capability to establish cyber situational awareness systems that could discover all unauthorised access and immediately prevent all cyber invasions into their space systems. Even with technical possibilities, meeting these cyber safety standards is expensive, particularly for private operators. Thus, a balance should be achieved between ensuring the peaceful purposes and the feasibility of space activities. However, the equilibrium point remains to be determined.

2.1.1.3 Article VI of the OST

Article VI contains both preventive dispositions and remedial and punitive provisions. The provisions for remedial and punitive purposes could be classified as secondary rules in the law of State responsibility, that is, rules on attribution issues, which are discussed in sub-section 2.2.1 of this chapter. The present sub-section focuses on the provisions imposing obligations on States Parties, envisioning that States Parties should ensure that their 'national [space] activities are carried out in conformity with the provisions set forth in the present Treaty' and that 'the activities of non-governmental entities in outer space . . . shall require authorisation and continuing supervision by the appropriate State Party to the Treaty'.

Interpreting 'national activities' is indispensable for deciding the responsible State Party to ensure compliance with the OST. Three approaches have been proposed to determine the 'nationality' of space activities. The first approach links it to the State of registry of space objects (Hobe et al., 2009). The irrationality of this approach has been approved, notably in cases of orbital transfer of space objects, where the initial State of registry and the transferee State are different, and the change of registration is not prompt. The State of registry retains *de jure* jurisdiction and control, whilst the transferee State has *de facto* jurisdiction and control (Dasgupta, 2016). It would be unreasonable to demand the initial State of registry to ensure that the space object transferred is operated in compliance with space law as it has no actual right or control over it. The second approach relates the 'nationality' of space activities to the nationalities of participants in space activities (UK, 1986), which originates from the provisions in Article VIII of the OST that the State of registry shall retain jurisdiction and control over the object registered and any personnel thereof. The limitation of this approach is apparent. The incremental international cooperation in the space sector would lead to situations where subjects of different nationalities are engaged in one space activity. Thus, the second approach proves to be completely helpless when facing a space object, the conception and manufacturing of which involve subjects from multiple States, including the more complex situation where some subjects are multinational. According to the third approach, the responsible State for a space activity should be the State to exercise jurisdiction over it (Cheng, 1998). Cheng distinguishes jurisfaction, a normative power of a State, and jurisaction, the internationally recognised competence of a State to physically 'exercise the functions of a State', and contends that a space activity carried on within a State's jurisaction, whether territorial, quasi-territorial, or personal, shall qualify as that State's national activity (Cheng, 1998). It is the approach most supported by State practice (Hobe et al., 2009). Cheng suggests that considering the principle that territorial jurisaction overrides quasi-territorial and personal jurisaction, and quasi-territorial jurisaction overrides personal jurisaction, all concerned States shall be, in principle, responsible for the space activity; however, the States enjoying quasi-territorial jurisaction or personal jurisaction should exert every possible effort, in good faith, to bring back those concerned under its own effective jurisaction to ensure the conformity of their national space activities with Article VI, 'unless other State is effectively doing so' (Cheng, 1998). This analysis is significant even for the complicated cases of MCASAs involving several States participating in space activities. Suppose an individual from State A participates in a space trip organised by a company established in State B and conducts an MCA while visiting a space station operated by State C, and all three States have acceded to the OST. According to Cheng's analysis, the space tourism activity in the hypothesis should be considered a national activity of all three States. State A should bear the burden of controlling all activities carried out in its space station, whilst the obligation to ensure compliance of States B and C appears to be exempted as they may, in good faith, believe that State A is performing its duties. If State A fails to fulfil its international obligations, and the fact is acknowledged by States B and C, whether State B or State C shall ensure the compliance relies on the acts of the other. However, judging whether the other State is effectively performing its duty could be difficult, and the standards are obscure. Reliance on other

States may trigger legal risks. It would be more appropriate to consider all involved States as responsible States, and all States should do their best to fulfil their obligations in good faith. The need of deciding the prevailing jurisaction facing several jurisactions shall intervene only when conflicts of jurisaction virtually occur.

A more detailed obligation imposed by Article VI is that the appropriate State should authorise and exercise continuing supervision over space activities conducted by its non-governmental activities. The term 'appropriate State' is critical for identifying the obligatory State and needs clarification, and 'authorisation and continuing supervision' requires further interpretation to determine the substantive content of the obligation. Cheng perceives appropriate States in a broad way, reckoning that every State Party concerned in the space activity is an appropriate State, and in practice there may be more than one appropriate State, *de facto* or even *de jure* (Cheng, 1998). A narrower approach to defining the appropriate State has also been proposed, referring it directly to the State with jurisdiction over the space activity (Hobe et al., 2009). State practice in this respect differs, which is clear from the diversity in the application scope of national space legislation. For instance, the United States (US) licensing system for launching activities adopts both territorial and personal jurisdiction, requiring a license or a permit for launching-related activities, including launching a vehicle, operating a launch site or re-entry site, or re-entering a re-entry vehicle in the US, and for launching-related activities carried out by US citizens outside the US, with some exceptions (US, n.d.). The United Kingdom (UK) adopts a single personal jurisdiction approach, providing that launching or procuring the launch of a space object, operating a space object and any activity in outer space carried out by UK nationals, bodies incorporated under the law of any the UK requires licensing (UK, 1986). International coordination and cooperation are inevitable in space activities involving multiple States, as more than one State may qualify as an appropriate State according to their national legislation. They shall decide whether a license in one State suffices; with a positive answer, which State shall have the jurisdiction to do so.

Discrepancies in the application scope of national space laws also testify to different understandings of the substantive content of the 'authorisation and continuing supervision' obligation. The duty to authorise 'ensures the State recognises the activity about to be undertaken by a commercial entity through an a priori licensing procedure', and the duty of continuing supervision guarantees the continual compliance of the space activity with the OST (Spencer, 2010). Neither the OST nor the subsequential non-binding documents hint at the concrete measures to be taken by States Parties for performing the duties. Many States, even most States Parties to the OST, have not enacted national regulations regarding this concern. Moreover, the existing national rules adopted by States vary significantly. Nonetheless, one of the purposes of these national rules is identical: to ensure the compliance of space activities with international law. Guaranteeing space cybersecurity is a critical element for fulfilling space law obligations. Incorporating relevant technical standards and measures in national regulations on licensing and continuing supervision can be a plausible approach. The US has taken the initiative to enhance space cybersecurity by issuing the Memorandum on Cybersecurity Principles for Space Systems (Administration of Donald J. Trump, 2020). It establishes cybersecurity principles and practices applicable to both terrestrial systems and space systems and directs related governmental agencies to work with the commercial space industry and other non-government space operators to further define best practices, develop cybersecurity-informed norms, and promote improved cybersecurity behaviours throughout the Nation's industrial base for space systems in conformity with the principles and practices. Nonetheless, more substantive norms, standards, and measures are to be determined, and space cybersecurity concerns have not yet been included in the US licensing and supervision regime. It would produce pioneering and enlightening effects for other States if the US integrated cybersecurity dispositions into its current regulatory regime of space activities.

2.1.1.4 Article IX of the OST

Several dispositions of Article IX of the OST are significant for combatting MCASAs. The article, in its first sentence, stipulates that States Parties shall 'conduct all their activities in outer space, including the Moon and other celestial bodies, with due regard to the corresponding interests of all other States Parties to the Treaty'. Scholars have proposed their own understandings of the term 'due regard'. Mineiro deems 'due regard' as an obligation to consider the legal rights of other States prior to and during space activities (Mineiro, 2010), whereas Marchisio regards it as an obligation to perform certain acts (Hobe et al., 2009). Both understandings demand States take action to avoid hindering other States' interests in their peaceful exploration and use of outer space. It is unnecessary to define the scope of the acts and the measures to be undertaken. As the impacts of space activities on the corresponding interests of other States Parties may significantly vary and there may be a myriad of ways to minimise or avoid the impacts, the State conducting the space activity shall make the choice. From the perspective of countering MCASAs, due regard obligation implies that States Parties should adopt measures to prevent MCASAs from occurring and to avoid the impacts of MCASAs that may hamper other States' corresponding interests. The purpose of due regard obligation in the realm of space cybersecurity is relatively clear, and it is possible to list the measures to adopt. Nonetheless, the exact measures to be undertaken and their effects remain undefined. Corresponding interests denote the interests and rights vested by space law (Hobe et al., 2009), notably the freedom to peacefully explore and use outer space without discrimination. This general provision is supplemented by the following provisions of Article IX concerning environmental protection and harmful interference.

The second sentence of Article IX is devoted to environmental protection issues, stipulating that States Parties should carry out their space activities in a manner 'to avoid their harmful contamination and also adverse changes in the environment of the Earth resulting from the introduction of extraterrestrial matter and, where necessary, shall adopt appropriate measures for this purpose'. Planetary protection and space debris are currently the two major issues related to this provision. The essential legal instruments to regulate these two issues comprise international soft law and national regulations and practices. The development of soft law and national regulations and practices have reified the requirements for environmental protection of outer space raised by Article IX. Regrettably, as demonstrated in subsection 2.1.2.1, at this stage, MCASAs, as a hazardous potential to contaminate outer space and generate new space debris, are not considered.

Third, the remaining part of Article IX establishes a consultation mechanism in case of potential harmful interference with other States Parties' space activities. Mineiro distinguishes three types of interferences, radio, physical, and observational interferences (Sandalinas, 2010), with the radio and physical types being closely related to space safety and security. MCASAs could cause both radio and physical interferences. International Telecommunications Union (ITU) defines radio interference as

> the effect of unwanted energy due to one or a combination of emissions, radiations, or inductions upon reception in a radiocommunication system, manifested by any performance degradation, misinterpretation, or loss of information which could be extracted in the absence of such unwanted energy,

and harmful interference as radio interference that 'endangers the functioning of a radio navigation service or of other safety services or seriously degrades, obstructs, or repeatedly interrupts a radiocommunication service operating in accordance with Radio Regulations' (ITU, 2020). ITU Radio Regulations are the most important legal source for preventing harmful radio interference. It is prescribed in its preamble that 'all stations . . . must be established and operated in such a manner as not to cause harmful interference to the radio services or communications' (ITU, 2020). Its Chapter IV is dedicated to interference issues. Physical harmful interference refers to threats to the normal functioning or even the existence of the space object by acts such as approaching the space object in outer space, and so on. Except for Article IX, there are no other preventive rules pertaining to physical harmful interference. From the context of Article IX, it can be presumed that the purposes of consultations reside in preserving the corresponding interests of other States Parties, implying that the State of origin of the harmful interference should adopt measures to avoid the interference. According to this article, the timing of the request for consultation is different for the State of origin of the activity or experiment and the State potentially affected, as the interfering State should enter into consultation prior to the commencement of the activity or experiment, whereas the affected State could request consultation before or during the activity or experiment. The harmful interference caused by MCASAs is unpredictable, rendering it generally unnecessary for the State of origin of the activity or experiment to consult with the potentially affected States in advance. The State potentially affected by harmful interference caused by MCASAs could request consultation at any time before or during the space activity. Nonetheless, space law is silent on appropriate international consultations and the procedure to follow (Mineiro, 2010). It can only be inferred from the provisions of Article IX that the State planning for space activities is procedurally obligated to contact the States Parties which are likely to be affected and substantively obligated to, at minimum, provide the information sufficient for the latter to take action to prevent potential harmful interference (Mineiro, 2010). It is also possible that the planning State will adopt technical measures to prevent harmful interference. Thus, whether the States should undertake measures, which State should act, and what measures should be undertaken to avoid harmful interferences depend on the circumstances of each case. In sum, the consultation mechanism established by Article IX does not provide for concrete obligations on States Parties to prevent and eliminate harmful interference caused by MCASAs, and the obligations to avoid radio harmful interference are primarily imposed by ITU Radio Regulations.

2.1.2 Non-Binding Soft Law

The difficulty in developing new binding international treaties, the diversity of States' interests, and the increasing importance of private actors at the international level have contributed to the prevalence of soft law in the space sector (Freeland, 2011). Although formal sources of international law will always play an important role, the benefits of soft law are undeniable (von der Dunk, 2012). Soft law functions as substitution for treaties, a choice and preference, and *lex ferenda* to avoid confrontations among States in different domains (Aoki, 2012). Particularly, it is submitted that technically based guidelines are suitable for certain types of space activities involving highly technical issues as political considerations are excluded (Aoki, 2012). Therefore, soft law appears to be an effective tool for preventing MCASAs, as MCASAs can be highly technical.

Non-binding international instruments have already been developed to cope with various aspects of space activities, such as space applications, the use of nuclear power sources in outer space, the exploration of outer space for the benefit of all States, space debris mitigation, the anti-proliferation of ballistic missile (UNIDIR, n.d.). Moreover, soft law instruments are burgeoning around issues such as the long-term sustainability (LTS) of outer space activities and space security and safety, which are most closely linked to space cybersecurity; and these issues intertwine. The LTS of outer space entails space debris mitigation and space security and safety, and space debris mitigation is indispensable for space security and safety. As soft law instruments cluster over these three issues, this sub-section addresses the soft law instruments concerning space debris mitigation, the LTS of outer space activities and space security and safety separately, and appraises whether they could contribute towards combatting MCASAs.

2.1.2.1 The Protection of Outer Space Environment

The soft law approach has been used for planetary protection and space debris mitigation. The Committee on Space Research (COSPAR) began issuing planetary protection standards in 1964 and the consolidated version of these standards—Planetary Protection Policy (PPP)—since 2002. These instruments serve as guidelines for planetary protection purposes. The PPP divides celestial bodies and mission types into five categories (Tennen, 2020) and offers implementation guidelines for each category (COSPAR, 2021). Typically, for Category III missions, which comprise 'certain types of missions (mostly flyby and orbiter) to a target body of chemical evolution and/or origin of life interest and for which scientific opinion provides a significant chance of contamination which could compromise future investigations', requirements regarding documentation and implementing procedures, including trajectory biasing, the use of cleanrooms during spacecraft assembly and testing, and possibly bioburden reduction, are all included in the PPP (COSPAR, 2021). Similarly, for Category IV missions comprising 'certain types of missions (mostly probe and lander) to a target body of chemical evolution and/or origin of life interest and for which scientific opinion provides a significant change of contamination which could compromise future investigations', more detailed and involved requirements on documentation and implementing procedures including trajectory biasing, cleanrooms, bioburden reduction, possible partial sterilisation of the direct contact hardware, and a bio shield for that hardware are established (COSPAR, 2021). The PPP sets international standards for avoiding organic-constituent and biological contamination in space exploration; however, it does not envision unexpected incidents that may cause contamination during space missions. For instance, biological extraction of Lunar/Martian regolith, involving using terrestrial microorganisms, is promising for in-situ resource utilisation and will probably be promoted extensively (Wang et al., 2022). Incidental collisions between the biomass reactors used to grow and store the microorganisms in outer space and other space objects, which MCASAs could cause, may result in the diffusion of the microorganisms and, thus, contamination of the outer space environment. Without guidance on preventing contamination in such cases, the PPP may not be effective in addressing the potential incidents caused by MCASAs.

Concerning space debris mitigation, the Inter-Agency Space Debris Coordination Committee (IADC) issued its Space Debris Mitigation in 2002 (IADC, 2021), which was also the basis of the Space Debris Mitigation Guidelines of the UN Committee on the Peaceful Uses of Outer Space (COPUOS) (UN COPUOS, 2007). Both the IADC and UN Space Debris Mitigation Guidelines limit the regeneration of space debris released during normal operations, minimise the potential for on-orbit break-ups and post-mission disposal, and prevent on-orbit collisions. Although the two guidelines shed light on the *lex ferenda* for mitigating space debris, they are far from flawless, as they do not envisage space debris resulting from incidents caused by, for instance, MCASAs (Li, 2023). The ITU also plays a role in mitigating space debris. The ITU Recommendation ITU-R S.1003.2, titled Environmental protection of the geostationary-satellite orbit, 'provides guidance about disposal orbits for satellites in the geostationary satellite orbit and comments on the increase in debris due to fragments resulting from increased numbers of satellites and their associated launches' (ITU, 2010). In addition, non-governmental entities attach importance to space debris issues as well and establish industrial standards, such as the International Organization for Standardization (ISO) and the ISO 24113, requiring collision risks to be actively managed and avoidance manoeuvres to be performed where appropriate (Stokes et al., 2020). Although these documents and actual mitigation practices generally incorporate measures to avoid collisions, the risks of collisions caused by MCASAs are not considered (Li, 2023).

2.1.2.2 The Long-Term Sustainability of Outer Space Activities

The LTS of outer space activities is defined as

> the ability to maintain the conduct of space activities into the future in a manner that realises the objectives of equitable access to the benefits of the exploration and use of outer space for peaceful purposes, to meet the needs of the present generations while preserving the outer space environment for future generations.
>
> (UN COPUOS, 2019a)

Currently, the most critical issues of the LTS of outer space activities are space debris that causes obstruction in the peaceful use of outer space and natural resource exploration in outer space that risks leading to overexploitation (Prasad, 2019). Given the threats to space activities in the long term posed by the proliferation of space debris, the increasing complexity of space operations, the emergence of large constellations, and the increasing risks of collision and interference with the operation of space objects, international cooperation is imperative, as the existing international instruments appear to be incompetent, whether binding and non-binding.

Confronting the threats to the LTS of space activities, the Scientific and Technical Subcommittee (STSC) of the COPUOS established the first Working Group on the LTS of Outer Space Activities in 2010, aiming to prepare a report on the LTS of space activities, examine the measures that could enhance the LTS of such activities, and prepare a set of best-practice guidelines (UN COPUOS, 2010). After eight years of discussions and negotiations, the Guidelines for the Long-term Sustainability of Outer Space Activities were adopted by the COPUOS in 2019. The LTS Guidelines aim to 'assist States and international intergovernmental organisations, both individually and collectively, to mitigate the risks associated with the conduct of outer space activities so that present benefits can be sustained and future opportunities realised' (Martinez, 2020). Several guidelines under Part B titled 'Safety of space operations' and Part C titled 'International cooperation, capacity-building and awareness' may be useful in combatting MCASAs, including Guideline B.1 on providing updated contact information and sharing information on space objects and orbital events; Guideline B.2 on improving accuracy of orbital data on space objects and enhancing the practice and utility of sharing orbital information on space objects; Guideline B.4 on performing conjunction assessment during all orbital phases of controlled flight; Guideline B.8 on design and operation of space objects regardless of their physical and operational characteristics; Guideline B.10 on observing measures of precaution when using sources of laser beams passing through outer space; Guideline C.3 on promoting and supporting capacity-building; Guideline C.4 on raising awareness of space activities.

However, none of the guidelines explicitly mention cybersecurity issues related to space activities. Although States may select to incorporate elements of the LTS Guidelines into their national legislation and enjoy the discretion to elaborate specific requirements and measures following the elements they select, owing to a lack of explicit guidance in the LTS Guidelines on space cybersecurity, States tend to ignore the relevance between the LTS and space cybersecurity, and thus, the effects of the LTS Guidelines in combatting MCASAs are inconspicuous.

A new working group under the agenda item on the LTS of outer space activities of the STSC was established in 2019 (UN COPUOS, 2019a). Several guidelines proposed by the first working group did not reach consensus during its mandate, including those relevant to ensuring space cybersecurity, notably Guidelines 18 and 19 on measures to identify, mitigate, and manage the risk to terrestrial infrastructure that supports the operation of orbital systems, launch vehicles, and spacecraft (UN COPUOS, 2019b). The new working group will continue working on reaching a consensus on these guidelines. Moreover, it is tasked to identify and study the challenges and consider new guidelines for the LTS of outer space activities, share experiences, practices, and lessons from the adopted guidelines, raise awareness, and build capacity (Martinez, 2020). Incorporating cybersecurity concerns into the negotiation of the working group is possible.

2.1.2.3 Space Security

The scope of space security has been broadened to encompass, aside from the military dimension, the economic, societal, and environmental dimensions (Sheehan, 2015). Two other soft law initiatives regarding space security have been considered within the UN system: the prevention of an arms race in outer space (PAROS) negotiated at the Conference on Disarmament (CD) and the transparency and confidence-building measures (TCBMs) in outer space activities, for which a Group of Governmental Experts has been established under the First Committee of the UN (Martinez, 2018).

The PAROS has been considered in the CD since 1982. Opinions diverge on the most effective manner to address the issue: whether to apply legally binding or non-binding instruments (Martinez, 2020). China and Russia confirmed their support for the legally binding instruments by proposing the Draft Treaty on the Prevention of the Placement of Weapons in Outer Space, the Threat or Use of Force against Outer Space Objects (PPWT) in 2008, and a revised version in 2014, which the US and its allies have poorly received. Hitherto, the major space powers remain deadlocked on the issues of legally binding instruments on PAROS. Contrary to the binding instrument approach, the UN General Assembly has witnessed the adoption of several resolutions related to PAROS, notably a series of Resolutions on the 'No first placement of weapons in outer space' (UNGA, 2014, 2015, 2016a), the Resolution on 'Prevention of an arms race in outer space' (UNGA, 2016b), the Resolution on 'Further practical measures for the prevention of an arms race in outer space' (UNGA, 2017), and so forth. Although these resolutions raise the awareness of the States of the urgency and significance of the PAROS, they have barely any relations with space cybersecurity. They can contribute minimally to combatting MCASAs, although MCASAs could turn ordinary space objects in outer space into devastating objects, producing similar effects as weapons.

TCBMs are a set of tools designed to display, predict, and discipline States' behaviour with respect to maintaining the security of space (Robinson, 2016). They could play a significant role in 'clarifying the intentions of space actors and reducing the risk of misperception and erroneous assessment of the activities of States in outer space, thus helping to foster regional and global stability' (Martinez et al., 2014). TCBMs could be developed unilaterally, bilaterally, and multilaterally in various forms, and the measures developed in multilateral frameworks are most likely to be adopted by the international community (Martinez et al., 2014). In addition to the binding TCBMs contained in Articles V, IX, and IX of the OST (Nardone, 2017), non-binding instruments have also been developed in the UN system. Since 2005, the UN General Assembly has been endorsing resolutions titled 'Transparency and Confidence-building Measures in Outer Space Activities' (UNGA, 2005, 2006, 2007), and established a Group of Governmental Experts on Transparency and Confidence-building Measures in Outer Space Activities (GGE on TCBMs) in 2011 (UNGA, 2011), which issued its report in 2013 (UNGA, 2013). The TCBMs proposed in the report of the GGE on TCBMs included information exchange on space policies and notifications related to outer space activities, risk reduction notifications, contact and visits to space launch sites and facilities, international cooperation, consultative mechanisms, outreach, and coordination. The report submits, under the title 'risk reduction notifications', more specific measures of notifications, including notifications and monitoring of uncontrolled high-risk re-entry events and notifications in the case of emergency situations, which are particularly relevant to MCASAs. Although these measures cannot contribute towards preventing the occurrence of MCASA, they could minimise the negative impacts of MCASAs. However, given their soft law nature, States enjoy the discretion as to whether to adopt such measures, which may significantly reduce their effects.

Moreover, initiatives outside the UN system are emerging. Regional initiatives could be best represented by the Code of Conduct for Outer Space Activities (CoC) adopted by the European Union (EU) in 2008. Several States joined the European CoC, including the US. These participating States decided to develop an International Code of Conduct for Outer Space (ICoC) together with the EU and other States. The ICoC aims to 'enhance the safety, security and sustainability of all outer space activities pertaining to space objects, as well as the space environment' (EU, 2014). The ICoC does not address space cybersecurity explicitly; however, some of the principles proposed appear promising for engaging subscribing States in the fight against MCASAs, including Clause 4 on measures on outer space operations and space debris mitigation, Clause 5 on notification of outer space activities, and Clause 7 on consultation mechanism. Typically, Clause 4.1 articulates that the subscribing States 'resolve to establish and implement policies and procedures to minimise the risk of accidents in space collisions between space objects, or any form of harmful interference with another State's peaceful exploration, and use, of outer space', implying the adoption of space debris mitigation regulations and practices by subscribing States, which could include measures to enhance cybersecurity of space systems to avoid collision or harmful interference caused by MCASAs. Clause 5.1 requires subscribing States to notify, in a timely manner and to the greatest extent practicable, all potentially affected States of any 'malfunctioning of space objects or loss of control that could result in a significantly increased probability of a high re-entry event or a collision between space objects', elucidating the measures that States should undertake in case of malfunctioning or loss of control of space objects owing to MCASAs. However, the preventive effects of the ICoC on MCASAs remain limited. Despite its non-binding nature, States are prudent regarding whether to subscribe to the ICoC, as the political cost of non-compliance can be very high (Su, 2015). In addition, the ICoC is only concerned with preventing specific dire impacts that may arise from MCASAs, such as the generation of space debris due to collisions and the malfunctioning and loss of control of space objects. It is not a comprehensive instrument dedicated to space cybersecurity and does not cover all preventive requirements for confronting MCASAs. Finally, owing to a lack of explicit reference to space cybersecurity, the ICoC can contribute minimally to promote the awareness of this issue among subscribing States.

2.1.3 Sub-Conclusion

Based on space law, two categories of preventive rules could be distinguished. The first category rests on preventing cyber intrusions, which could be deduced from Article VI of the OST. Most other rules aim to prevent or minimise the devastating aftermaths of MCASAs. Both categories of rules imply certain specific measures to undertake, such as cybersecurity requirements in the development and construction of space systems, enhancing situational awareness capabilities, developing and adopting technical measures to prevent manipulations by malicious cyber actors, and notifying and entering into consultations with possibly affected states. However, the unclear terminology of the provisions of hard law, the non-binding nature of soft law instruments, and the incoherent national practices only establish an empty legal framework for preventing MCASAs without any substantive or unequivocal content, rendering space law incompetent for preventing MCASAs and their aftermaths.

2.2 The Remedial and Punitive Rules

The remedial and punitive rules determine the legal consequences that should be borne by the States conducting space activities in case of MCASAs, particularly when the States fail to prevent the MCASAs and their negative impacts. Space law has not only established a unique attribution rule for acts violating space law but also established a liability regime for damages, regardless of whether international wrongful acts exist. However, the effectiveness of the attribution rule and liability regime of space law for tackling MCASAs is questionable.

2.2.1 Attribution

Attribution is 'the process by which international law establishes whether the conduct of a natural person or other such intermediary can be considered an "act of State", and thus be capable of giving rise to State responsibility' (Crawford, 2013). Although it does not give rise to remedial or punitive effect *per se*, it is one of the two inevitable steps to decide the existence of an internationally wrongful act leading to remedial and/or punitive legal consequences (ILC, 2001). Space law is endowed with a special set of attribution rules, crystallised in Article VI of the OST. Unlike the attribution rules in general international law, which demands establishing a certain degree of influence of a State over the wrongdoer, space law prescribes that States Parties shall bear international responsibility for national space activities, whether they are conducted by governmental agencies or non-governmental entities. The only link that space law requires for attributing a space activity to a State Party is that the activity is a national activity of the State. When MCASAs qualify as space activities, Article VI shall apply.

As analysed above, controversies on deciding the 'nationality' of space activities exist, with the prevailing view of holding the State to exercise jurisdiction over a space activity responsible. However, applying the attribution rules of international space law does not always conform to the objectives of international space law. For example, the hypothesis provided in subsection 2.1.1.3. An individual from State A participates in a space trip organised by a company established in State B and conducts an MCA while visiting a space station operated by State C, and all three States have acceded to the OST. According to the principle that quasi-territorial jurisaction prevails over personal jurisaction, the MCASA should only be attributed to State C. The national State of the malicious cyber actor would be exempted from any legal consequence, despite the actor exercising elements of the governmental authority of the State, meeting the requirements of Article 5 of the Articles on Responsibility of States for Internationally Wrongful Acts (ARSIWA). Similarly, State B will be exempted from international responsibility, even if the company concerts with the individual under the instruction of State B. Applying this attribution rule to MCASAs may lead to unreasonable conclusions on some occasions, notably when the MCASAs from outer space involve multiple States. Furthermore, this would particularly discourage States' enthusiasm in enacting regulations on commercial space tourism, resulting in a chaotic commercial tourism sector threatening the overall space safety and security. The consequences of relying on the attribution rules of space law in some cases of MCASAs may be incongruent with the objectives of *iuris spatialis*, thus igniting the application of the attribution rules of general international law.

In addition, States responsible for space activities may fulfil their duties, however, via the space activities and provide aid or assistance to the MCASAs. According to Article VI, the contributory effect of space activities is not legally assessed. The approach to pursue States' secondary responsibility when they fulfil their duties but still help with the occurrence of MCASAs is not provided for in space law. A loophole exists in the attribution rules of space law, rendering the attribution rules of general international law applicable.

2.2.2 Liability Regime

The liability regime of space law is enshrined in Article VII of the OST and specified in the Liability Convention of 1972. It shall apply once eligible damages occur, regardless of whether the State causing the damages has committed international wrongful acts. The Liability Convention distinguishes two types of liability based on the location of damages, providing that a launching State shall bear absolute liability for 'damage caused by its space object on the surface of the Earth or to aircraft in flight' and liability for fault if the damage has been 'caused elsewhere than on the surface of the Earth to a space object of one launching State or to persons or property on board such a space object by a space object of another launching State'.

The Liability regime of space law does not have any punitive effects; its remedial effects in cases of MCASAs are questionable. First, not all compensation issues resulting from damages caused by space activities are covered by the liability regime of space law. The primary reason lies in the scope of damages. Article I of the Liability Convention defines damage as 'loss of life, personal injury or other impairment of health' or 'loss of or damage to property of States or of persons, natural or juridical, or property of intergovernmental organisations'. This definition does not hint at the causal links between damages and space activities, that is, whether the link should be direct or indirect. Although most scholars support that only the damages directly caused by the space object itself are eligible (Hobe et al., 2009; Smith & Kerrest, 2013), doubts regarding this issue continue to surface, particularly concerning its applicability to damages inflicted by space application systems such as the global navigation satellite systems (Kong, 2019). However, rashly integrating indirect damages into the current liability regime remains unfeasible, in the absence of State practice or a new consensus among States. MCASAs could cause collisions, leading to direct damages and interruption of satellite services, resulting in other losses, which could be qualified as direct or indirect damages on a case-by-case basis (Kong, 2019). Therefore, not all damages caused by MCASAs are covered by the liability regime of space law (Das, 2020).

Second, proving fault for damages in outer space is challenging. From a technical viewpoint, space activities are ultra-hazardous, highly technological activities, and normally, victims only have limited or even no access to information and data regarding space operations of foreign operators (Capurso et al., 2023), let alone in the case of MCASAs. In addition, owing to the lack of a specific definition of fault, the standards for proving fault are unclear. As there are no inevitable connections between States' violation of their obligations under international law and the fault, it would be unreasonable to link the obligations to the standards to establish fault.[1] Adopting the duty of care standard appears to be more appropriate (Capurso et al., 2023). However, the standard remains to be established without prominent judicial precedents in this respect.

Failure to receive compensation through the liability regime of space law will compel the victims to resort to other remedies. The first alternative is to prove that the State conducting the space activities has committed an internationally wrongful act, which will be followed by legal consequences, including compensation.

The second alternative lies in applying the law of State responsibility as well. The victim could prove that the State of origin of the MCA has committed international wrongful acts. However, this approach can be rather tough. Apart from the difficulties in technically (Dederer & Singer, 2019) and legally attributing the act to the State, it could be more difficult to confirm violations of international obligations by the State as States' international obligations in cyberspace are indeterminate, as demonstrated in Chapter 3. In addition, not all MCAs are conducted under a link with States; many of them are conducted entirely by private groups or individuals. The third alternative lies in domestic remedies (Smith & Kerrest, 2013). When MCAs are carried out by private entities without a link with the State, and if the State in which the activities are performed has enacted national laws to prohibit and punish such activities, domestic remedies appear to be promising. However, considering the fact that domestic regulations in this respect may significantly vary, it is possible that the victim cannot be compensated at all.

2.2.3 Sub-Conclusion

The remedial and punitive effects of space law on MCASAs are limited. First, it does not encompass a comprehensive regime to cope with States' violation of international law. The obligations prescribed by space law are ambiguous, and the attribution rules envisioned by Article VI may achieve unreasonable results confronting MCASAs. No specific space law rules are provided to deal with the content of States' responsibility. Second, the liability regime of space law is incomplete, as it only applies to limited types of damages. The regulatory loopholes in space law to punish wrongdoers and compensate the victims are evident, and therefore, reference to general international law is imperative.

2.3 Conclusion

Regulatory gaps exist in both preventive rules and remedial and punitive rules of space law facing MCASAs. Owing to several reasons, including the ambiguous terminology of the space treaties, the lack of binding force of relevant soft law instruments, and the incoherent national practices, the preventive rules have ill-defined States' substantive international obligations for preventing MCASAs. The remedial and punitive rules in space law only deal with certain aspects of State responsibility and subsequent legal consequences. Reference to general international law is imperative.

Note

1 There are scholarly propositions to link due regard obligations under Article IX of the OST to the fault standard, which are inappropriate. The liability regime of space law is somewhat independent from other provisions in that it has no inherent relation with the international obligations imposed on States. For the propositions, see for instance, Doucet, G. (2017). Fault in space: proposed approach for liability assessments in the event of accidental collisions in outer space. *Annals of Air and Space Law*, *42*, 293–316.

References

Administration of Donald J. Trump. (2020). Memorandum on cybersecurity principles for space systems. *Daily Compilation of Presidential Documents*, 1–4.

Aoki, S. (2012). The function of 'soft law' in the development of international space law. In I. Marboe (Ed.), *Soft law in outer space: The function of non-binding norms in international space law* (pp. 57–85). Böhlau Verlag.

Berman, F. (2005). Preemption and weapons of mass destruction. *International Peacekeeping*, (9), 173–182. https://doi.org/10.1163/18754112-90000037

Betts, R. K. (1998). The new threat of mass destruction. *Foreign Affairs*, *77*(26), 26–41. https://doi.org/10.2307/20048360

Byers, M. (2021). Still agreeing to disagree: International security and constructive ambiguity. *Journal on the Use of Force and International Law*, *8*(1), 91–114. https://doi.org/10.1080/20531702.2020.1761656

Capurso, A., Marzioli, P., & Boscia, M. (2023). Questions of fault liability: A case study analysis of in-orbit collisions with debris. *Journal of Space Safety Engineering*, *10*(4), 439–446. https://doi.org/10.1016/j.jsse.2023.08.001

Chartier, G. (2010). Natural law and non-aggression. *Acta Juridica Hungarica*, *51*(2), 79–96. https://doi.org/10.1556/ajur.51.2010.2.1

Cheng, B. (1998). Article VI of the 1967 space treaty revisited: "International responsibility", "national activities", and "the appropriate state". *Journal of Space Law*, *26*, 7–30.

Cheng, B. (2000). Properly speaking, only celestial bodies have been reserved for use exclusively for peaceful (Non-Military) purposes, but not outer void space. *International Law Studies Series. US Naval War College*, *75*, 81–118.

Committee on Space Research (COSPAR). (2021). *COSPAR planetary protection policy*. https://cosparhq.cnes.fr/assets/uploads/2021/07/PPPolicy_2021_3-June.pdf

Crawford, J. (2013). *State responsibility: The general part*. Cambridge University Press.

Das, I. (2020). Outer space and cyber-attacks: Attributing responsibility under international space law. *Proceedings of the International Institute of Space Law*, *63*, 309–320.

Dasgupta, U. (2016). On-orbit transfer of satellites between states legal issues with special emphasis on liability and registration. *Proceedings of the International Institute of Space Law*, *59*, 641–666.

Dederer, H., & Singer, T. (2019). Adverse cyber operations: Causality, attribution, evidence, and due diligence. *International Law Studies Series. US Naval War College*, *95*, 430–[i].

European Union (EU). (2014). *Draft international code of conduct for outer space activities*. www.eeas.europa.eu/sites/default/files/space_code_conduct_draft_vers_31-march-2014_en.pdf

Felix, K. A. (2003). Weapons of mass destruction: The changing threat and evolving solution. *McGeorge Law Review*, *34*(2), 391–397.

Freeland, S. (2011). The use of soft law within the international legal regulation of outer space. *Annals of Air and Space Law*, *36*, 409–446.

Hobe, S. (2015). The meaning of peaceful purposes in Article IV of the outer space treaty. *Annals of Air and Space Law*, *40*, 9–24.

Hobe, S., Schmidt-Tedd, B., & Schrogl, K. (Eds.) (2009). *Cologne commentary on space law, Vol. I, outer space treaty*. Carl Heymanns Verlag.

Inter-Agency Space Debris Coordination Committee (IADC). (2021). *IADC space debris mitigation guidelines*. IADC-02–1. www.iadc-home.org/documents_public/file_down/id/5249

International Law Commission (ILC). (2001). *Articles on responsibility of states for internationally wrongful acts*. ILC Yearbook, II, Part 2.

International Telecommunications Union (ITU). (2010). *Environmental protection of the geostationary-satellite orbit*. (Recommendation ITU-R S.1003–2).

ITU. (2020). *ITU radio regulations*. www.itu.int/en/publications/ITU-R/pages/publications.aspx?parent=R-REG-RR-2020&media=electronic

Kong, D. (2019). International space law for GNSS civil liability: A possible solution? *Space Policy*, *48*, 76–86. https://doi.org/10.1016/j.spacepol.2019.01.001
Lachs, M. (2010). *The law of outer space: An experience in contemporary law-making*. Nijhoff.
Lee, R. J. (2012). *Law and regulation of commercial mining of minerals in outer space*. Springer.
Li, D. (2023). upgrading space debris mitigation measures to cope with proliferating cyber threats to space activities. *Advances in Space Research*, *71*, 4185–4195. https://doi.org/10.1016/j.asr.2022.12.055
Martinez, P. (2018). Development of an international compendium of guidelines for the long-term sustainability of outer space activities. *Space Policy*, *43*, 13–17. https://doi.org/10.1016/j.spacepol.2018.01.002
Martinez, P. (2020). The role of soft law in promoting the sustainability and security of space activities. *Journal of Space Law*, *44*(2), 522–564.
Martinez, P., Crowther, R., Marchisio, S., & Brachet, G. (2014). Criteria for developing and testing transparency and confidence-building measures (TCBMs) for outer space activities. *Space Policy*, *30*, 91–97. https://doi.org/10.1016/j.spacepol.2014.03.006
Mineiro, M. C. (2010). Article IX's principle of due regard and international consultations: An assessment in light of the European draft space code-of-conduct. *Proceedings of the International Institute of Space Law*, *53*, 674–686.
Mosteshar, S. (2004). Militarization of outer space: Legality and implications for the future of space law. *Proceedings on the Law of Outer Space*, *47*, 473–480.
Nardone, V. (2017). The implementation of TCBMs in outer space activities: From the OST principles to the international space governance action. *Proceedings of the International Institute of Space Law*, *60*, 119–134.
Prasad, D. (2019). Relevance of the sustainable development concept for international space law: An analysis. *Space Policy*, *47*, 166–174. https://doi.org/10.1016/j.spacepol.2018.12.001
Robinson, J. (2016). Transparency and confidence-building measures for space security. *Space Policy*, *37*, 134–144. https://doi.org/10.1016/j.spacepol.2016.11.003
Sandalinas, J. (2010). Art IX of the outer space treaty and peaceful purposes: Issues and implementation. *Proceedings of the International Institute of Space Law*, *53*, 639–645.
Sheehan, M. (2015). Defining space security. In K-U. Schrogl, P. L. Hays, J. Robinson, D. Moura & C. Giannopapa (Eds.), *Handbook of space security: Policies, applications and programs*(pp. 7–22). Springer. https://doi.org/10.1007/978-1-4614-2029-3_47
Smith, L. J., & Kerrest, A. (2013). The 1972 convention on international liability for damages caused by space objects. In S. Hobe, B. Schmidt-Tedd & K. Schrogl (Eds.), *Cologne commentary on space law, Vol. II, rescue agreement, liability convention, registration convention, Moon agreement* (pp. 83–226). Carl Heymanns Verlag.
Spencer Jr., R. L (2010). International space law: A basis for national regulation. In R. S. Jakhu (Ed.), *National regulation of space activities*. Springer. https://doi.org/10.1007/978-90-481-9008-9_1
Stokes, H., Akahshi, Y., Bonnal, C., Destefanis, R., Gu, Y., Kato, A., Kutomanov, A., Lacroix, A., Lemmens, S., Lohvynenko, A., Oltrogge, D., Omaly, P., Opiela, J., Quan, H., Sato, K., Sorge, M., & Tang, M. (2020). Evolution of ISO's space debris mitigation standards. *Journal of Space Safety Engineering*, *7*, 325–331. https://doi.org/10.1016/j.jsse.2020.07.004
Su, J. (2010). Use of outer space for peaceful purposes: Non-militarization, non-aggression and prevention of weaponization. *Journal of Space Law*, *36*(1), 253–272.
Su, J. (2015). Space arms control: Lex lata and currently active proposals. *Asian Journal of International Law*, *7*, 61–95. https://doi.org/10.1017/S2044251315000223
Taghdiri, A. (2013). Flags of convenience and the commercial space flight industry: The inadequacy of current international law to address the opportune registration of space vehicles in flag states. *Boston University Journal of Science & Technology Law*, *19*(2), 405–431.
Tennen, L. I. (2020). The role of COSPAR for space security and planetary protection. In K-U. Schrogl (Ed.), *Handbook of space security: Policies, applications and programs*(2nd ed., pp. 1559–1580). Springer. https://doi.org/10.1007/978-3-030-22786-9_145-1

Tronchetti, F. (2009). *The exploitation of natural resources of the Moon and other celestial bodies: A proposal for a legal regime*. Nijhoff.
UN. (1945). *Charter of the United Nations.* https://treaties.un.org/doc/Publication/CTC/uncharter.pdf
UN COPUOS. (2007). *Space debris mitigation guidelines of the committee on the peaceful uses of outer space.* (UN Doc. A/62/20).
UN COPUOS. (2010). *Report of the scientific and technical subcommittee.* (UN Doc. A/AC.105/958).
UN COPUOS. (2019a). *Report of the committee on the peaceful uses of outer space.* (UNGA Resolution. A/74/20).
UN COPUOS. (2019b). *Draft guidelines for the long-term sustainability of outer space activities.* (UN Doc. A/AC.105/C.1/L.367).
UNGA. (1968). *Agreement on the rescue of astronauts, the return of astronauts and return of objects launched into outer space.* (UNGA Resolution 2345 (XXII)). UNTS. (672, No. 9574).
UNGA. (1972). *Convention on international liability for damage caused by space objects.* (UNGA Resolution 2777 (XXVI)). UNTS. (961, No. 13810).
UNGA. (1975). *Convention on registration of objects launched into outer space.* (UNGA Resolution 3235 (XXIX)). UNTS. (1023, No. 15020).
UNGA. (1977). *Prohibition of the development and manufacture of new types of weapons of mass destruction and new systems of such weapons.* (UNGA Resolution 32/84-B).
UNGA. (1979). *Agreement governing the activities of states on the moon and other celestial bodies.* (UNGA Resolution 34/68). UNTS. (1363, No. 23002).
UNGA. (2005). *Transparency and confidence-building measures in outer space activities.* (UNGA Resolution 60/66).
UNGA. (2006). *Transparency and confidence-building measures in outer space activities.* (UNGA Resolution 61/75).
UNGA. (2007). *Transparency and confidence-building measures in outer space activities.* (UNGA Resolution 62/43).
UNGA. (2011). *Transparency and confidence-building measures in outer space activities.* (UNGA Resolution 65/68).
UNGA. (2013). *Group of governmental experts on transparency and confidence-building measures in outer space activities.* (UN Doc. A/68/189).
UNGA. (2014). *No first placement of weapons in outer space.* (UNGA Resolution 69/32).
UNGA. (2015). *No first placement of weapons in outer space.* (UNGA Resolution 70/27).
UNGA. (2016a). *No first placement of weapons in outer space.* (UNGA Resolution 71/32).
UNGA. (2016b). *Prevention of an arms race in outer space.* (UNGA Resolution 71/31).
UNGA. (2017). *Further practical measures for the prevention of an arms race in outer space.* (UNGA Resolution 72/250).
UN Institute for Disarmament Research (UNIDIR). (n.d.). *A brief overview of norms development in outer space.* https://unidir.org/sites/default/files/publication/pdfs//a-brief-overview-of-norms-development-in-outer-space-en-462.pdf
UN Office for Disarmament Affairs (UNODA). (n.d.). Weapons of mass destruction. www.unrcpd.org/wmd/
United Kingdom (UK). (1986, July 18). *Outer space act of the United Kingdom.* www.legislation.gov.uk/ukpga/1986/38/contents
United Nations General Assembly (UNGA). (1967). *Treaty on principles governing the activities of states in the exploration and use of outer space, including the Moon and the other celestial bodies.* (UNGA Resolution 2222 (XXI)). UNTS. (610, No. 8843).
United States (US). (n.d.). 51 U.S. *Code § 50904—restrictions on launches, operations, and reentries.* https://uscode.house.gov/view.xhtml?req=granuleid:USC-prelim-title51-section50904&num=0&edition=prelim

von der Dunk, F. (2012). *Contradictio in terminis* or Realpolitik? A qualified plea for a role of "soft law" in the context of space activities. In I. Marboe (Ed.), *Soft law in outer space: The function of non-binding norms in international space law*(pp. 31–55). Böhlau Verlag.

Wang, Y., Hao, L., Li, Y., Sun, Q., Sun, M., Huang, Y., Li, Z., Tang, D., Wang, Y., & Xiao, L. (2022). In-situ utilization of regolith resource and future exploration of additive manufacturing for lunar/Martian habitats: A review. *Applied Clay Science*, *229*, 106673. https://doi.org/10.1016/j.clay.2022.106673

Ziemblicki, B., & Oralova, Y. (2021). Private entities in outer space activities: Liability regime reconsidered. *Space Policy*, *56*, 101427. https://doi.org/10.1016/j.spacepol.2021.101427

3 The Limitations of the Emerging Cybersecurity Norms in Combatting MCASAs

Hitherto, no internationally binding rules have been specifically devoted to cybersecurity. However, 'a thick web of international law norms suffuses cyberspace', outlawing many malevolent cyber activities and allowing States to mount robust responses (Schmitt, 2012–2013). Whilst there are debates on the conceptual aspects of international norms concerning whether they are modal forms of State behaviour that do not concern what is right or obligatory or standards of proper behaviour (Raymond, 2021), this study takes another perspective, emphasising the regulatory nature of norms. From a functional perspective, international norms related to cybersecurity could be divided into preventive and reparatory and punitive norms. For space activities, ensuring cybersecurity is essential for protecting space assets, space systems, and space missions against malicious cyber activities (MCAs), which should be realised through the joint efforts of two types of subjects: the States of origin of the MCAs and the States conducting space activities. Thus, in the context of space cybersecurity, at the international level, the preventive norms aim to establish duties or guidelines on State actions to prevent MCAs and defend space activities against MCAs. The preventive norms aim to establish duties or guidelines on State actions to prevent malicious cyber MCAs and their aftermaths. The adverse effects of MCAs may significantly vary. The most severe MCAs may amount to cybercrime, which refers to criminal activities in which a computer or information system is either the primary tool or target of attack and includes various offences (Bagdasarova, 2015). Hence, in addition to the legal consequences following the establishment of State responsibility, individual responsibility for cybercrimes may also be investigated. The rules on State responsibility and the emerging norms tackling cybercrimes constitute the reparatory and punitive norms related to cybersecurity.

Nonetheless, the effectiveness of both types of norms in combatting malicious cyber activities against space activities (MCASAs) is limited. This chapter analyses the two types of norms and argues that they are incompetent to counter MCASAs.

DOI: 10.4324/9781003561996-5

3.1 The Preventive Norms

3.1.1 Hard Law Rules

Owing to a lack of binding rules specifically dedicated to cybersecurity, referring to general international law and some *lex specialis* of international law is justified (Schmitt, 2017). Most of the rules applicable to cybersecurity for the prevention of MCAs are included in *jus ad bellum* and *jus in bello*. In addition, other principles of international law, such as sovereign equality, the protection of human rights, the cooperation principle, and the due diligence principle, are relevant as well (Kettemann, 2017). Chapter 4 provides more detailed discussions in this regard. Without specific international treaties prescribing States' international obligations for ensuring and promoting cybersecurity, the lacunae of hard law for preventing MCAs is evident.

Despite the absence of preventive hard law at the international level for securing cybersecurity, regional treaties in this respect are mushrooming. These include the Agreement between the Governments of State Members of the Shanghai Cooperation Organization (SCO) on Cooperation in the Field of Ensuring the International Information Security (Agreement of the SCO) of 2009, 'aiming to limit threats of the international information security, to provide interests of information security of Parties and to create the international information environment of which are characteristic the world, cooperation and harmony', and 'wishing to create legal and organizational basis of cooperation of the Parties in the field of ensuring the international information security' (SCO, 2009); the African Union Convention on Cyber Security and Personal Data Protection (the AUC) of 2014, aiming at 'defining the objectives and broad orientations of the Information Society in Africa and strengthening the existing legislations on ICTs (information and communications technologies) of Member States and the Regional Economic Communities' (AU, 2014); the European Union (EU) Directive on Cybersecurity of Network and Information Systems, setting out a common cybersecurity regulatory framework aiming to enhance the level of cybersecurity in the EU, requiring EU member States to strengthen cybersecurity capabilities, and introducing cybersecurity risk-management measures and reporting in critical sectors, along with rules on cooperation, information sharing, supervision, and enforcement (EU, 2022); the EU General Data Protection Regulation of 2016, which 'lays down rules relating to the protection of natural persons with regard to the processing of personal data and rules relating to the free movement of personal data' and 'protects fundamental rights and freedoms of natural persons and in particular their right to the protection of personal data' (EU, 2016); and so forth. These regional efforts for promoting cybersecurity vary significantly in terms of purposes and contents. They contribute towards ensuring regional cybersecurity; however, they result in diversification and fragmentation of preventive rules dealing with cybersecurity. For instance, the Agreement of the SCO requires State members to perform cooperation in 16 listed directions, including the 'creation of monitoring system and joint response to the threats arising in the field' of ensuring international information security, 'development of joint efforts on development of rules of international law in the field of restriction of distribution and use of the information weapon creating threats of defence capability, homeland and public security', and so on (SCO, 2009). It does not demand State members to adopt domestic measures, such as enacting domestic laws. Contrarily, the AUC stipulates expressly that

> each State Party shall commit itself to establishing a legal framework aimed at strengthening fundamental rights and public freedoms, particularly the protection of physical data, and punish any violation of privacy without prejudice to the principle of free flow of personal data
>
> (AU, 2014)

requiring States Parties to undertake national legislative measures.

3.1.2 Soft Law

Despite the absence of specific hard law, the international community is exerting efforts to enhance cybersecurity. Concerns about cybersecurity in the United States (UN) system arose early. After the acceptance by the UN General Assembly (UNGA) to include an item 'Developments in the field of information and telecommunications in the context of international security' in its agenda in 1998 (UNGA, 1999), six Governmental Groups of Experts (GGEs) have been established since 2004, among which four GGEs have agreed on substantive reports with conclusions and recommendations that all UN member States have welcomed (UNODA, n.d.). Moreover, the UNGA established two Open-Ended Working Groups (OEWG) open to all States in 2018 and 2020. The first OEWG adopted its report by consensus in 2021, which the UNGA endorsed (UNODA, n.d.). The Report of the GGE of 2021 on Advancing Responsible State Behaviour in Cyberspace in the Context of International Security, built upon the assessments and recommendations of the previous three consensus reports of the GGEs, adopted in 2010, 2013, and 2015, contains findings on the existing and emerging threats, norms, rules, and principles of responsible State behaviour, international law, confidence-building and international cooperation, and capacity-building (UNGGE, 2021). It adds an additional layer of understanding to the norms of responsible State behaviour submitted in the 2015 GGE report,

> underscoring their value with regard to the expected behaviour of States in their use of ICTs in the context of international peace and security and providing examples of the kinds of institutional arrangements that States can put in place at the national and regional levels to support their implementation.
>
> (UNGGE, 2021)

These norms concern the consistency with the purposes of the UN, including to maintain international peace and security (Norm 13(a)); the attribution issues (Norm 13 (b)); the due diligence obligations (Norm 13 (c)); the prevention of cyber-terrorism and cybercrimes (Norm 13 (d)); the protection of human rights in the cyber sphere (Norm 13 (e)); the protection of critical infrastructure against ICT operations (Norms 13 (f), (g), and (h)); the assurance of the integrity of the supply chain of ICT products and the prevention of proliferation of malicious ICT tools and techniques (Norm 13 (i)); information sharing (Norm 13 (j)); and the protection of the information systems of the authorised emergency response teams (Norm 13 (k)) (UNGGE, 2021). Under these norms, recommendations on the measures that States could adopt have been proposed. Although the norms are voluntary and non-binding, States tend to consider them as guidance regarding applying international law in cyberspace (Moynihan, 2019). For instance, under Norm 13 (a), it is suggested that States 'put in place or strengthen the existing mechanisms, structures and procedures at the national level such as relevant policy, legislation and corresponding review processes', and so forth; under Norm 13 (f),

> States are encouraged to put in place relevant policy and legislative measures at the national level to ensure that ICT activities conducted or supported by a State and that may impact the critical infrastructure of or the delivery of essential public services in another State are consistent with this norm.

Similarly, the recommendations in the OEWG report do not purport to replace or alter States' obligations or rights under international law. Instead, they provide additional specific guidance on what constitutes responsible State behaviour in the use of ICTs (OEWG, 2021). They are attempts to define States' international obligations under the current international law rather than create new duties for States.

All these efforts aim to establish behaviour standards for the States from which the ICT activities originate and the States that are involved in ICT activities. In the context of MCASAs, although the States of origin of the MCAs are the major addressees of the norms, the State responsible for the space activities involved is also concerned, notably by Norm 13 (c) on the due diligence obligations in cyberspace articulated in the Report of the GGE of 2021. The due diligence obligation is defined in the Corfu Channel case as 'every State's obligation not to allow knowingly its territory to be used for acts contrary to the rights of other States' (ICJ, 1949). According to the Corfu Channel case, due diligence obligation is a well-recognised principle of international law applicable generally to all States (ICJ, 1949), aiming to prevent, stop, or redress various harms or risks to persons, property, or territory, ranging from internationally wrongful acts to lawful activities or even accidents (Dias & Coco, 2021). However, the nature of due diligence is controversial as it is deemed as a self-standing obligation or a standard of conduct (Dias & Coco, 2021). In the cyber context, the extent to which States accept due diligence as either a principle of general international law or as a rule of conduct, whether States owe due diligence obligations and the content of such an obligation remains to be determined (Liu, 2017; Jensen & Watts, 2021). Norm 13 (c), which articulates that 'States should not knowingly allow their territory to be used for internationally wrongful acts using ICTs' contributes to clarifying these issues. It

> reflects an expectation that if a State is aware of or is notified in good faith that an internationally wrongful act conducted using ICTs is emanating from

> or transiting through its territory it will take all appropriate and reasonably available and feasible steps to detect, investigate and address the situation.
> (UNGGE, 2021)

Under this norm, it is expected that a State will 'take reasonable steps within its capacity' to stop the ongoing activity in its territory and, in case of incapacity, to seek assistance from other States or the private sector in conformity with international and domestic law. It hints at the measures that a State should undertake when an MCA is conducted in its territory or is transiting through its territory. This norm is inspiring for understanding the content of the due diligence obligations in the case of MCASAs, not only for the States from which the MCASA is conducted but also for the State responsible for the space activities involved. Particularly, for the State responsible for space activities, this norm would mean that when its space activities are manipulated for the accomplishment of an MCASA, the State should take 'proportionate, appropriate and effective' means to end the ongoing cyber invasion. Nonetheless, as indicated in the 2021 report of the GGE, 'it is not expected that States could or should monitor all ICT activities within its territory', it would be unrealistic to expect that all ongoing MCASAs be ended by the States of origin or by the States responsible for space activities. All that is required to establish that the due diligence obligations have been performed is to adopt 'proportionate, appropriate and effective' means. The meanings of the words 'proportionate', 'appropriate', and 'effective' necessitate further clarification. They should be interpreted in a balanced manner, considering both the need to ensure space cybersecurity and the technical and economic feasibility for the States involved.

Efforts made by other international governmental organisations to ensure cybersecurity could be best represented by the Global Cybersecurity Agenda (GCA) launched in 2007 by the International Telecommunications Union (ITU), aiming to encourage collaboration amongst all relevant partners in building confidence and security in the use of ICTs (Schjølberg, 2008). The GCA functions as a framework for international cooperation in the area of cybersecurity. It is built upon five strategic pillars: legal measures (Work Area one, WA 1), technical & procedural measures (Work Area two, WA 2), organisational structures (Work Area three, WA 3), capacity building (Work Area four, WA 4) and international cooperation (Work Area five, WA 5). Extensive discussions are spread over WA 1, which seeks to 'promote cooperation and provide strategic advice to the ITU Secretary-General on legislative responses to address evolving legal issues in cybersecurity', and WA 2, focusing on 'key measures for addressing vulnerabilities in software products, including accreditation schemes, protocols and standards' (Schjølberg, 2008). Concerning WA 1, consensus was reached only on a few recommendations. States agreed on the significance of cooperation among the police, governments and other elements of the criminal justice system, the International Criminal Police Organisation and other international organisations, the public, the private sector and non-governmental organisations, and the obligation to preserve the fundamental rights to privacy and human rights when conducting cybercrime investigation and prosecution (Schjølberg, 2008). No consensus was achieved on the recommendations of WA 2. General consensus has been achieved on the recommendations of WAs 3, 4, and 5. The recommendations included in the Chairman's Report of the 2008 High-Level Experts Group (HLEG) remain relevant today, whereas further elaboration of appropriate guidelines of the GCA may be required to bring better clarity and effectiveness in implementing the GCA recommendations, considering the complexity of the issues involved in the fast-changing ICT ecosystem, as the ICT landscape has changed drastically since 2008 (ITU, 2019a). Pursuant to the instructions of the ITU Council (ITU, 2019b) and after several years of preparation and consultations, a report explaining how the ITU is currently using the GCA framework was developed by the ITU secretariat (ITU, 2021a), and the guidelines for utilisation of the GCA were formulated (ITU, 2021b). Concerning WA 1 on legal measures, the report highlights as an example of ITU's activities that ITU collaborates with partners to assist member States in understanding the legal aspects of cybersecurity through its ITU Cybercrime Legislation Resources aiming to help to harmonise their legal frameworks, as it is deemed an integral component of any national cybersecurity strategy 'the adoption of appropriate legislation against the misuse of ICTs for criminal purposes and harmonised with regional and international policy and practices' (ITU, 2021a). As for WA 2 on technical and procedural measures, the report indicates that ITU study groups provide a neutral, global platform for ITU's membership to collaborate on security-related standardisation on a variety of topics, and highlights that ITU should continue its efforts to develop and disseminate cybersecurity guidelines and recommendations (ITU, 2021b). The Guidelines for Utilisation of the GCA emphasise the significance of international cooperation in all WAs without furthering any substantial recommendations (ITU, 2021b). The work of the ITU in terms of cybersecurity is remarkable, covering both preventive and punitive approaches for tackling this issue of global concern. It helps to foster new standards and best practices in this regard. As cybersecurity issues are relevant to various interests, notably those cherished at the national level, such as defence and national security interests, harmonising relevant national legislation would be tough. Although the work of the GCA sheds some light on the measures that States should undertake to counter cybercrimes, such as national legislations and procedural tools, the GCA remains a suggested non-binding framework (Bagdasarova,2015), with various factors deciding its effectiveness.

Moreover, efforts to ensure cybersecurity at the regional level are remarkable. Cybersecurity considerations are included in the Strategic Action Plans 2016–2020 and 2021–2025 of the Asia-Pacific Economic Cooperation (APEC) Telecommunications and Information Working Group (TEL WG) (APEC TEL, 2015, 2020). The TEL WG continues to promote the importance of cybersecurity through engaging in capacity building on preventing and combatting cybercrime, responding to computer security incidents, and implementing cybersecurity awareness initiatives (APEC TEL, 2020). At the Paris Peace Forum of 2018, a declaration titled the Paris Call for Trust and Security in Cyberspace (the Paris Call) was made by France and has been endorsed by about 80 States, 35 public authorities and local governments, more than 700 companies, and almost 400 civil society entities (The Paris

Call, 2021). Aiming to develop common principles for securing cybersecurity, the Paris Call provides a platform for a multistakeholder approach to tackle cybersecurity issues and develops recommendations on nine principles, including protecting individuals and infrastructure, protecting the Internet, defending electoral processes, defending intellectual property, non-proliferation, lifecycle security and supply chain security, cyber hygiene, no private hack back, and international norms (The Paris Call, 2021). Recognising the powerful contribution to the economic, social, cultural, and political life of the Commonwealth made by the development of cyberspace and the interest in protecting the security of the networks, security of data, the people that use them, and the services that run on them, participants to the Commonwealth Heads of Governments Meeting of 2018 unanimously agreed upon the Commonwealth Cyber Declaration, establishing the commitments made by Heads of Government purporting to build the foundations of an effective national cybersecurity response and to promote stability in cyberspace through international cooperation (The Commonwealth Heads of Governments Meeting, 2018). To implement the commitments made in the Commonwealth Cyber Declaration, four projects, centred respectively on African cyber resilience, electronic evident training in the Caribbean, international cooperation, and election cybersecurity, have been launched. Moreover, cybersecurity is addressed in some comprehensive instruments, such as the 10th BRICS Summit Johannesburg Declaration (BRICs Summit, 2018) and the G-20 Leaders Declaration of the G-20 Summit 2018 titled 'Building Consensus for Fair and Sustainable Development' (G-20 Summit, 2018). The regional initiatives help to enrich the norms to guarantee cybersecurity; nonetheless, as most initiatives are macroscopical and the participants are usually subject to regional restrictions, the contribution of these efforts to developing international cybersecurity norms is fragmented and limited.

Private entities are contributing to the formation of international norms on cybersecurity as well. In 2018, 34 global technology and security companies signed the Cybersecurity Tech Accord, which gathers more than 150 signatories and countless engagements and consultations with governments, civil society, and private sector partners (Tech Accord, 2023). Signatories are committed to protecting all users and customers everywhere, opposing cyberattacks on innocent citizens and enterprises from anywhere, helping empower users, customers, and developers to strengthen cybersecurity protection and partnering with each other and with like-minded groups to enhance cybersecurity (Tech Accord, 2023).

3.1.3 Sub-Conclusion

Preventive hard and soft laws for ensuring cybersecurity are surging; however, their drawbacks for preventing MCASAs are apparent. First, the current international cybersecurity rules and norms are fragmented horizontally and vertically. No universally binding instruments have been adopted at the international level, whereas several conventions or legislations have been adopted at the regional level. Soft law instruments are adopted globally and regionally on governmental platforms and by the private sector. The focuses and contents of these instruments differ significantly, with some covering several issues in the scope of cybersecurity, some only dealing with specific aspects, and some more comprehensive instruments only recognising the importance of cybersecurity. The mushrooming national legislation further intensifies the fragmentation, leading to difficulties in implementing the international and regional instruments. Second, the international legislation on cybersecurity is at its primitive stage, and the content is incomplete. Although recommendations have been made by the UN GGEs and the principles have been announced in the Paris Call, they remain general and cannot be applied directly. Their substantive content remains to be developed and enriched through practice. Third, in the context of space cybersecurity, most of the preventive norms only apply to the States of origin of MCAs. The few rules that are applicable to the State conducting space activities may not be entirely appropriate. For instance, the due diligence principle, as addressed in Norm 13 (c) of the UN GGE reports. As enormous gaps exist even among spacefaring States in terms of cyber technologies, and technical loopholes are left to malicious cyber actors by obsolete space objects that continue to function (Li, 2023), ending MCASAs in a proportionate, appropriate, and effective manner is not always possible or may be excessively expensive. The interpretation of the 2021 report of the due diligence principle in cyberspace would impose excessive burden on States carrying out space activities.

3.2 The Punitive Norms

3.2.1. Hard Law

With the absence of an international definition of cybercrime or cyberattacks, cyber offences typically cluster around the following categories according to the UN Office on Drugs and Crime (UNODC): computer-related offences, content-related offences, and offences related to infringement of copyright and related rights (UNODC, n.d.a). Legal measures are crucial to the prevention and combatting of cybercrime and are necessary in all related areas, covering criminalisation, procedural powers, jurisdiction, international cooperation, and Internet service provider responsibility and liability (UNODC, 2013). The current conventions on cybercrimes, whether regional or international, adopted or in process, are mostly comprehensive instruments comprising punitive rules, preventive measures, procedural requirements, and so on. The punitive rules on cybercrimes, typically seeking to criminalise certain cyber offences so that the wrongdoers will bear the harshest legal consequences, are significant for deterring the potential wrongdoers in the cyberspace realm.

Initiatives to adopt conventions on cybercrimes originate from the regional level. The Convention on Cybercrime (the Budapest Convention), adopted by the Council of Europe in 2001, could best represent the results of regional efforts. It is a treaty designed to police cybercrimes through international cooperation (Council of Europe, 2001). State parties to the Budapest Convention are committed to adopting 'such legislative and other measures as may be necessary to establish as criminal offences under its domestic law' the following offences:

offences against the confidentiality, integrity, and availability of computer data and systems, including illegal access, illegal interception, data interference, system interference, and misuse of devices; computer-related offences, including computer-related forgery and computer-related fraud; content-related offences, including offences related to child pornography and offences related to infringements of copyright and related rights; the acts of aiding or abetting intentionally the commission of the above established offences; and intentional attempts to commit any of the offences established in accordance with Articles 3 through 5, 7, 8, and 9.1.a and c of the Convention (Council of Europe, 2001). Moreover, it requires State parties to ensure that the criminal offences established are punishable by effective, proportionate, and dissuasive sanctions, including deprivation of liberty, and that liable legal persons are subject to effective, proportionate, and dissuasive criminal or non-criminal sanctions or measures, including monetary sanctions (Council of Europe, 2001). The 1st Additional Protocol to the Budapest Convention adds acts of a racist and xenophobic nature committed through computer systems to the list of offences that should be criminalised (Council of Europe, 2003). Unlike the Rome Statute of the International Criminal Court, which directly addresses crimes (UNGA, 1998), the Budapest Convention adopts an indirect approach by imposing on State parties the obligations to criminalise and punish certain offences domestically. This approach echoes the Convention's aim to harmonise international laws by prescribing a number of uniform offences, which makes it a pioneering text of wide legal scope (O'Herlihy, 2003). The Budapest Convention now gathers 68 parties and 21 countries that have signed or been invited to accede, most of which are European countries, with only a small number of States from other regions of the world, including notably Canada, Japan, and the United States (Council of Europe, n.d.). Without global participation, the Budapest Convention largely remains a regional instrument rather than an international one.

In addition, other regions have attempted to address cybercrimes through regional treaties. The Arab Convention on Combatting Information Technology Offences requires State parties to criminalise offences by means of information technology of illicit access, illicit interception, misuse of information technology means, forger, fraud, and pornography, offences against privacy, offences related to terrorism, organised crime committed by means of information technology, offences related to copyright and adjacent rights, illicit use of electronic payment tools, and attempt at and participation in the commission of offences and to arrange for the penal responsibility of the wrongdoers (League of Arab States, 2010). Further, the EU adopted a Directive on attacks against information systems, aiming to harmonise national legislation of member States in the specific area of attacks against information systems by establishing minimum rules concerning the definition of criminal offences and the relevant sanctions and to improve cooperation between competent authorities (EU, 2013).

These regional efforts represent a good starting point for combatting cybercrimes and thus ensuring cybersecurity. Nonetheless, their drawbacks are apparent. Inconsistency among regional treaties would result in inconsistency of national legislation, possibly leading to conflict of laws. Moreover, considering the transboundary feature of cyber offences, instruments on the international level continue to be indispensable.

Concerned with the need to address cybercrimes internationally with hard law instruments, the UNGA adopted Resolution 74/247, which established an Ad Hoc Committee to Elaborate a Comprehensive International Convention on Countering the Use of Information and Communications Technologies for Criminal Purposes (Ad Hoc Committee), comprising experts and representatives of all regions (UNGA, 2019). The sessions convened by the Ad Hoc Committee on creating the international convention were planned to take three years. With the first session held in 2022, the Ad Hoc Committee completed its tasks at the beginning of 2024 as scheduled. A draft resolution for consideration by the General Assembly (UN Ad Hoc Committee, 2023) and a draft convention against cybercrimes have been finalised (UN Ad Hoc Committee, 2024). The draft convention contains nine chapters: in addition to a preamble, they are dedicated to general provisions, criminalisation, jurisdiction, procedural measures and law enforcement, international cooperation, preventive measures, technical assistance and information exchange, mechanism of implementation, and final provisions, respectively (UN Ad Hoc Committee, 2024). The draft convention adopts a similar approach to the Budapest Convention in that it requires State parties to criminalise and punish cyber offences through domestic legislation and measures. The cyber offences addressed in the draft convention include illegal access, illegal interception, interference with electronic data, interference with an information and communications technology system, misuse of devices, information and communications technology system-related forgery, information and communications technology system-related theft or fraud, several content-related offences, laundering of proceeds of crime, offences relating to other international treaties, and participation and attempt to the offences listed (UN Ad Hoc Committee, 2024). It requests States Parties to adopt legislative and other measures to combat these crimes, establish liability, and prescribe sanctions to the wrongdoers (UN Ad Hoc Committee, 2024). Moreover, the draft convention requires States Parties to establish their territorial and personal jurisdiction over the cyber offences addressed in the convention (UN Ad Hoc Committee, 2024). It is noteworthy that Article 22 expressly stipulates that a State Party should extend their jurisdiction over offences which are 'committed on board a vessel that is flying the flag of that State Party or an aircraft that is registered under the laws of that State Party at the time when the offence is committed', ignoring the case where the offence is conducted in a spacecraft. For a better implementation of the convention, a mechanism of implementation should be framed: a Conference of the States Parties shall be established 'to improve the capacity of and cooperation between States Parties to achieve the objectives set forth in this Convention and to promote and review its implementation' (UN Ad Hoc Committee, 2024). The draft resolution submitted that all States and competent regional economic integration organisations are urged 'to sign and ratify the [convention] as soon as possible in order to ensure its rapid entry into force' (UN Ad Hoc Committee, 2023).

Several cyber offences that are included in the Budapest Convention and the Draft Convention against Cybercrimes are relevant to MCASAs, notably offences of illegal access, illegal interception, interference with computer systems and data, misuse of devices, and so forth. These two instruments help enhance States' awareness of the threats of cyber offences, urge States to undertake domestic measures, and harmonise national legislation in this respect. The more States criminalise and sentence these offences, the more deterred the potential wrongdoers would be. Nonetheless, the prevailing approach of elaborating cybercrime-related conventions has not only received praise; it is submitted that it would be more beneficial if the Convention itself contained the crime elements instead of requiring the parties to create their own (Hopkins, 2003). The approach of the Rome Statute of the International Criminal Court would be more plausible, as it could better guarantee the coherence of implementation and avoid problems arising out of jurisdictional and procedural issues. Regrettably, considering the subtleness of cyber issues, conceptual uncertainties in some respects, and the multitude of relevant entities (Kerekes, 2021), adopting the approach of the Rome Statute would be highly challenging.

3.2.2. Other Instruments

In addition to developing a comprehensive international treaty on cybercrime, the UN adopted other initiatives. In 2009, the UNGA drew attention to cybercrime as an emerging policy issue and invited the UNODC to explore, within its mandate, ways and means of addressing this issue (UNGA, 2009). In 2011, the UNGA, by Resolution 65/230, requested the UNODC to aim for sustainable and long-lasting results in the prevention, prosecution, and punishment of crime, in particular by building, modernising, and strengthening criminal justice systems, as well as promoting the rule of law, increasing the capacity of requesting States to prevent and suppress the various types of crime affecting societies, including cybercrime (UNGA, 2011). Following the UNGA's requests, the Commission on Crime Prevention and Criminal Justice (CCPCJ) adopted Resolutions 22/7 and 22/8, requesting the UNODC to continue to provide, upon request, technical assistance and training to States, based on national needs, particularly with regard to prevention, detection, investigation, and prosecution of cybercrime in all its forms (CCPCJ, 2011a, 2011b). In response to these requests, the UNODC launched the Global Programme on Cybercrime in 2013 to assist member States in their combat against cyber-related crimes through capacity building and technical assistance. Considering the dimensions of cybercrime risks, the specialised areas involving and traversing this type of criminality, and the different capacities that member States possess to counter it, the Global Programme on Cybercrime promotes long-term, sustainable capacity building to prevent and counter cybercrime through supporting national structures (UNODC, n.d.b). In addition to efforts to achieve normative consensus, the Programme applies a programmatic approach, delivering technical assistance drawn upon the specialised expertise on criminal justice systems response of the UNODC to capacity building/technical assistance, cooperation, and normative assistance/legal framework and prevention (UNODC, n.d.b).

Moreover, the UNGA Resolution 65/230 requests the CCPCJ to establish an open-ended intergovernmental expert group to conduct a comprehensive study of the problem of cybercrime and different Stakeholder responses to it, including the exchange of information on national legislation, best practices, technical assistance, and international cooperation (UNGA, 2011). The report was finalised in 2013, covering eight topics: connectivity and cybercrime, the global picture, legislation and frameworks, criminalisation, law enforcement and investigations, electronic evidence and criminal justice, international cooperation, and prevention (UNODC, 2013). The major findings of the report demonstrate that the international rules to counter cybercrimes are fragmented, whereas national rules are limited. They include (1) fragmentation at the international level and diversity of national cybercrime laws; correlating with the existence of multiple instruments with different thematic and geographic scope may lead to the emergence of country cooperation 'clusters' that are not always suited to the global nature of cybercrime; (2) reliance on traditional means of formal international cooperation in cybercrime matters is not currently able to offer the timely response needed for obtaining volatile electronic evidence; (3) the role of evidence 'location' needs to be reconceptualised; (4) there is insufficient harmonisation of 'core' cybercrime offences, investigative power, and admissibility of electronic evidence among national legal frameworks; (5) law enforcement authorities, prosecutors, and judiciary in developing countries require long-term, sustainable comprehensive technical support and assistance; (6) cybercrime prevention activities in all countries require strengthening (UNODC, 2013). This report reveals the significance of the regulatory approach in combatting cybercrimes and confirms the necessity to harmonise national laws and enhance international cooperation in this respect. Based on the responses of States, the report summarises four options to strengthen the existing and proposed new national and international legal or other responses to cybercrime: the development of international model provisions, a multilateral instrument on international cooperation regarding electronic evidence in criminal matters, a comprehensive multilateral instrument on cybercrime, and the delivery of enhanced technical assistance for the prevention and combatting of cybercrime in developing countries (UNODC, 2013). The report received comments from 22 States and the EU (UNODC, n.d.c). According to the status quo of international legislation on cybercrime, all options have been considered and implemented or are in the process of implementation.

Other international organisations are also concerned with cybercrime problems besides the UN. The Association of Southeast Asian Nations (ASEAN) adopted the ASEAN Declaration to Prevent and Combat Cybercrime in 2017, aiming at strengthening the commitment of ASEAN member States to cooperate at the regional level in preventing and combatting cybercrime through several measures, including acknowledging the importance of harmonisation of laws related to cybercrime and electronic evidence, encouraging ASEAN member States to explore the feasibility of acceding to the existing regional and international instruments in combatting cybercrime, and so on (ASEAN, 2017). Moreover, some general instruments on cyberspace contain norms combatting cybercrime, such as the Strategic Action Plans of the APEC TEL WG and the Paris Call.

3.2.3 Sub-Conclusion

The current punitive norms, binding and non-binding, are characterised by several features. First, they adopt an indirect approach, promoting the criminalisation and punishment of cyber offences through harmonising domestic laws and practices without prescribing uniform constitutive elements, penalty measurements, procedural requirements, and so forth. They rely on national legislation and practice to combat cybercrime. Second, most of the instruments are comprehensive documents comprising, in addition to punitive rules, preventive rules and international cooperation requirements. The preventive rules contained in these instruments generally request States to adopt national measures and standards. Third, the cyber offences addressed in the instruments are similar, covering computer-related offences, content-related offences, and offences related to infringement of copyright and related rights. All these types of cybercrimes are relevant to MCASAs. As in MCASAs, malicious cyber actors access the space system illegally, with various intentions, including but not limited to intercepting the transmission of space data, interfering with space data and other space systems, disseminating unlawful content, and so forth. Fourth, all these instruments focus on the obligations to adopt national measures of the State of origin or the State victim of cyber offences. They ignore the specific situation where the cyber offences are conducted in outer space. In the case of MCASAs, whether the States responsible for space activities should also adopt national measures to punish the operators of space activities if the operators fail in their duties, deliberately or negligently, leading to the occurrence of cyber offences on or in their space objects or transmitted through their space systems, is not considered.

3.3 Conclusion

International norms regarding cybersecurity remain in the process of formation and reification. No globally binding preventive or punitive instruments have been adopted yet. It appears that binding preventive instruments will have a longer period to wait, notably considering the severe fragmentation of the existing norms and the participation of multi-stakeholders. Preventive soft law instruments elucidate States' obligations to promote cybersecurity. However, given the particularities of space activities, they may not be entirely suitable for determining States' standard conduct in MCASAs, notably the States responsible for the space activities involved. In addition, their non-binding nature further undermines their applicability. Punitive instruments focus on combatting cybercrimes through punishing the wrongdoers. With a regional binding treaty on cybercrime already gathering more than 60 States Parties and an international treaty on cybercrime in process under the auspices of the UN, a globally binding punitive instrument is likely to become a reality soon. However, almost all punitive instruments, regional or international, binding or non-binding, adopt the same indirect approach of harmonising domestic laws and practices, leaving the choice to individual States. The punitive effects of national legislation may differ significantly. The fact that not all actors engaged in MCASAs are addressed by the current punitive instruments countering cybercrimes strengthens the deficiency of the latter in ensuring space cybersecurity.

To conclude, the emerging cybersecurity norms are important for regulating States' activities in cyberspace. However, their lack of binding force and the fact that the 'space' factor is not considered during their conception render them insufficient for promoting space cybersecurity.

References

African Union (AU). (2014). *African Union convention on cyber security and personal data protection.* https://au.int/sites/default/files/treaties/29560-treaty-0048_-_african_union_convention_on_cyber_security_and_personal_data_protection_e.pdf

APEC TEL. (2020). APEC TEL WG strategic action plan 2021–2025. www.apec.org/docs/default-source/groups/tel/tel-sap-2021–2025.docx

Asia-Pacific Economic Cooperation Telecommunications and Information Working Group (APEC TEL). (2015). *APEC TEL WG strategic action plan 2016–2020.* www.apec.org/docs/default-source/Groups/TEL/APEC_TEL_Strategic_Action_Plan_2016–2020.pdf?la=en&hash=6CB6B7DB14210FB8435DEBBC23CB55ABE9936896

Association of Southeast Asian Nations (ASEAN). (2017). The ASEAN declaration to prevent and combat cybercrime. https://asean.org/wp-content/uploads/2017/11/ASEAN-Declaration-to-Combat-Cybercrime.pdf

Bagdasarova, S. (2015). Brave new world: Challenges in international cybersecurity strategy and the need for centralized governance. *Penn State Law Review, 119*(4), 1005–1032.

BRICs Summit. (2018). *10th BRICS summit Johannesburg declaration.* www.ilo.org/wcmsp5/groups/public/—dgreports/—cabinet/documents/Statement/wcms_771296.pdf

CCPCJ. (2011b). *Promoting technical assistance and capacity-building to strengthen national measures and international cooperation against cybercrime. commission resolution 22/8.* www.unodc.org/documents/commissions/CCPCJ/Crime_Resolutions/2010–2019/2013/CCPCJ/Resolution_22–8.pdf

Commission on Crime Prevention and Criminal Justice (CCPCJ). (2011a). *Strengthening international cooperation to combat cybercrime.* commission resolution 22/7. www.unodc.org/documents/commissions/CCPCJ/Crime_Resolutions/2010–2019/2013/CCPCJ/Resolution_22–7.pdf

The Commonwealth Heads of Governments Meeting. (2018). *Commonwealth cyber declaration.* https://production-new-commonwealth-files.s3.eu-west-2.amazonaws.com/s3fs-public/2022–01/2%20Commonwealth%20Cyber%20Declaration%20.pdf?VersionId=AW6.eNDNfAtLT0gXO.oKQv3JgGN3LXEO

Council of Europe. (n.d.). Parties/observers to the Budapest convention and observer organizations to the T-CY. www.coe.int/en/web/cybercrime/parties-observers

Council of Europe. (2001). *Convention on cybercrime.* European Treaty Series. (No.185).

Council of Europe. (2003). *Addiction protocol to the convention on cybercrime, concerning the criminalization of acts of a racist and xenophobic nature committed through computer systems.* European Treaty Series. (No.189).

Dias, T., & Coco, A. (2021). 'Cyber due diligence': A patchwork of protective obligations in international law. *EJIL, 32*(3), 771–805. https://doi.org/10.1093/ejil/chab056

European Union (EU). (2013). Directive 2013/40/EU of the European parliament and of the council of 12 August 2013 on attacks against information systems and replacing council framework decision 2005/222/JHA. *OJL, 218*, 8–14.

EU. (2016). Regulation (EU) 2016/679 of the European parliament and of the council O of 27 April 2016 on the protection of natural persons with regard to the processing of personal data and on the free movement of such data, and repealing directive 95/46/EC (General Data Protection Regulation). *Official Journal of the EU, 119*, 1–88.

EU. (2022). Directive (EU) 2022/2555 of the European parliament and of the council of 14 December 2022 on measures for a high common level of cybersecurity across the union, amending regulation (EU) No 910/2014 and directive (EU) 2018/1972, and repealing directive (EU) 2016/1148 (NIS 2 Directive). *Official Journal of the EU, 333*, 80–152.

G-20 Summit. (2018). *G-20 leaders' declaration: Building consensus for fair and sustainable development.* www.consilium.europa.eu/media/37247/buenos_aires_leaders_declaration.pdf

Hopkins, S. L. (2003). Cybercrime convention: A positive beginning to long road ahead. *Journal of High Technology Law, 2*(1), 101–122.

International Court of Justice (ICJ). (1949, December 15). Corfu channel (United Kingdom of Great Britain and Northern Ireland v. Albania). Merits judgment of. *ICJ Reports*, 4.

International Telecommunications Union (ITU). (2019a). *Report by the secretary-general: Transmission of the report from the former chairman of GCA high-level experts group.* ITU Document. (C19/58-E).

ITU. (2019b). *Summary record of the sixth plenary meeting.* ITU Document. (C19/117-E).

ITU. (2021a). *Report by the secretary-general: A report explaining how the ITU Is currently utilizing the global cybersecurity agenda (GCA) framework.* ITU Document. (C21/36-E).

ITU. (2021b). *Report by the secretary-general: Guidelines for utilization of the global cybersecurity agenda.* ITU Document. (C21/71-E).

Jensen, E., & Watts, S. (2021). Cyber due diligence. *Oklahoma Law Review, 73*(4), 645–710.

Kerekes, L. (2021). 'Waiting for godot': The challenges of codifying convention against cybercrime. *Debreceni Jogi Muhely Legal Workshop of Debrecen, 2021*(3–4), 32–41.

Kettemann, M. C. (2017). Ensuring cybersecurity through international law. *Revista Española de Derecho Internacional, 69*(2), 281–289. https://doi.org/10.17103/redi.69.2.2017.2.01

League of Arab States. (2010). Arab convention on combatting information technology offences. www.asianlaws.org/gcld/cyberlawdb/GCC/Arab%20Convention%20on%20Combating%20Information%20Technology%20Offences.pdf

Li, D. (2023). Cyber-attacks on space activities: Revisiting the responsibility regime of Article VI of the outer space treaty. *Space Policy, 63*, 101522. https://doi.org/10.1016/j.spacepol.2022.101522

Liu, I. (2017). State responsibility and cyberattacks: Defining due diligence obligations. *Indonesian Journal of International & Comparative Law, 4*(2), 191–260.

Moynihan, H. (2019, December). *The application of international law to state cyberattacks: Sovereignty and non-intervention.* www.chathamhouse.org/sites/default/files/publications/research/2019-11-29-Intl-Law-Cyberattacks.pdf

O'Herlihy, E. (2003). The cybercrime convention: Pioneering text of international legal scope. *Hibernian Law Journal, 4*, 145–176.

The Paris Call. (2021). *Advancing international cyber norms: Multistakeholder recommendations.* https://pariscall.international/assets/files/WG4-Final-Report-101121.pdf

Raymond, G. A. (2021). International norms. In *International norms and the resort to war* (pp. 23–48). Palgrave Macmillan. https://doi.org/10.1007/978–3-030–54012–8_2

Schjølberg, S. (2008). *Report of the chairman of high-level experts group to ITU secretary-general.* www.itu.int/en/action/cybersecurity/Documents/gca-chairman-report.pdf

Schmitt, M. N. (2012–2013). Cyberspace and international law: The penumbral mist of uncertainty. *Harvard Law Review Forum, 126*, 176–180.

Schmitt, M. N. (Ed.). (2017). *Tallinn manual 2.0 on the international law applicable to cyber warfare.* Cambridge University Press. https://doi.org/10.1017/9781316822524

Shanghai Cooperation Organization (SCO). (2009). *The agreement between the governments of state members of the Shanghai cooperation organization on cooperation in the field of ensuring the international information security.* https://cis-legislation.com/document.fwx?rgn=28340

Tech Accord. (2023). *Building a voice for peace and security online: The cybersecurity tech accord's first five years.* https://cybertechaccord.org/building-a-voice-for-peace-and-security-online-the-cybersecurity-tech-accords-first-five-years/

UN Ad Hoc Committee. (2023). *Draft resolution for consideration by the general assembly*. (UN Doc. A/AC.291/25).
UN Ad Hoc Committee. (2024, February 6). *Further revised draft text of the convention*. (UN Doc. A/AC.291/22/Rev.2).
UNGA. (1999). *Developments in the field of information and telecommunications in the context of international security*. (UNGA Resolution A/RES/53/70).
UNGA. (2009). *Strengthening the United Nations crime prevention and criminal justice programme in particular its technical cooperation capacity*. (UNGA Resolution A/RES/64/179).
UNGA. (2011). *Twelfth United nations congress on crime prevention and criminal justice*. (UNGA Resolution A/RES/65/230).
UNGA. (2019). *Countering the use of information and communications technologies for criminal purposes*. (UNGA Resolution 74/247).
UN General Assembly (UNGA). (1998). *Rome statute of the international criminal court*. UNTS. (2187, 3).
UN Group of Governmental Experts (UNGGE). (2021). *Report of the group of governmental experts on advancing responsible state behaviour in cyberspace in the context of international security*. (UN Doc. A/76/135).
UNODC. (n.d.a). *Cybercrime*. www.unodc.org/e4j/en/mun/crime-prevention/cybercrime.html
UNODC. (n.d.b). *UNODC global programme on cybercrime: Our approach*. www.unodc.org/unodc/en/cybercrime/our-approach
UNODC. (n.d.c). *Comments to the comprehensive study on cybercrime*. www.unodc.org/unodc/en/organized-crime/comments-to-the-comprehensive-study-on-cybercrime.html
UN Office for Disarmament Affairs (UNODA) (n.d.). Developments in the field of information and telecommunications in the context of international security. https://disarmament.unoda.org/ict-security/
UN Office on Drugs and Crime (UNODC). (2013). *Comprehensive study on cybercrime*. www.unodc.org/documents/organized-crime/UNODC_CCPCJ_EG.4_2013/CYBERCRIME_STUDY_210213.pdf
UN Open-ended Working Group on Developments in the Field of Information and Telecommunications in the Context of International Security (OEWG). (2021). *Report of the open-ended working group on developments in the field of information and telecommunications in the context of international security*. (UN Doc. A/75/816).

4 The Applicability of Other Branches of International Law

In addition to international space law and cyber law, other branches of international law may apply to combat malicious cyber activities against space activities (MCASAs); however, only under particular circumstances to cope with specific aspects of MCASAs: where MCASAs risk polluting the outer space environment, some principles of international environmental law may intervene; when MCASAs are used in an armed conflict or constitute use of force, the law of armed conflicts shall be applicable; where MCASAs threaten the health or lives of human beings in outer space or other people's human rights on earth, human rights law may apply; conducting MCACAs may also constitute international crimes where the criteria are satisfied. They complement international space law and cyber law, notably for preventing some dire consequences of MCASAs. Nonetheless, their contribution to reducing the challenges of international space law and the existing cyber norms in ensuring space cybersecurity is minimal.

4.1 The Applicability of International Environmental Law

International environmental law was developed in the late twentieth century when serious scientific, public, and political attention focused on the world's environmental problems (Nanda & Pring, 2013). It is founded on multiple sources listed in Article 38 of the Statute of the International Court of Justice (ICJ), comprising international conventions and customs, the general principles of law recognised by civilised nations, judicial decisions, and the teachings of the most highly qualified publicists of the various nations (ICJ, 1946). Statistics reveal that by the beginning of the second decade of the twenty-first century, this branch of international law already consisted of over 1000 multilateral agreements and 1500 bilateral agreements, as well as declarations, resolutions, judicial decisions, and other legal authorities (Nanda & Pring, 2013). Despite the bulk of international treaties on environmental protection, they are not directly applicable to space activities as they scarcely specifically and expressly address the environmental problems elicited by space activities.

Only a few environmental rules have been accepted as customary international law, and they have remained largely unchanged over time, revolving around the duty to prevent transboundary harm and related procedural obligations of States (Brunnée, 2017). The core of these customary rules are summarised in the Costa Rica v. Nicaragua judgement:

DOI: 10.4324/9781003561996-6

> to fulfil its obligation to exercise due diligence in preventing significant transboundary environmental harm, a State must, before embarking on an activity having the potential adversely to affect the environment of another State, ascertain if there is a risk of significant transboundary harm, which would trigger the requirement to carry out an environmental impact assessment. . . . If the environmental impact assessment confirms that there is a risk of significant transboundary harm, the State planning to undertake the activity is required, in conformity with its due diligence obligation, to notify and consult in good faith with the potentially affected State, where that is necessary to determine the appropriate measures to prevent or mitigate that risk.
> (ICJ, 2015)

They include the prohibition against transboundary harms, the requirements of prior notice and consultation for projects and activities with potential transboundary impacts (Nanda & Pring, 2013), the obligation to 'undertake an environmental assessment where there is a risk that the proposed industrial activity may have a significant adverse impact in a transboundary context, in particular, on a shared resource' (ICJ, 2010), and so on. Some of these customary rules have crystallised into principles of international environmental law, the existence of which has been confirmed in the Iron Rhine case (PCA, 2005). These principles, potentially applicable to all members of the international community, may contribute to the protection of the outer space environment.

A distinction between general principles of law and those of international environmental law should be made: the general principles of law are of limited utility in the international environmental context (Mbanugo & Ifemeje, 2021), whereas the general principles of international environmental law are 'potentially applicable to all members of the international community across the range of activities that they carry out or authorise and in respect of the protection of all aspects of the environment' (Sands et al., 2018), including the outer space environment. Recognised principles of international environmental law encompass the principles of sovereignty, good neighbourliness and international cooperation, sustainable development, preventive action, common but differentiated responsibility, the precautionary principle, and the polluter pays principle (Khare, 2021). Some of the principles are derived from principles of general international law; others are unique to environmental issues. They are reflected in relevant treaties, binding acts of international organisations, State practice, and soft law instruments (Khare, 2021) and may apply to the protection of the outer space environment. This section aims to appraise the applicability and effects of these principles for protecting the outer space environment in the case of MCASAs.

4.1.1 The Principle of Sovereignty

In the realm of international environmental law, the principle of sovereignty, as reflected in Principle 21 of the Declaration of the United Nations (UN) Conference on the Human Environment (Stockholm Declaration) (UNGA, 1972a) and Principle 2 of the Rio Declaration on Environment and Development (Rio Declaration)

(UN Conference on Environment and Development, 1992a), means that States have sovereignty over their natural resources and bear the responsibility not to cause transboundary environmental damage. The second element of the principle, 'the responsibility to ensure that the activities within their jurisdiction or control do not cause damage to the environment of other States or of areas beyond the limits of national jurisdiction', as stated in Principle 21 of the Stockholm Declaration and Principle 2 of the Rio Declaration, reveals its possible relevance with outer space.

In the outer space context, this element may imply that States should bear the responsibility not to harm the outer space environment during their peaceful use and exploration of outer space. Nonetheless, the formulation provided by Principle 21 omits two important requirements: the characterisation of the harm as 'significant' and the requirement to minimise the 'risk' thereof (Brunnée, 2017). These two requirements have been supplemented by Article 3 of the Draft Articles on Prevention of Transboundary Harm from Hazardous Activities (Draft Articles) adopted by the International Law Commission (ILC) in 2001 (ILC, 2001b), which articulates that '[t]he State of origin shall take all appropriate measures to prevent significant transboundary harm or at any event to minimise the risk thereof'. However, the Draft Articles only apply to transboundary circumstances, and rashly extending the document's application scope to outer space is inappropriate. In all, the principle of sovereignty imposes a stricter criterion than the environmental-protection-related dispositions contained in Article IX of the Treaty on Principles Governing the Activities of States in the Exploration and Use of Outer Space, including the Moon and the Other Celestial Bodies (OST) (UNGA, 1967), as the latter only requires States to adopt measures to 'avoid their harmful contamination and also adverse changes in the environment of the Earth resulting from the introduction of extraterrestrial matter'. Were the second element of the principle of sovereignty to apply to outer space, all States shall be held internationally responsible for the space debris generated owing to their space activities. Apparently, it may better protect the outer space environment. However, it would undermine the development of the space sector, as per the status quo of relevant technologies, the chances of producing new space debris remain significant, and the only way for States to avoid international responsibility is to cease all space activities.

4.1.2 The Principle of Good Neighbourliness and International Cooperation

The principle of good neighbourliness enshrined in the maxim *sic utere tuo ut alienum non laedas* is borrowed from general international law. It is crystallised in Article 74 of the UN Charter, which provides that

> Members of the United Nations also agree that their policy in respect of the territories to which this Chapter applies, no less than in respect of their metropolitan areas, must be based on the general principle of good-neighbourliness, due account being taken of the interests and well-being of the rest of the world, in social, economic, and commercial matters.

In the Corfu Channel case, the principle was understood as 'the obligation of every State not to allow its territory to be used for acts contrary to the rights of other States' (ICJ, 1949a). The principle of good neighbourliness has been integrated into international environmental law from the beginning and translated into the development and application of rules promoting international environmental cooperation (Sands, 2018), as stated in Principle 24 of the Stockholm Declaration,

> [c]ooperation through multilateral or bilateral arrangements or other appropriate means is essential to effectively control, prevent, reduce and eliminate adverse environmental effects resulting from activities conducted in all spheres, in such a way that due account is taken of the sovereignty and interests of all States.

It also implies that a State, 'in exercising rights to utilise its territory and resources within its control as it deems fit, should not inflict harm to the environment within another State and areas beyond State jurisdiction, including outer space' (Fadahunsi-Banjo, 2015). As the State of registry exercises jurisdiction and control over the space object that it registers (UNGA, 1967), this implication could be further adapted to the following version in the realm of space activities: the State of registry of a space object, in using the space object as it deems fit, should not inflict harm to the outer space environment. The extent of the implications of the principle of good neighbourliness in international space law is broader, possibly including the duty of non-interference, due diligence, the obligation to cooperate on international issues, space debris mitigation, and so on (Fadahunsi-Banjo, 2015). Several norms articulated in the Report of the Group of Governmental Experts on Advancing Responsible State Behaviour in Cyberspace in the Context of International Security (UNGGE, 2021) are relevant for understanding the principle of good neighbourliness and international cooperation in the sphere of cyberspace. Norms 13 (a), 13 (d), 13(h), and 13(j) reflect the international cooperation requirements, whereas Norm 13(c) regarding the due diligence obligations corresponds to the general meaning of the principle of good neighbourliness. The connotations of the principle in international environmental law overlap with those in international space law and the norms on cybersecurity.

4.1.3 The Principle of Sustainable Development

Sustainable development has been defined in the Brundtland Report as 'development that meets the needs of the present without compromising the ability of future generations to meet their own needs' (World Commission on Environment and Development, 1987). It is a global principle that "includes and implies a balance between economic development and environmental protection" (Damjanovic et al., 2021). Other than the attempt of the Brundtland Report to define the concept, no proper definition was provided by other international instruments. As striving to adopt a precise definition of sustainable development may prove futile, identifying and providing content to its components may be more constructive (Atapattu,

2007). The Rio Declaration seeks to reify its content and incorporates substantive elements of sustainable development in Principles 2, 3, and 4; procedural elements in Principles 10, 18, and 19; tools that can be utilised to achieve sustainable development in Principles 15, 16, and 17; and issues related to and integrated with sustainable development in Principles 5, 6, 7, 8, 12, 23, 24, and 25 (Atapattu, 2007). Agenda 21 (UN Conference on Environment and Development, 1992b), as 'the blueprint for action for global sustainable development', embodies a set of ambitious guidelines and action plans to implement sustainable development at both the national and international levels (Atapattu, 2007). Moreover, a report issued in 1996 by the Expert Group convened by the Commission on Sustainable Development to identify the principles of international law for sustainable development contributes to clarifying the connotations of the principle by subdividing it into several sub-principles: interrelationship and integration, the right to development, the right to a healthy environment, the eradication of poverty, equity, sovereignty over natural resources and responsibility not to cause damage to other States, the sustainable use of natural resources, the prevention of environmental harm, the precautionary principle, peaceful settlement of disputes, and so on (UN Commission on Sustainable Development, 1996). In 2015, the international community adopted the 2030 Agenda, with 17 Sustainable Development Goals as its core, including no poverty, zero hunger, good health and well-being, quality education, gender equality, clean water, affordable and clean energy, decent work and economic growth, industry, innovation and infrastructure, reduced inequalities, sustainable cities and communities, responsible consumption and production, climate action, life below water, life on land, peace, justice, and strong institutions and partnerships (UNGA, 2015). The principle of sustainable development is no doubt anthropocentric and development-centred instead of ecocentric and environment-centred. Today, the concept of sustainable development is a much broader concept than mere environmental protection. It has evolved into 'an umbrella concept' (Atapattu, 2019). The principle of sustainable development has also been integrated into space law, with a focus on environmental protection. The instruments of space law on the long-term sustainability of space activities may be better adapted to protecting the outer space environment. As analysed in Chapter 2 of this study, space cybersecurity considerations are absent from the existing instruments, and the effect of the sustainable development principle on minimising the negative effects of MCASAs on the environment is trivial.

4.1.4 The Principle of Preventive Action

The principle of preventive action 'is based on the idea that it is better to prevent environmental damage than to employ measures to restore the environment thereafter' (Louka, 2006). It is closely related to the second element of the principle of sovereignty, that is, States are responsible for ensuring that the activities within their jurisdiction or control do not cause extra-territorial environmental damage, but differs from it in two ways: minimising environmental damage is an inherent objective of the former, whereas the latter is derived from 'respect for the principle of sovereignty'; and the area subject to environmental protection under the former is larger, as a State should also prevent environmental damages to its own jurisdiction (Sands et al., 2018). Thus, the scope of the principle of preventive action is broader than that of Principle 21 of the Stockholm Declaration. The principle of preventive action is supported by an extensive body of domestic environmental protection legislation and relied upon by several international treaties (Sands et al., 2018). The obligation to undertake an environmental assessment, as a customary norm of international environmental law, is an important way to achieve the objective the principle of preventive action (Atapattu, 2007). The principle itself offers nothing concrete for the protection of the outer space environment. Nonetheless, Article IX of the OST, stipulating that States parties shall conduct exploration of outer space, including the Moon and other celestial bodies, 'so as to avoid their harmful contamination and also adverse changes in the environment of the Earth resulting from the introduction of extraterrestrial matter, and, where necessary, shall adopt appropriate measures for this purpose', corresponds to the core of the principle. In practice, the measures already undertaken to avoid 'back' and 'forward' contamination could be considered preventive actions, including the planetary protection measures and the measures to mitigate space debris. However, environmental assessment is rarely demanded in space activities.

4.1.5 The Precautionary Principle

The precautionary principle stems from domestic legal systems and began to appear in international legal instruments only in the mid-1980s (Fisher, 2001). The core of the principle is reflected in Principle 15 of the Rio Declaration, stating that 'where there are threats of serious or irreversible damage, lack of full scientific certainty shall not be used as a reason for postponing cost-effective measures to prevent environmental degradation'. Although various formulations of the principle have been proposed, they share the similarity in calling for actions to prevent possible harm even when uncertainties exist (MacLeod, 2004). Thus, it is different from the situation where the risk reduction policy is followed to prevent known environmental risks (Fisher, 2001). The threats of MCASAs to the outer space environment, particularly in generating new space debris, can be proved scientifically and practically. Almost no scientific uncertainty exists in the context of MCASAs as to whether they could produce space debris and threaten the environment of and persons in outer space. The precautionary principle can barely apply.

4.1.6 The Principle of Common but Differentiated Responsibility

Human beings rely on a healthy climate for their survival. Thus, the Earth's climate has been recognised by the General Assembly as a 'common concern' of humankind (UNGA, 1988), and the necessity of international cooperation and responsibility on the part of countries to protect it is justified (Harris, 1999). Therefore, who is responsible for climate pollution? The answer lies partly in the principle of common but differentiated responsibility (CDR). The notion of CDR appeared prior to the 1992 UN Conference on Environment and Development in Rio de Janeiro; however, it was not until the Rio Conference that it was formally articulated as a principle. Principle 7 of the Rio Declaration enunciates that '[i]n view of the different contributions to global environmental degradation, States have common but differentiated responsibilities'. It further states that '[t]he developed countries acknowledge the responsibility that they bear in the international pursuit of sustainable development in view of the pressures their societies place on the global environment and of the technologies and financial resources they command'. The principle of CDR considers States' varying degrees of responsibility for causing the climate problems and their divergent capacities to address them (Bufundo, 2006). Following the essence of the principle, a series of agreements have divided States Parties into different groups to take on divergent responsibility for acting (Bushey & Jinnah, 2010). For instance, the United Nations Framework Convention on Climate Change (UNFCCC) applies the implementation method of differentiation (UN Conference on Environment and Development, 1992c), dividing State parties into three groups, developed countries, countries undergoing a transition to a market economy, and developing countries, and apportioning responsibility between these different groups, thus providing a 'readily discernible structure' to the principle of CDR (Bushey & Jinnah, 2010). The Kyoto Protocol to the UNFCCC (Conference of the Parties of the UNFCCC, 1997) adopts both the obligation and implementation of differentiation, applying differential obligations based on industrial or non-industrial status of countries and individual differential targets for industrial countries (Maguire, 2014). Broad consensus has been achieved among States in favour of differentiation by implementation; however, the differentiated obligations for each group of States remain to be defined. It has been submitted by scholars that applying the principle of CDR to space debris issues is feasible and may even contribute towards solving the legal dilemma of space debris removal (Prasad & Lochan, 2007; Gopalakrishnan & Prasad, 2013). However, the common recognition of the applicability of the principle of CDR to the protection of the outer space environment is yet to be confirmed by States. In addition, in the realm of space activities, tackling the questions of how to categorise States and define the obligations and/or the responsibility of different groups of States will create new arduous tasks for the international community.

4.1.7 The Polluter Pays Principle

The polluter pays principle originated as an economic principle articulated by the Organisation for Economic Cooperation and Development (OECD) in its Guiding Principles Concerning International Economic Aspects of Environmental Policies of 1972 as a principle 'to be used for allocating costs of pollution prevention and control measures to encourage rational use of scares environmental resources and to avoid distortions in international trade and investment' (OECD, 1972). It is incorporated into Principle 16 of the Rio Declaration as well. In the OECD context, the polluter pays principle is 'a cost allocation or non-subsidisation principle intended to guide governments' (Stevens, 1994) to allocate the costs of pollution prevention and control measures, spreading the cost of environmental harm to all stakeholders, and thereby enhance the efficiency of resource use at all levels (Mamlyuk, 2009). The polluter pays principle also seeks to 'internalise the cost of polluting activity', placing them on the polluter rather than on the governments or the public generally (Anderson, 2012). In addition, polluters are expected to restore the damage that occurred despite the application of measures undertaken under the spirit of the polluter pays principle. In the absence of a commonly accepted definition of the polluter pays principle, the principle is sufficiently flexible for domestic interpretation. Regrettably, implementing the principle outside the OECD countries and the European Union is rare, rendering it only a candidate for regional customs (Atapattu, 2007). Although theoretically, extending the application scope of the polluter pays principle to outer space is to be confirmed, the current State practice to protect the outer space environment, primarily comprising preventive measures, corresponds well to this principle's objective and requirements. For example, space debris mitigation. Although States' legislation and practices differ significantly in terms of space debris mitigation, the costs of the preventive measures are undoubtedly borne by the entities conducting space activities. Nonetheless, as the polluter pays principle is an abstract and flexible notion without a universally agreed concrete definition, from a preventive perspective, its connotations for space activities are yet to be clarified. This principle is more enlightening when dealing with cases where space debris has already been generated. When the principle is applied to outer space, States conducting space activities that generate space debris are responsible for restoring the damage made to the outer space environment. This may imply removing the space debris at the States' own expense. However, that will not be easy, as active space debris removal triggers both technical and controversial legal issues (Force, 2012; Langlade, 2018; Sheer & Li, 2019). Addressing these legal issues would be a primary step towards active space debris removal. Thus, for the time being, the polluter pays principle does not contribute substantially to tackling the outer space environmental crisis prompted by MCASAs, as it neither offers more detailed measures for preventing the generation of space debris caused by MCASAs, nor provides substantive solutions to restore damage done to the outer space environment.

4.1.8 Sub-Conclusion

As some MCASAs may lead to the generation of space debris and thus undermine the outer space environment, international environmental law is expected to contribute to coping with this potential. Treaties of international environmental law seldom mention outer space, leading to their inapplicability to this area beyond national jurisdiction. Instead, general principles of international environmental law, enshrined in customary norms, rules of relevant treaties, binding acts of international organisations, State practice, and soft law instruments may play a role in protecting the outer space environment. Some of these principles are also absorbed into space law, such as the principles of international cooperation and sustainable development. The adapted version of these principles caters better to the specific circumstances of space activities. Other principles of international environmental law are more specifically formed for environmental issues. Their applicability to outer space is uncertain. Even if they could apply, their contributions towards space debris issues are trivial, not considering their effects on preventing or minimising the potential negative effects on the outer space environment of the MCASAs.

4.2 Difficulties in Applying *jus ad bellum*

Jus ad bellum 'prohibits States from using cross-border force' except 'with the consent of the territorial State', 'pursuant to the authorisation of the United Nations Security Council', or 'in individual or collective self-defence' (Hakimi, 2018). The UN Charter has been the centrepiece of *jus ad bellum* since 1945, including the non-intervention norm envisioned in Article 2(4), which provides that 'all members shall refrain in their international relations from the threat or use of force against the territorial integrity or political independence of any State, or in any other manner inconsistent with the purposes of the United Nations', and an enforcement mechanism prescribed in Chapter VII (Stromseth, 2006). These dispositions enshrine a complete prohibition on the threat or use of force in international relations, except for the exercise of the right to self-defence or under the authorisation of the UN Security Council.

Whether MCASAs are prohibited by *jus ad bellum* depends on whether they constitute threats or use of force. As it is clarified that Article 2(4) applies to 'any use of force, regardless of the weapons employed' (ICJ, 1996), cyber activities may fall under this article. Therefore, what cyber activities may qualify threat or use of force? It necessitates interpreting the terms 'use of force' and 'threat of force'. However, controversies exist over their meanings. Scholars have proposed different approaches to determine what constitutes the use of force. The instrument-based approach focuses on the means used for launching an attack. The prohibition on using military force against another State by Article 2(4) is owing to the close correlation between severe physical destruction and injuries and the use of armed forces, as these consequences are unlikely to be caused by economic or political coercion (Silver, 2002). MCASAs are not inherently lethal; however, they have the potential to lead to similar reprobated consequences that military force would result in. Thus, according to the instrument-based approach, they are tantamount to weapons when used with the aim of physical destruction or injury and constitute the use of force in such circumstances. According to the strict liability approach, a malicious cyber activity (MCA) would be automatically deemed an armed attack when it targets critical national infrastructure, considering the dire consequences that attacks on this type of infrastructure could lead to (Graham, 2010). As States define critical national infrastructure differently, the indeterminacy of whether conducting MCASAs constitutes the use or threat of force in terms of Article 2(4) increases. The most supported approach is the effect-based approach, which may qualify MCASAs as the use of force if they cause or are likely to cause the same damaging consequences as kinetic weapons (Roscini, 2014). This approach stems from the Military and Paramilitary Activities in and Against Nicaragua case (Military and Paramilitary Activities case), which adopted a 'scale and effects' standard for deciding which actions may amount to an armed attack (ICJ, 1986). As judicial precedents have not provided a way to evaluate the scale and effects, appraising models have been submitted, among which the most influential criteria are proposed in the Tallinn Manual. Tallinn Manual proposed severity, immediacy, directness, invasiveness, measurability of effects, military character, State involvement, and presumptive legality as consideration factors (Schmitt, 2013). Nonetheless, implementing the criteria proves to be difficult, particularly because it lacks guidance on the weight of each factor (Gervais, 2012) and the appraising methods of these factors.

Opposing views exist as to whether the threat of force is subject to the same parameters as the use of force itself. One view relates the threat of force with the use of force, whereas the other holds that the threat of force is an independent concept from use of force (Stürchler, 2007). The first view, proposed by Ian Brownlie (Brownlie, 1963) based on his pre-Charter practice regarding threats, has been widely repeated and endorsed as authoritative, and embraced by the ICJ (Stürchler, 2007). It is declared in the Legality of the Threat or Use of Nuclear Weapons case that

> [t]he notions of 'threat' and 'use' of force under Article 2, Paragraph 4, of the Charter stand together in the sense that if the use of force itself in a given case is illegal . . . the threat to use such force will likewise be illegal.
>
> (ICJ, 1996)

Tallinn Manual followed the logic of this view and submitted in Rule 12 that '[a] cyber operation, or threatened cyber operation, constitutes an unlawful threat of force when the threatened action, if carried out, would be an unlawful use of force' (Schmitt, 2013). Actions of threat of force could be classified into several categories: 'the clear communication, oral or by communiqué, that failure to comply with a request, obligation or ultimatum will result in force being employed'; the entrance into a defensive alliance; and certain positive actions (Green & Grimal, 2011). According to State practice, troop buildups and other forms of military posturing are positive actions and can constitute the threat of force (Green & Grimal, 2011). Developing the capability to conduct massive MCAs is not inherently military, and it is unlikely that this type of activity can qualify as a positive action. It appears reasonable to conclude that only express communication may constitute the threat of force in cyberspace. However, as highlighted by Stürchler, the first view has a fatal drawback as it may be difficult to apply in reality (Stürchler, 2007). When a State threatens to use cyber ways to deter another, predicting whether the MCAs that it may conduct constitute the use of force is a difficult task. Thus, whether threats to use cyber means violate Article 2(4) remains uncertain.

The second view holds that threat and force are uncoupled. Although with fewer supporters, this view has led to extensive discussions. From a realistic perspective, threats are two-sided as they may lead to escalation but also prevent conflicts.

International relations scholars have developed the deterrence and spiral models to explain this phenomenon. According to the deterrence model, military threats may dissuade the adversary from entering into conflicts by conveying to it the message that the costs of conflicts would be extremely high or that conflicts would be detrimental to its own interests (Stürchler, 2007), which conforms to UN's aim to maintain international peace and security, as enshrined in Article 1 of the UN Charter. The spiral model asserts that military threats would escalate into war (Stürchler, 2007). According to different models, military threats lead to different results, and the violation of the threat of force of Article 2(4) remains indeterminate. If the threat of force is considered uncoupled with force, it would be unreasonable and rash to consider Article 2(4) as a comprehensive threat ban, as the effects of threats are uncertain. Therefore, directly qualifying a State's threat to conduct massive MCAs against another as violating Article 2(4) is imprudent, as the consequences remain unknown.

According to Article 51 of the UN Charter, a State may exercise the right of self-defence when an armed attack is launched against it, 'until the Security Council has taken necessary measures to maintain international peace and security'. When MCASAs are involved in self-defence issues, two problems arise. The first problem is the type of MCASAs that may invoke the right of self-defence, which lies in interpreting the term 'armed attack'. Without a definition of the term provided by the Charter, reference to other international documents is necessary. Jean Pictet's proposed criteria to determine the existence of an international armed conflict under Common Article 2 of the 1949 Geneva Conventions (DCG, 1949a, 1949b, 1949c, 1949d), deeming a use of force as an armed attack when the force is of sufficient scope, duration, and intensity, contribute to identifying armed attacks (Graham, 2010). However, no uniform criteria have been established to decide and appraise the scope, duration, and intensity of the use of force amounting to an armed attack. Whether the cyber activities disrupting the adversary's military operation without causing similar effects to classic kinetic operations could be considered a resort to armed force in terms of these criteria remains an open question (Dörmann, 2016). International judicial decisions assist with identifying armed attacks as well. An armed attack is described in the Military and Paramilitary Activities case as the 'most grave form of the use of force' (ICJ, 1986). Similarly, deciding whether an act is an armed attack could be even more tricky than identifying the use of force, as what is the gravest form is yet to be determined. It is commonly agreed that at least some types of MCAs may constitute an armed attack justifying the use of force in self-defence (Hayward, 2017), notably those that cause injuries or kill persons or damage or destroy property (Schmitt, 2013). Nonetheless, whether the MCAs leading to large-scale political or economic crises or other adverse effects are armed attacks is uncertain (Hayward, 2017).

The second problem is whether the attacked State could use MCASAs to legally exercise its right of self-defence. Reactions in self-defence should comply with the principles of necessity and proportionality, which have been recognised as customary rules of international law, as reflected in several international judicial precedents (Schmitt, 2017). Necessity requires that the State under armed attack undertake self-defence only as a 'last resort and the only effective way to repel the armed attack' (Roscini, 2014). It implies that force is only appropriate when non-forceful measures are insufficient (Schmitt, 2017). According to the principle of necessity, if passive cyber defences such as firewalls and installing antivirus software and active cyber activities under the threshold of use of force may reliably and completely curb an armed attack, the use of force in self-defence is impermissible; if the measures are insufficient to defeat an armed attack, MCASAs amounting to the use of force and other forms of use of force could be conducted against the attacking State (Schmitt, 2017). The crux again resides in the MCASAs that qualify the use of force. When the use of force is necessary for self-defence purposes, the measures adopted by the victim State are limited by the principle of proportionality. The principle of proportionality suggests that the response to armed attacks, which ought to be commensurate with permissible objectives of self-defence, should not exceed what is necessary in terms of intensity and magnitude (Culapa, 2004). Appraising the proportionality of using MCASAs could be difficult, owing to the hardship in determining the magnitude and consequences of MCASAs (Roscini, 2014).

In addition, *jus ad bellum* is continuously changing, boosted by several significant developments in the international situation and law: the emergence of weapons of mass destruction of various types, the rise of global terrorism, the elevation of the person to a central place in the realm of international law, the inability of all States to accept the Security Council as a disinterested arbiter, and the continuing erosion of the sanctity of the sovereign State (Murphy, 2009). These factors risk undermining the role of maintaining international peace and security of *jus ad bellum*. The potential consequences of MCASAs differ significantly, from unnoticeable theft of space data to physical, economic, and political damage at large scale. Some of the consequences are comparable to or even more serious than the results that weapons of mass destruction could produce. Applying *jus ad bellum* to combat MCASAs is necessary. However, the circumstances under which it could be applied remains to be determined. It is suggested to accommodate these new challenges through actions at the international level and academic efforts (Murphy, 2009). As cyber and space technologies play an increasingly important role in the modern battlefield, State practice may also influence the development of the law of war. It is noteworthy that applying *jus ad bellum* to MCASAs should be prudent as well. A low threshold of identifying the key terms, such as 'use or threat of force' and 'armed attack', would lead to many MCASAs being considered violations of *jus ad bellum*. This might incite the escalation of conflicts instead of promoting international peace and security.

To sum up, the prohibition of resorting to force and the rules on self-defence apply to cyber activities, including MCASAs. However, owing to the uncertainties in interpreting critical terms, such as the use of force, the threat of force, and armed attacks, and the lack of uniform criteria to evaluate the magnitude and intensity of the use of force in self-defence, the application of *jus ad bellum* in the cyber context proves to be difficult.

4.3 Difficulties in Applying *jus in bello*

Customs and treaties are the major sources of the law of armed conflict (Solis, 2010). Customary international law rules are difficult to describe, whereas the treaties on *jus in bello* are numerous, typically the Geneva Conventions and their Additional Protocols.[1] The existence of armed conflict triggers the application of the law of armed conflict. The Geneva Conventions and the Additional Protocols have refrained from defining armed conflict to avoid similar political and legal controversies that had occurred over the legal definition of war and collateral difficulties in distinguishing a state of war, a police action, and other forms of hostile action. Thus, determining the existence of armed conflicts is intended to be factual rather than legal (Dinniss, 2012).

It is commonly agreed that the law of armed conflicts applies to MCAs undertaken in the context of armed conflicts (ICRC, 2020), which is implied in the Legality of the Threat or Use of Nuclear Weapons case, where the Court recalled that the rules and principles of the law of armed conflict apply to 'all forms of warfare and to all kinds of weapons, those of the past, those of the present and those of the future' (ICJ, 1996). The term 'armed conflict' and the nexus between MCAs and armed conflicts have already invoked extensive discussions (Piatkowski, 2017; Schmitt, 2012; Serbanescu, 2017), whilst the obligations bearing on States participating in armed conflicts derived from the *jus in bello* when the States use cyber means are even more obscure. In addition to the lengthy international treaties, represented by the 1949 Geneva Conventions and the Additional Protocols, special agreements between belligerents, customary norms, general principles, and hybrid soft law documents contribute to founding the law of armed conflict (Sassòli, 2019). Owing to space limitations, this sub-section discusses only the basic principles that combatants must follow to protect civilian populations and objects against the effects of hostilities as an illustration of the difficulties in applying this branch of international law to MCAs, and does not explore the application of every specific rule of the law of armed conflict in the cyber context. These principles, deriving from treaties, customs, and general principles of law (Sassòli, 2019), include the principles of distinction and proportionality, and the prohibition to inflict unnecessary suffering and military necessity.

4.3.1 The Principle of Distinction

The principle of distinction requires that the parties to armed conflicts distinguish at all times between civilians and combatants and between civilian and military objects and direct their attacks only against military objectives. This principle excludes indiscriminate attacks that do not target any particular persons or objects, whether civilian or combatant (Dinstein, 2012). The possibility of MCASAs being indiscriminate can be rather high, notably owing to the dual-use nature of most space assets. As more space objects are simultaneously used for civilian and military purposes, MCAs against them may indiscriminately affect both civilian and military end-users. However, whether MCASAs violate the principle of distinction remains to be determined, as traditional attacks directed against military objects can also result in collateral impacts on civilian objects nearby. It can be inferred from Article 51(5)(a) of the Additional Protocol I, which considers indiscriminate an attack 'which treats as a single military objective a number of clearly separated and distinct military objectives located in a city, town, village of other area containing a similar concentration of civilians or civilian objects', that attacks are not indiscriminate when the military objectives are not clearly separated and distinct (Dinstein, 2012). Similarly, using cyber means to attack military space assets, dual-use space assets, and civilian space assets used exclusively for military purposes during armed conflicts does not violate the principle of distinction. However, the MCASAs against dual-space assets may impact civilian populations, even civilians far from the battlefield. For instance, the cyberattack launched against Viasat's KA-SAT network in 2022 during the Russo-Ukrainian crisis impacted not only several thousands of customers in Ukraine but also tens of thousands of other customers across Europe (Viasat, 2022). The spill-over effects of such MCASAs are severe. Deeming them lawful based on the aforementioned inference that attacking military and civilian objectives that are not clearly separated and distinct do not violate the principle of distinction would lead to undesirable repercussions. Proposals for applying the principle of distinction to dual-use infrastructures have been proposed, such as the exemption of central infrastructure components that serve important civilian functions, the creation of 'digital safe havens', and possible precautionary obligations based on Article 58 of Additional Protocol I (Geiß & Lahmann, 2012), the adoption of the 'effective contribution' and 'definite military advantage criteria' (Huang & Ying, 2020), and so on. Nonetheless, further evolution of the law of armed conflict and State practice is necessary for resolving the dilemma.

4.3.2 The Principle of Proportionality

MCASAs risk breaching the principle of proportionality as well. The Viasat incident is not pertinent to the principle of proportionality as it does not cause loss of life, injury to human beings, or damage to property (Dinstein, 2012). However, some MCASAs may be tainted with illegality for breaching the principle of proportionality, which regulates side effects over civilian persons or objects of attacks on military objectives (Crowe & Weston-Scheuber, 2015). The principle of proportionality, as a customary norm, is codified in Article 51(5)(b) of Additional Protocol as prohibiting 'an attack which may be expected to cause incidental loss of civilian life, injury to civilians, damage to civilian objects, or a combination thereof, which would be excessive in relation to the concrete and direct military advantage anticipated'. Military attacks causing collateral damage are sometimes inevitable and not necessarily illegal. For military attacks to be lawful, the commander must take all reasonable precautions based on the available information to balance the need to accomplish the mission and the need to minimise harm to civilians and their property (Doyle Jr, 2002). Therefore, the legality of military attacks should be evaluated through the proportionality test, the core of which lies in evaluating the relationship between the collateral damage attackers reasonably expect to cause and the military advantage they anticipate as a result of the attack (Schmitt, 2017). The 'excessiveness', which is the essence of the proportionality calculation, plays a central role in the test (Clarke, 2012). However, as no detailed guidance has been offered by the law of armed conflict regarding determining damage and assessing military advantage, appraising the excessiveness and applying the principle of proportionality are virtually difficult, which has been recognised by the International Criminal Tribunal for the former Yugoslavia (ICTY) (ICTY, 2000). This situation would be exacerbated when using MCASAs as a means for military attack, as MCASAs introduce new difficulties in applying the proportionality principle, typically owing to the dual-use nature of most space assets and the potential knock-on effects, that is, 'the indirect consequences that flow from the direct results of a given action' (Boylan, 2017). MCAs against dual-use space assets may cause direct damage to the assets which also serve civilian functions. Knock-on effects can be common in the case of MCASAs as well. For instance, the belligerents conduct MCAs against the global navigation satellite system (GNSS) used by their opponents and other civilian end-users. Such MCASAs only temporarily disrupt GNSS services but cause civilian losses and irreparable damage to civilian infrastructures, such as resulting in the crash of a civilian aircraft which relies on the navigation services provided by the GNSS. The principle of proportionality requires the commander to ensure that the expected damage and injuries from the attack, 'given the circumstances as known to him at the time after taking all feasible measures to ascertain those circumstances, is not excessive to the concrete and direct military advantage anticipated', before conducting MCASAs (Jensen, 2003). This implies that the commander should do everything feasible to gather information, learn the specific circumstances of the object of his attack, and consider and evaluate all factors and the existing possibilities that may cause civilian losses before deciding to initiate MCASAs (Jensen, 2003). Nonetheless, given the broad customer base of space application services and the fact that the vast majority of the Internet consists of civilian objects (Jensen, 2013), considering and evaluating the factors and possibilities would be extremely challenging.

4.3.3 The Prohibition to Inflict Unnecessary Suffering

The prohibition to inflict unnecessary suffering proscribes injuries to opposing combatants that are beyond what is necessary to remove them from active combat (Crowe & Weston-Scheuber, 2015). This principle aims to prevent the use of 'weapons, projectiles and materials and methods of warfare of a nature to cause superfluous injury or unnecessary suffering', as proclaimed in Article 35(2) of Protocol I to the Geneva Conventions (DCG, 1977). It is also articulated in Article 22 of the Hague Regulations concerning the Laws and Customs of War on Land (Hague Regulations) as '[t]he right of belligerents to adopt means of injuring the enemy is not unlimited' (International Peace Conference, 1907), and in Article 35(1) of Additional Protocol I, which states that '[i]t is prohibited to employ weapons, projectiles and material and methods of warfare of a nature to cause superfluous injury or unnecessary suffering'. The principle of the prohibition on unnecessary suffering focuses on the weapons and warfare methods applied. Thus, whether this prohibition applies to MCASAs depends on whether MCASAs constitute weapons or methods of warfare that would result in unnecessary effects that outweigh their military utility. Historically, several weapons have been banned or criticised for causing unnecessary suffering, including crossbows, explosive bullets, dum-dum bullets, landmines, cluster munitions, chemical weapons, and nuclear weapons (Crowe & Weston-Scheuber, 2015). Other weapons have been added to the list in practice as causing unnecessary suffering if used in certain or all contexts, such as expanding and explosive bullets, poison and poisoned weapons, chemical and biological weapons, and so forth (Henckaerts & Doswald-Beck, 2005). Some of these weapons are expressly prohibited by customary norms or specific treaties, notably the Convention on Prohibition on the Use of Certain Conventional Weapons, which may be deemed to be Excessively Injurious or to have Indiscriminate Effects (UNGA, 1980). Whether other weapons or methods of warfare outside the list of weapons are prohibited is uncertain and should be examined specifically. However, views differ on the approach to determine a weapon or warfare method that could cause unnecessary suffering. There is a general consensus among States that suffering without military purpose violates the principle (Henckaerts & Doswald-Beck, 2005). If military purposes exist, many States underline the importance of a balance between military necessity and the expected suffering inflicted on a person (Henckaerts & Doswald-Beck, 2005). From a utilitarian perspective, a weapon is outlawed if an alternative weapon that causes less suffering and has the same military effects exists (Sassòli, 2019). International judicial decisions contribute to this issue by defining unnecessary suffering as any suffering that is 'greater than that unavoidable to achieve military objectives' (ICJ, 1996). However, the proposed standards of deciding whether a weapon is of a nature to cause superfluous injury or unnecessary suffering remain obscure, necessitating specific analysis facing new weapons.

Using cyber means in armed conflicts is gaining popularity, considering their capacity to offer military advantage with reduced risk of civilian losses and their lower cost compared with conventional weapons (Fenton, 2019). In many cases, the adverse effects of MCASAs are less than those of conventional weapons and are generally not of a nature to cause superfluous injury or unnecessary suffering, and thus, conducting MCASAs does not breach the prohibition to inflict unnecessary suffering. However, as the consequences of MCASAs may differ significantly, rigidly deeming them as non-violative of the prohibition on inflicting unnecessary suffering would be fallacious. The method of conducting MCASAs, the target, and the purpose are all vital for judging the conformity of the activities with the law of armed conflict. Therefore, MCASAs are not inherently lethal but could still be used to cause physical injury and damage. Although most MCASAs do not breach the principle of prohibition to inflict unnecessary suffering, evaluating the legality of MCASAs in terms of this principle should remain case specific.

4.3.4 The Principle of Military Necessity

The principle of military necessity permits the use of the force only to a degree necessary to achieve the anticipated military objective with minimum loss of life and property (Crowe & Weston-Scheuber, 2015). This principle is closely linked to the principle of proportionality and the prohibition of inflicting unnecessary suffering, which are positive rules of law incorporating absolute prohibitions. However, their conditions of application are different: military necessity cannot justify the use of force when positive rules apply (Downey, 1953). Being historically a general circumstance precluding unlawfulness, today, it is a restrictive and exceptional principle justifying conduct contrary to the law of armed conflicts when it is expressly stipulated so (Sassòli et al., 2011). It is prescribed in some articles of the foundational treaties of the law of armed conflict. For instance, Article 23 (g) of the Hague Regulations permits the destruction or seizure of the enemy's property imperatively demanded by the necessities of war. These properties should be military objects, which are defined in Article 52 of Protocol I as 'those objects which by their nature, location, purpose or use make an effective contribution to military action and whose total or partial destruction, capture or neutralisation, in the circumstances ruling at the time, offers a definite military advantage'. In MCASA cases, deciding whether the targeted space systems or assets offer a definite military advantage for the belligerents can be complicated. The military space systems used in the armed conflicts are undoubtedly military objects, and MCASAs against such systems could be justified, whereas it would be more challenging to decide whether dual-use systems are military objects. Moreover, judging ex-ante the military advantage of destroying or suspending the service of a space system or asset may lead to opposite conclusions as the definitiveness of the military advantage is apparent only if the MCASA is successful (Gervais, 2012).

4.3.5 Sub-Conclusion

Owing to the virtues of cyber technologies, attacks through cyber means, notably MCAs, are becoming popular on battlefields and contributing to achieving the military objectives anticipated in international and non-international armed conflicts. *Jus in bello* applies to MCASAs when they are used in armed conflicts. However, the uncertainty of the meanings of critical principles and terms and the lack of State practice sometimes render States' obligations under the *jus in bello* challenging to determine, complicating their implementation. Similarly, applying them to MCASAs is challenging, which is even exacerbated by the dual-use nature of space assets and the broadly diversifying, indirect repercussions that could result from MCASAs. Scholars have proposed various approaches for alleviating the issue, such as specific ways to interpret the norms, developing special standards for applying the rules in the cyber context, and even elaborating treaties for cyber warfare (Boylan, 2017; Fenton, 2019; Geiß & Lahmann, 2012; Jensen, 2003; Petkis, 2016). Nonetheless, international consensus on this issue is yet to be achieved.

4.4 Difficulties in Applying International Human Rights Law

MCAs have resulted in the closure of hospitals, rupture of electric power, standstills of major cities and even affected the integrity of the democratic process (Brown & Esterhuysen, 2023), posing threats to human rights. MCASAs may infringe upon human rights primarily in three ways: threatening human lives in outer space, interrupting the services that space systems offer, such as the various communication services and navigation positioning service, and manipulating space data, such as jamming and spoofing of data. The potentially impacted human rights are extensive, ranging from the most fundamental right to life, liberty, and the security of person, the right to free expression of belief, political opinion, art and written texts, and the protection of privacy issues, the right of free and equal access to information, to the right to enjoy scientific progress. The applicability of international human rights law in the cyber context has received wide recognition, whereas applying the law remains difficult. Several reasons exist for this predicament.

The first reason is the uncertainties about the exact scope and content of human rights. International human rights law primarily comprises treaties, customary norms, judicial decisions, soft law, and *jus cogens*. Treaty law protects the human rights codified therein. Despite overlap in the categories of human rights protected under different treaties, their specific scope and content differ, indicating that their connotations in the cyber context may be different. In addition to the universal human rights treaties, regional human rights treaties play an important role as well, represented by the European Convention for the Protection of Human Rights and Fundamental Freedoms (ECHR) (Council of Europe, 1950), American Convention on Human Rights (Organization of American States, 1969), and the African Charter on Human and Peoples' Rights (Organisation of African Unity, 1981). Unlike the universal treaties and other regional treaties on human rights, which only protect natural persons, the ECHR also endows legal persons with the right to peaceful enjoyment of their possessions. Regarding customary norms, there is growing consensus that most rights enumerated in the Universal Declaration of Human Rights (UDHR) (UNGA, 1948) have acquired customary law status in international law (de Schutter, 2019). Typically, these include the rights to life, liberty, and security of persons, the prohibition of slavery and torture, and so forth. However, other than the listed rights that have been recognised as customary norms, considerable uncertainty exists regarding the customary status of other rights (Bantekas & Oette, 2020). It is generally accepted that to obtain the status of customary law, a rule must undergo a double test of practice or behaviour and *opinio juris*. A bulk of the literature contributes to the discussion on determining the existence of a customary rule of international human rights law based on this test (Meron, 1991; Paust, 1995 Simma & Alston, 1988–1989). Judicial decisions, as a subsidiary means for determining rules of law, demonstrate the status and content of norms by interpreting them in a given case (Bantekas & Oette, 2020). They do not create obligations bearing on States but contribute to reifying them. *Jus cogens* is defined in Article 53 of the Vienna Convention on the Law of Treaties (VCLT) as 'a norm from which no derogation is permitted and which can be modified only by a subsequent norm of general international law having the same character' (UNGA, 1969). However, its source, contents, and legal consequences are not fully settled (Bantekas & Oette, 2020). Recognised peremptory norms include the prohibition of aggression, slavery and the slave trade, genocide, racial discrimination, apartheid and torture, basic rules of international humanitarian law applicable in armed conflict, and the right to self-determination (de Schutter, 2019). As limited progress has been made on the doctrine of *jus cogens* identification and the justification for the status of peremptory norms, the methods for determining whether a new norm has acquired the status of *jus cogens* remain inchoate (Saul, 2015), and whether there are other peremptory norms of international human rights law is uncertain. Without an international consensus on the scope and content of human rights, the scope and content of human rights admitted by different States vary. As the cyber world is interconnected, a single MCA impacting several States could be considered violative of human rights by some States and non-violative by others.

In addition, the allegedly emerging fourth generation of human rights increases legal uncertainties in applying international human rights law to MCASAs. It is contended that a new type of human rights—the fourth generation of human rights—has emerged between the twentieth and the twenty-first centuries, which may encompass the right to die, the right to dispose of organs and body, reproductive rights, the right to change sex, and digital rights (Perepolkin et al., 2021), such as the right to information. However, the opposing view exists, holding that new human rights norms or standards are not required with the development of cyber technologies (Mihr, 2014). Although the existence of the right to information could be evidenced, to some extent, by State practice, international human rights instruments, and decisions of judicial authorities (McDonagh, 2013), its implementation may be difficult owing to its controversial nature. In practice, the right to information is often invoked with other human rights, such as the right to freedom of expression, the right to take part in public affairs, the right to respect for private life, and so on (McDonagh, 2013). Nonetheless, it is deemed by some scholars as an intrinsic right, which should be unlimited in terms of the context of invocation, the requester, the nature of the information sought, and the purpose for which access may be sought (McDonagh, 2013). Other fundamental human rights, such as the dignity or privacy of others, may also limit the enjoyment of the right to information (Mihr, 2016). MCASAs may negatively impact the right to access to information, whether through suspending the internet services or damaging the information. However, owing to the uncertainty about the recognition of the right to information and the doubts on its implementation, whether and under what circumstances MCASAs violate the new type of human right are unclear.

Second, inconsistencies in interpreting international human rights law suffuse. For instance, it is difficult to reach consensus on understanding the foundational aspirations such as equality, justice, and peace, criteria of limitation such as the necessities of 'a democratic society', judicial tests of reasonableness or proportionality, structural principles such as subsidiarity or the common good, and so forth (Carozza, 2008). The first reason that have led to these inconsistencies reside in the values accorded to the rights by different stakeholders. Human rights are pertinent to eight values people cherish, including respect, power, enlightenment, well-being, wealth, skill, affection, and rectitude (Chen, 1982). The specific connotations accorded to different human rights vary across States, as they differ in the way they measure these values and the weight they assign to them. The second reason lies in the various interpretation techniques used by different judicial authorities. Different interpretation techniques may lead to different understandings of international human rights rules. It is contended that the interpretation rules laid out in the VCLT are insufficient for understanding human rights norms, considering the peculiar nature of human rights (Çali, 2012; Craven, 2000). In addition, the ICJ adopted other interpretation techniques, such as purposive interpretation, evolutive interpretation, and the principle of effectiveness when dealing with human rights-related cases (Crawford & Keene, 2019). Furthermore, incoherence exists not only at the international level but also at the regional level. Realising that the meanings of many terms are not static and may change over time through the living instrument approach, the African and Inter-American human rights tribunals have also largely followed a universalistic approach by extensively relying on UN and regional human rights instruments; the European Court of Human Rights is shifting from assuming the existence of a regional consensus to adopting a universalistic approach (Killander, 2010). As States and regional bodies may accord varied interpretations to the same human right codified, and thus, they may impose different limitations on the exercise and enjoyment of certain rights to protect other rights and maintain national security and public order (Schmitt, 2017), an MCASA that is likely to be considered as violating the human rights in one State or region could be justified in other States or regions.

Third, the responsible parties for human rights infringement may be complex to determine. Human rights imply 'the responsibility to prevent violations of human rights, to react to violations and to help to rebuild societies that have experienced gross violations of human rights' (Ramcharan, 2009). Unlike other branches of international law, which primarily focus on States' responsibility, the scope of the responsible subjects involved in the realm of international human rights law is expanding to include non-State actors (NSAs), such as private individuals, groups of individuals, associations, companies, and so on. The allocation of responsibilities among these different subjects is unclear. For States, international human rights law addresses both governmental action and inaction, creating positive obligations for States to exercise control over certain activities of private individuals so as to protect against human rights abuses (Farrior, 1998). To fulfil these obligations, States should establish a regulatory and institutional framework for the protection of these rights, the prosecution and punishment of the perpetrators, and the provision of remedies for the victim (McBeth, 2008). More specifically, it is contended that national governments should establish national protection systems with six dimensions: 'a constitutional order that faithfully reflects international human rights law, legislation that gives effect to international legal obligations, courts, specific institutions, preventive arrangements to head off potential conflicts and including human rights education in schools and universities' (Ramcharan, 2009). However, the substantive obligations of States are ambiguous and interpreted differently. Under what circumstances a State should be responsible for failing to ensure the conformity of the conduct of NSAs on its territory with human rights requirements remains to be determined. For instance, can a single failure to act constitute a breach of obligation? In case of fault, what is required from the subjective aspects (Farrior, 1998)? Even if States have in place such protection systems, it does not necessarily imply that States could satisfy the human rights protection requirements, let alone the possibility of inappropriate national legislation, inefficient national judicial bodies, and ineffective institutions. Moreover, as envisaged in the International Law Commission's Articles on Responsibility of States for Internationally Wrongful Acts (ARSIWA) (ILC, 2001a), third-State obligations may be invoked in the case of breaching certain international human rights norms, such as *jus cogens* and the obligation not to render aid or assistance to a State that has violated international human rights law (Bird, 2010). With the uncertainties in the scope and content of the peremptory norms in the realm of international human rights law, holding a State responsible based on the third-State responsibility theory takes work.

In the context of MCASAs, international human rights law requires States to ensure the conformity of their cyber activities and the cyber activities conducted by the NSAs under their jurisdiction with international human rights law without prescribing specific obligations. The States responsible for the space activities involved are also required to ensure that the space activities do not violate human rights. However, it is noteworthy that imposing an absolute obligation on States responsible for space activities to prevent human rights-violative MCASAs would be technically unrealistic. Furthermore, as in most MCASAs, human rights violations do not arise out of space activities per se, but rather, space activities are manipulated to the detriment of human rights; pinpointing the specific obligations that these States should bear under international human rights law is also difficult.

The fact that States bear primary obligations for human rights protection does not necessarily preclude the responsibility of other actors. The UDHR Preamble states that every individual and organ of society shall strive to promote respect for fundamental human rights and freedoms and secure their universal and effective recognition and observance, in accordance with which many scholars conceive that it is a universal duty extending to all entities, including NSAs (Onuoha, 2021). Although the current international legal system remains largely State-centred, and neither the customary norms nor treaty law pertaining to human rights expressly extend beyond States, the possibility of directly imposing obligations on NSAs by international human rights law is rooted in international judicial decisions. The ICJ denoted that '[t]he subjects of law in any legal system are not necessarily identical in their nature or in the extent of their rights, and their nature depends on the needs of the community' (ICJ, 1949b). Similarly, if a subject is capable of acting on the international plane, it may be considered to have an international legal personality that is limited by the 'needs of the international community' (McBeth, 2008). Clapham highlighted four forces that recur as background elements for including NSAs as obligation bearers for human rights protection: the globalisation of the world economy, the privatisation of sectors, the increase in internal armed conflict situations involving the fragmentation of States, and the developments surrounding the international human rights of women (Clapham, 2006). Moreover, States are not always capable or willing to hold a given entity accountable (McBeth, 2008). These factors may justify NSAs' status as the subject of international human rights law. Scholars have analysed the possibility of direct responsibility for human rights abuses of different NSAs, such as peace operations, *de facto* regimes, and the NSAs that exercise effective territorial control to the exclusion of a government, transnational corporations, and individuals (Berkes, 2021; Clapham, 2006; Ronen, 2013). However, without international consensus, imposition of human rights obligations directly on NSAs would require 'the careful delineation of the contours of such NSAs and their pertinent obligations' (Ronen, 2013). NSAs are of particular significance in the cyber context, as MCAs could be easily and almost inexpensively conducted by individuals or groups of individuals with and without specific legal status. Similarly, in MCASAs violating human rights, various NSAs may become involved. For instance, a space tourist intrudes on the monitoring system of a communication satellite system to disseminate information, infringing on the right to privacy of others. Whether and under what conditions the individual and the space tourist company bear the responsibility for the direct invasion of privacy remains to be determined based on the specific circumstances of the MCASA.

Scholars have made abundant suggestions confronting the difficulties in applying international human rights law in the cyber context (Chan, 2019; Hathaway et al., 2017; Mihr, 2014; Schmitt, 2017). However, no international consensus has been reached yet. Cyber activities pose few new challenges to the application of international human rights law. Instead, it is the persistent uncertainties of this branch of international law itself which render its application in the cyber context more complex. MCASAs may violate various human rights, as terrestrial cyber activities do. Applying international human rights law in cases of MCASAs would encounter similar difficulties but raise more complexities in determining the responsible bodies.

4.5 The Applicability of International Criminal Law

Cybercrimes remain regulated primarily at the domestic level, as most of them, such as those included in the Convention on Cybercrime adopted by the Council of Europe (Council of Europe, 2001), have not been recognised as international crimes. Universally recognised international crimes include first-generation crimes, such as piracy, slavery, and terrorism, and core crimes, typically encompassing genocide, crimes against humanity, war crimes, and crime of aggression. Although how to conceptualise international crimes and identify the differences between international and domestic crimes are yet to be determined (Greenawalt, 2020), the scope of international crimes could be most directly depicted through the sources of international criminal law, notably relevant treaties and jurisprudence. The elements of an international crime, including *actus reus* and *mens rea*, are also prescribed in treaties and by adjudicatory bodies. MCASAs can be used as tools by perpetrators during their commission of an international crime. For instance, the criminal of war crime may use MCASAs during armed conflicts. Some cyber activities which are *malum in se* have the potential to constitute an international crime, necessitating reference to international criminal law. Likewise, an MCASA itself can also constitute an international crime, such as terrorism and the crime of aggression, when it fulfils its constitutive requirements.

Being a transnational crime with historical roots, terrorism is nonetheless tackled on an international level in a 'piecemeal fashion' (Stahn, 2019). It is understandable because terrorism represents several difficulties of legal categorisation, such as definitional difficulty, difficulty in deciding whether criminalising terrorist acts suffices, or armed force should be used against terrorists (Cyber et al., 2019). Thus, despite all the international efforts exerted,[2] no specific agreement on anti-terrorism has been approved. Instead, a 'thematic' approach has been adopted to prevent and criminalise terrorist acts, leading to the emergence of sectoral anti-terrorist rules (Cyber et al., 2019). Following terrorist attacks against diplomats and civilians, numerous sectoral antiterrorism treaties have been adopted (Cyber et al., 2019), such as the Hague Convention for the Suppression of Unlawful Seizure of Aircraft (UNGA, 1970) and the Montreal Convention for the Suppression of Unlawful Acts Against the Safety of Civil Aviation (UNGA, 1971). The increasing recognition that terrorist attacks affect not only States and political processes but also individual human rights and international peace and security leads to the adoption of treaties coping with specific terrorist activities (Stahn, 2019), such as the International Convention for the Suppression of Terrorist Bombings (UNGA, 1997) and the International Convention on the Suppression of the Financing of Terrorism (UNGA, 1999). Nearly 50 offences have been categorised as terrorist offences (Stahn, 2019), which can be prosecuted in an international court only if they amount to war crimes or crimes against humanity owing to the limited jurisdictional scope of the courts (Cyber et al., 2019). Cyberterrorism, a new form of terrorism denoting the use of cyber technology to achieve terror agendas, can result in both virtual and physical losses (Singh, 2021). It could be defined in a comprehensive way as

> the use, making preparations for, or threat of action designed to cause a social order change, to create a climate of fear or intimidation amongst the general public, or to influence political decision-making by the government or international governmental organisation; made for the purposes of advancing a political, religious, racial or ideological cause; by affecting the integrity, confidentiality, and/or availability of information, information systems and networks, or by unauthorised actions affecting information and communication technology-based control of real-world physical processes,

involving or causing serious physical and virtual damages (Luiif, 2014). As an international offence, cyberterrorism demands a transnational response, necessitating international cooperation (Tehrani et al., 2013). This need has been recognised in a report of the UN Office on Drugs and Crime (UNODC) titled 'The Use of the Internet for Terrorist Purposes', which admits that the lack of a universal instrument related to cybercrime or terrorism imposing specific obligations on States to cooperate internationally is 'an impediment to international cooperation in some terrorism-related investigations and prosecutions' (UNODC, 2012). Nonetheless, currently, no remedy is available for the adoption of a specific instrument countering cyberterrorism. MCASAs could be used for terrorist purposes. They can also constitute cyberterrorism by themselves, typically when the intent and consequences conform to the crime's constitutive elements. According to the status quo of international legislation on cyber terrorism, it is only when the use of MCASAs for terrorist purposes or when they fall under the scope of other crimes, such as the crime of war and the crime of aggression, could such activities be addressed at the international level in accordance with the international criminal law.

Although amongst the earliest crimes prosecuted by international tribunals, the crime of aggression has faced significant acceptance problems owing to

> the relatively abstract nature of the protected interests, the highly political nature of findings on aggression, ambiguities in the law, the overlap with powers of the Security Council, limited State practice and concerns about the role of the International Criminal Court (ICC).
>
> (Stahn, 2019)

Despite all these difficulties, concerns about categorising some cybercrimes as crimes of aggression are increasing, as cybercrimes are considered as 'a threat to the peaceful coexistence and harmony of the international community' (Ogbe, 2022). The Rome Statute of the ICC (Rome Statute) (UNGA, 1998) is deemed promising in addressing the threat of cybercrimes, typically with its provisions concerning the crime of aggression (Ophardt, 2010–2011; Ogbe, 2023). Article 8*bis* of the Rome Statute defines the crime of aggression as

> the planning, preparation, initiation or execution, by a person in a position effectively to exercise control over or to direct the political or military action of a State, of an act of aggression which, by its character, gravity and scale, constitutes a manifest violation of the Charter of the United Nations,

and the 'act of aggression' as 'the use of armed force by a State against the sovereignty, territorial integrity or political independence of another State, or in any other manner inconsistent with the Charter of the United Nations', thus distinguishing the crime of aggression under the jurisdiction of the ICC and the aggression that should be dealt with in the Security Council. It is suggested that the definition of the crime of aggression could be interpreted flexibly by the ICC to encompass cyber-aggression (Miller, 2014). However, the definition given in the Rome Statute has triggered considerable debate (Glennon, 2010; Mancini, 2012; Solera, 2010; Trahan, 2012). Uncertainties exist on applying Article 8*bis* to determine whether an MCA or an MCASA qualifies as a crime of aggression. Furthermore, the Rome Statute only applies to its States Parties, indicating that the definition has not received universal acceptance.

In addition to the core crimes, the criminalisation of other acts is under discussion, such as organised economic crime, crimes against the environment, and famine-related crimes. Criminalising the offences that cause severe impacts on the environment is promising for punishing those conducting MCASAs that cause severe environmental damage in outer space and on Earth. The necessity to criminalise environmental and ecological insults has long been recognised, particularly considering the strong evidence of an environmental norm and the practically universal condemnation of pollution implicated in international and State practice (van Niekerk, 1976). Environmental insults, possibly impacting globally and harming the well-being of future generations, demand an international response. Currently, five types of international environmental offences have been attached major importance, including illegal trade in wildlife; illegal logging and its associated timber trade; illegal, unreported, and unregulated fishing; illegal trade in controlled chemicals; and illegal disposal of hazardous waste (van Niekerk, 1976), which are often driven by financial incentives, low detection rates, and limited enforcement (Stahn, 2019). However, they do not sufficiently address the most severe environmental pollution. Several initiatives have been undertaken in support of stronger international criminalisation of environmental crimes. The ILC considered this issue while drafting the ARSIWA and the Draft Code for an International Criminal Court, however, failed to include the crime against the environment in the two documents. Scholars have suggested the creation of the crime of ecocide (Gray, 1996; Jenkin, 2022), 'literally a killing of the Earth" and "the environmental counterpart of genocide', implies that 'significantly harming the natural environment constitutes the breach of a duty of care, and this breach insists in tortious or delictual conduct and, when undertaken with wilfulness, recklessness, or negligence, ought to constitute a crime' (Kausar, 2001). Others advocated for holding individuals responsible in international criminal law to ensure enforcement and compliance with international environmental law (McLaughlin, 2000). Moreover, it is suggested that the Rome Statute and the ICC may play a significant role in criminalising environment-devastating acts (Bustami & Hecken, 2021; McLaughlin, 2000). The establishment of an international environmental court has also been advocated (Murphy, 2000; Condor Salazar, 2017). Despite all these scholarly efforts, the development of a strong international criminal law regime for the protection of the environment stagnates, which is ascribable to various factors, including the problematic distinctiveness of environmental damage compared to other types of damage prescribed by international criminal law, the diffused character of much of the harm on the environment, the debatable common culpability involved in some crime against the environment, the fact that much of the environmental damage may result from negligence rather than intentional behaviour, the vagueness and broadness of many environmental law obligations, and problems on the limitations of individual liability (Pathal, 2016). Although the concept of crimes against the environment is promising for addressing the negative consequences on the environment that MCASAs could produce, the relevant rules, as in the status quo, could barely help to deter potential criminals. In addition, when the adverse effects of MCASAs occur in outer space, human survival and well-being are not directly impacted; it is doubtful whether this type of pollution, typically the generation of space debris, would be considered constituting an environmental crime, as the perception of considering massive pollution of the atmosphere or the sea as a State crime was rejected while drafting the ARSIWA (Stahn, 2019).

4.6 Conclusion

Several branches of international law may apply to MCASAs with variant application circumstances: international environmental law may be applicable to prevent adverse environmental impacts of MCASAs, *jus ad bellum* regulates the MCASAs that constitute the use or threat of forces and the use of MCASAs in self-defence, the law of armed conflict applies to the use of MCASAs in armed conflicts, international human rights law is relevant when MCASAs violate human rights, and international criminal law applies when MCASAs are used for international crimes or MCASAs constitute international crimes. However, their preventive, remedial, and punitive effects for countering MCASAs are weak. In addition to their lack of universal applicability to all MCASA cases, their application may present specific difficulties. As no treaty in international environmental law explicitly extends its scope to outer space, the more specific and detailed treaty provisions are unlikely to apply. Instead, general principles of international environmental law will apply. Owing to the ambiguity of these principles, it is challenging to determine the obligations of States in MCASAs. A similar dilemma lies in applying *jus ad bellum* and the law of armed conflicts to MCASAs. In addition, the lack of universally agreed definitions of some critical terms adds to the complexity. Implementing international human rights law is inherently challenging as the range of recognised human rights differs among States and regions, which may have different understandings of the same human right. The direct obligations of NSAs not to violate human rights are also under debate. International criminal law could be applied to punish the subjects responsible for MCASAs. The qualification of MCASA as an international crime, such as terrorism, the crime of aggression, or even a crime against the environment, depends on the application of relevant rules by adjudicative bodies. Considering the status quo of these branches of international law, no substantive obligations for States to combat MCASAs could be derived from them, and applying international criminal law to punish those responsible for MCASAs is subject to specific and strict conditions. The overall contribution of these laws to ensuring space cybersecurity is limited.

Notes

1 The 1949 Geneva Conventions include the Convention (I) for the Amelioration of the Condition of the Wounded and Sick in Armed Forces, the Convention (II) for the Amelioration of the Condition of Wounded, Sick and Shipwrecked Members of Armed Forces at Sea, the Convention (III) relative to the Treatment of Prisoners of War and the Convention (IV) relative to the Protection of Civilian Persons in Time of War. The Additional Protocols are the Protocol Additional to the Geneva Conventions of 12 August 1949, and relating to the Protection of Victims of International Armed Conflicts (Protocol I), the Protocol

Additional to the Geneva Conventions of 12 August 1949, and relating to the Protection of Victims of Non-International Armed Conflicts (Protocol II) and Protocol additional to the Geneva Conventions of 12 August 1949, and relating to the Adoption of an Additional Distinctive Emblem (Protocol III).

2 The first transnational efforts to criminalise terrorism were marked by the Convention for the Punishment and Prevention of Terrorism of 1937 [League of Nations Doc. C. 546 (I).M.383(I)1937.V)], which defined terrorism as '[c]riminal acts directed against a State and intended or calculated to create a State of terror in the minds of particular persons, or a group of persons or the general public'. The Convention never entered into force owing to insufficient ratifications. In 1972, the Secretary-General of the UN requested the UNGA to include in its 1972 session an additional agenda item titled 'Measures to prevent terrorism and other forms of violence which endanger or take innocent human lives or jeopardize fundamental freedom'. [UNGA (1972b). Request for the Inclusion of An Additional Item in the Agenda of the Twenty-Seventh Session. UN Doc. A/8791]. Following this, the UNGA considered the item biennially at its thirty-fourth to fourth-eighth sessions and annually thereafter. However, although several resolutions and reports have been adopted, including the Declaration on Measures to Eliminate International Terrorism [UNGA (1995). Measures to Eliminate International Terrorism. UN Resolution. A/RES/49/60.], and a draft Comprehensive Convention against International Terrorism [UNGA (2005). Annex to the Letter Dated 3 August 2005 from the Chairman of the Sixth Committee Addressed to the President of the General Assembly. UN Doc. A/59/894.], no comprehensive agreement devoted to the suppression of terrorism has been reached. See also the Sixth Committee of the UNGA (2023). *Session information of the 78th session.* www.un.org/en/ga/sixth/78/int_terrorism.shtml

References

Anderson, C. B. (2012). Marine pollution and the polluter pays principe: Should the polluter also pay punitive damages. *Journal of Maritime Law and Commerce, 43*(1), 43–58.

Atapattu, S. A. (2007). *Emerging principles of international environmental law.* Transnational Publishers.

Atapattu, S. A. (2019). From 'our common future' to sustainable development goals: Evolution of sustainable development under international law. *Wisconsin International Law Journal, 36*(2), 215–246.

Bantekas, I., & Oette, L. (2020). *International human rights law and practice.* Cambridge University Press. https://doi.org/10.1017/9781108612524

Berkes, A. (2021). *International human rights law beyond state territorial control.* Cambridge University Press. https://doi.org/10.1017/9781108886543

Bird, A. (2010). Third state responsibility for human rights violations. *European Journal of International Law, 21*(4), 883–900. https://doi.org/10.1093/ejil/chq066

Boylan, E. (2017). Applying the law of proportionality to cyber conflict: Suggestions for practitioners. *Vanderbilt Journal of Transnational Law, 50*(1), 217–246.

Brown, D., & Esterhuysen, A. (2023, April 28). *Why cybersecurity is a human rights issue, and it is time to start treating it like one.* www.apc.org/en/news/why-cybersecurity-human-rights-issue-and-it-time-start-treating-it-one

Brownlie, I. (1963). *International law and the use of force by states.* Oxford University Press. https://doi.org/10.1093/acprof:oso/9780198251583.001.0001

Brunnée, J. (2017). The sources of international environmental law: Interactional law. In S. Besson & J. D'aspremont (Eds.), *The Oxford handbook on the sources of international law* (pp. 960–985). Oxford University Press. https://doi.org/10.1093/law/9780198745365.001.0001

Bufundo, N. E. (2006). Compliance with the Ozone treaty: Weak states and the principle of common but differentiated responsibility. *American University International Law Review, 21*(3), 461–496.

Bushey, D., & Jinnah, S. (2010). Evolving responsibility the principle of common but differentiated responsibility in the UNFCCC. *Publicist*, *6*(1), 1–10.

Bustami, A., & Hecken, M. (2021). Perspectives for new international crime against the environment: International criminal responsibility for environmental degradation under the Rome statute. *Goettingen Journal of International Law*, *11*(1), 145–190.

Çali, B. (2012). Specialized rules of treaty interpretation: Human rights. In D. B. Hollis (Ed.), *The Oxford guide to treaties*. Oxford University Press. https://doi.org/10.1093/law/9780199601813.001.0001

Carozza, P. G. (2008). Human dignity and judicial interpretation of human rights: A reply. *European Journal of International Law*, *19*(5), 931–944. https://doi.org/10.1093/ejil/chn059

Chan, A. W. (2019). The need for shared responsibility regime between state and non-state actors to prevent human rights violations caused by cyber-surveillance spyware. *Brooklyn Journal of International Law*, *44*(2), 795–830.

Chen, L. (1982). Human rights and the free flow of information. *New York Law School Journal of International and Comparative Law*, *4*(1), 37–50.

Clapham, A. (2006). *Human rights obligations of non-state actors*. Oxford University Press. https://doi.org/10.1093/acprof:oso/9780199288465.001.0001

Clarke, B. (2012). Proportionality in armed conflicts: A principle in need of clarification? *Journal of International Humanitarian Legal Studies*, *3*(1), 73–123. https://doi.org/10.1163/18781527-00301003

Condor Salazar, M. (2017). Towards the creation of the international environmental court. *Revista Temas Socio-Juridicos*, *72*, 197–212.

Conference of the Parties of the United Nations Framework Convention on Climate Change (UNFCCC). (1997). *The protocol to the United Nations framework convention on climate change.*UNTS. (2303, 162).

Council of Europe. (1950). *Convention for the protection of human rights and fundamental freedoms*. UNTS. (213, 221).

Council of Europe. (2001). *Convention on cybercrime*. European Treaty Series. (No.185).

Craven, M. (2000). Legal differentiation and the concept of the human rights treaty in international law. *European Journal of International Law*, *11*(3), 489–519. https://doi.org/10.1093/ejil/11.3.489

Crawford, C., & Keene, A. (2019). Interpretation of the human rights treaties by the international court of justice. *The International Journal of Human Rights*, *24*(7), 935–956. https://doi.org/10.1080/13642987.2019.1600509

Crowe, J., & Weston-Scheuber, K. (2015). *Principles of international humanitarian law*. Edward Elgar Publishing.

Culapa, A. L. (2004). Cyberattacks, cyberterrorism and cyber-use of force: Countering the unconventional under international law. *Ateneo Law Journal*, *48*(4), 1051–1163.

Cyber, R., Friman, H., Robinson, D., & Wilmshurst, E. (2019). *An introduction to international criminal law and procedure*. Cambridge University Press. https://doi.org/10.1017/9781108680455

Damjanovic, A., Vasilkov, Z., & Petrovic, S. (2021). Sustainable development as principle of environmental law. *Economic and Social Development. International Scientific Conference on Economic and Social Development*, *75*, 250–255.

DCG. (1949b). *Convention (II) for the amelioration of the condition of wounded, sick and shipwrecked members of armed forces at sea*. UNTS. (75, 86).

DCG. (1949c). *Convention (III) relative to the treatment of prisoners of war.* UNTS. (75, 135).

DCG. (1949d). *Convention (IV) relative to the protection of civilian persons in time of war*. UNTS. (75, 287).

DCG. (1977). *Protocol additional to the Geneva conventions of 12 August 1949, and relating to the protection of victims of international armed conflicts*. UNTS. (1125, 3).

de Schutter, O. (2019). *International human rights law: Cases, materials, commentary*. Cambridge University Press. https://doi.org/10.1017/9781108564588

Dinniss, H. H. (2012). *Cyber warfare and the laws of war*. Cambridge University Press. https://doi.org/10.1017/CBO9780511894527

Dinstein, Y. (2012). The principle of distinction and cyber war in international armed conflicts. *Journal of Conflict and Security Law*, *17*(2), 261–277. https://doi.org/10.1093/jcsl/krs015

Diplomatic Conference of Geneva (DCG). (1949a). *Convention (I) for the amelioration of the condition of the wounded and sick in armed forces in the field*. UNTS. (75, 31).

Dörmann, K. (2016). *Commentary on the first Geneva convention*. Cambridge University. https://doi.org/10.1017/9781316755709

Downey, W. (1953). Law of war and military necessity. *American Journal of International Law*, *47*(2), 251–262.

Doyle Jr, J. H. (2002). Computer networks, proportionality, and military operations. *International Law Studies*, *76*, 147–161.

Fadahunsi-Banjo, M. (2015). Extending the international law principle of good neighborliness to outer space. *Proceedings of the International Institute of Space Law*, *58*, 211–222.

Farrior, S. (1998). State responsibility for human rights abuses by non-state actors. *American Society of International Law Proceedings*, *92*, 299–302.

Fenton, H. (2019). Proportionality and Its applicability in the realm of cyber-attacks. *Duke Journal of Comparative and International Law*, *29*(2), 335–359.

Fisher, E. (2001). Is the precautionary principle justiciable? *Journal of Environmental Law*, *13*(3), 315–334. https://doi.org/10.1093/jel/13.3.315

Force, M. K. (2012). Legal implications of debris removal. *Proceedings of the International Institute of Space Law*, *55*, 727–744.

Geiß, R., & Lahmann, H. (2012). Cyber warfare: Applying the principle of distinction in an interconnected space. *IsraelLaw Review*, *45*(3), 381–399. https://doi.org/10.1017/s0021223712000179

Gervais, M. (2012). Cyber attacks and the law of war. *Berkeley Journal of International Law*, *30*, 525–579. https://doi.org/10.2139/ssrn.1939615

Glennon, M. J. (2010). The blank-prose crime of aggression. *Yale Journal of International Law*, *35*(1), 71–114.

Gopalakrishnan, V. V., & Prasad, M. (2013). Space debris remediation common but differentiated responsibility. *Proceedings of the International Institute of Space Law*, *56*, 379–394.

Graham, D. E. (2010). Cyber threats and the law of war. *Journal of National Security Law & Policy*, *4*, 87–102.

Gray, M. (1996). The international crime of ecocide. *California Western International Law Journal*, *26*(2), 215–272.

Green, J. A., & Grimal, F. (2011). The threat of force as an action in self-defense under international law. *Vanderbilt Journal of Transnational Law*, *44*(2), 285–330.

Greenawalt, A. K. A. (2020). What is an international crime? In K. Jon Heller, F. Mégret, S. MH. Nouwen, J. D. Ohlin & D. Robinson (Eds.), *The Oxford handbook of international criminal law*(pp. 293–316). Oxford University Press. https://doi.org/10.1093/law/9780198825203.003.0013

Hakimi, M. (2018). The *Jus ad Bellum*'s regulatory form. *The American Society of International Law*, *112*(2), 151–190. https://doi.org/10.1017/ajil.2018.23

Harris, P. G. (1999). Common but differentiated responsibility: The Kyoto Protocol and United States policy. *New York University Environmental Law Journal*, *7*(1), 27–48.

Hathaway, O. A., Chertoff, E., Dominguez, L., Manfredi, Z., & Tzeng, P. (2017). Ensuring responsibility: Common Article 1 and state responsibility for non-state actors. *Texas Law Review*, *95*(3), 539–590.

Hayward, R. J. (2017). Evaluating the imminence of cyber attack for purposes of anticipatory self-defense. *Columbia Law Review*, *117*(2), 399–434.

Henckaerts, J., & Doswald-Beck, L. (Eds.) (2005). *Customary international humanitarian law, Vol 1: Rules*. Cambridge University Press. https://doi.org/10.1017/CBO9780511804700

Huang, Z., & Ying, Y. (2020). The application of the principle of distinction in the cyber context: A Chinese perspective. *International Review of the Red Cross*, *102*(913), 335–365. https://doi.org/10.1017/s1816383121000023

ICJ. (1949a). Corfu channel (United Kingdom of Great Britain and Northern Ireland v. Albania). Merits judgment. *ICJ Reports*, 4.

ICJ. (1949b). Reparations for injuries suffered in the service of the United Nations. advisory opinion, *ICJ Reports*, 174.

ICJ. (1986). Military and paramilitary activities in and against Nicaragua (Nicaragua v. United States of America). Merits judgment, *ICJ Reports*, 14.

ICJ. (1996). Legality of the threat or use of nuclear weapons. Advisory opinions, *ICJ Reports*, 226.

ICJ. (2010). Pulp Mills on the River Uruguay (Argentina v. Uruguay). Merit judgment, *ICJ Reports*, 14.

ICJ. (2015). Certain activities carried out by Nicaragua in the border area (Costa Rica v. Nicaragua) and construction of a road in Costa Rica along the San Juan River (Nicaragua v. Costa Rica). Merit judgment, *ICJ Reports*, 664.

ILC. (2001b). *Draft articles on prevention of transboundary harm from hazardous activities*. Yearbook of the International Law Commission, II, Part Two.

International Committee of the Red Cross (ICRC). (2020). International humanitarian law and cyber operations during armed conflicts. *International Review of the Red Cross*, *102*(913), 481–492–494.

International Court of Justice (ICJ). (1946). *Statute of the international court of justice*. UNTS. (XV, 355).

International Criminal Tribunal for the former Yugoslavia (ICTY). (2000). *Final report to the prosecutor by the committee established to review the Nato bombing campaign against the federal republic of Yugoslavia*. www.icty.org/x/file/Press/nato061300.pdf

International Law Commission (ILC). (2001a). *Articles on responsibility of states for internationally wrongful acts*. ILC Yearbook 2001/II(2).

International Peace Conference. (1907). *Regulations concerning the laws and customs of war on land*. https://ihl-databases.icrc.org/assets/treaties/195-IHL-19-EN.pdf

Jenkin, A. (2022). The case for an international crime of ecocide. *New ZealandJournal of Environmental Law*, *26*, 221–244.

Jensen, E. T. (2003). Unexpected consequences from knock-on effects: A different standard for computer network operations?*American University International Law Review*, *18*(5), 1145–1188.

Jensen, E. T. (2013). Cyber attacks: Proportionality and precautions in attack.*International Law Studies Series. US Naval War College*, *89*, 198–[i]. https://doi.org/10.2139/ssrn.2154938

Kausar, T. (2001). International environmental crime: Concept, scope and possibility. *Pakistan Law Review*, *1*, 104–137.

Khare, A. (2021). Fundamental principles governing international environmental law. *International Journal of Law Management & Humanities*, *4*, 1874–1884.

Killander, M. (2010). Interpreting regional human rights treaties. *International Journal on Human Rights*, *7*(13), 145–169.

Langlade, J. (2018). The danger of space debris: Legal issues and solutions associated with active debris removal. *Proceedings of the International Institute of Space Law*, *61*, 977–986

Louka, E. (2006). *International environmental law: Fairness, effectiveness, and world order*. Cambridge University Press.

Luiif, E. (2014). Definitions of cyber terrorism. In B. Akhgar, A. Staniforth & F. Bosco (Eds), *Cyber crime and cyber terrorism investigator's handbook* (pp. 11–17). Syngress.

MacLeod, J. (2004). Unifying the precautionary principle. *Environmental Law Reporter News & Analysis*, *34*(10), 10891–10896.

Maguire, R. (2014). The role of common but differentiated responsibility in the 2020 Climate Regime. *Carbon & Climate Law Review*, *7*(4), 260–269. https://doi.org/10.21552/cclr/2013/4/269
Mamlyuk, B. N. (2009). Analyzing the polluter pays principle through law and economics. *Southeastern Environmental Law Journal*, *18*(1), 39–80.
Mancini, M. (2012). A brand new definition for the crime of aggression: The Kampala outcome. *Nordic Journal of International Law*, *81*(2), 227–248. https://doi.org/10.1163/157181012x638098
Mbanugo, O., & Ifemeje, S. (2021). Conscientizing the history, nature and sources of international environmental law. *International Review of Law and Jurisprudence*, *3*(2), 134–144.
McBeth, A. (2008). Every organ of society: The responsibility of non-state actors for the realization of human rights. *Hamline Journal of Public Law & Policy*, *30*(1), 33–88.
McDonagh, M. (2013). The right to information in international human rights law. *Human Rights Law Review*, *13*(1), 25–55. https://doi.org/10.1093/hrlr/ngs045
McLaughlin, R. (2000). Improving compliance: Making non-state international actors responsible for environmental crimes. *Colorado Journal of International Environmental Law and Policy*, *11*(2), 377–410.
Meron, T. (1991). *Human rights and humanitarian norms as customary law*. Oxford University Press. https://doi.org/10.1093/acprof:oso/9780198257455.001.0001
Mihr, A. (2014). Good cyber governance: The human rights and multi-stakeholder approach. *Georgetown Journal of International Affairs*, *15*(3), 24–34.
Mihr, A. (2016). Cyber justice: Cyber governance through human rights and rule of law in the internet. *US-China Law Review*, *13*(4), 314–336. https://doi.org/10.17265/1548-6605/2016.04.002
Miller, K. L. (2014). The Kampala compromise and cyberattacks: Can there be an international crime of cyber-aggression. *Southern California Interdisciplinary Law Journal*, *23*(2), 217–260.
Murphy, S. D. (2000). Does the world need new international environmental court. *George-WashingtonJournal of International Law and Economics*, *32*(3), 333–350.
Murphy, S. D. (2009). Protean jus ad bellum. *Berkeley Journal of International Law*, *27*(1), 22–52. https://doi.org/10.15779/z387h2z
Nanda, V. P., & Pring, G. (2013). *International environmental law and policy for the 21st century*. Martinus Nijhoff.
Ogbe, R. (2022). The legal justification of cyber crime as crime of aggression in international law. *International Review of Law and Jurisprudence*, *4*(2), 145–150.
Ogbe, R. (2023). International law, cyber crime and crime of aggression. *African Journal of Criminal Law and Jurisprudence*, *8*, 24–29.
Onuoha, A. (2021). Non-state actors and their obligations under international human rights treaties. *South Asian Law & Economics Review*, *6*, 97–108.
Ophardt, J. A. (2010–2011). Cyber warfare and the crime of aggression: The need for individual accountability on tomorrow's battlefield. *Duke Law & Technology Review*, *9*, 1–27.
Organisation For Economic Cooperation and Development (OECD). (1972). *Recommendation of the council on guiding principles concerning international economic aspects of environmental policies*. OECD/LEGAL/0102. https://legalinstruments.oecd.org/public/doc/4/4.en.pdf
Organisation of African Unity. (1981). *African charter on human and peoples' rights*. UNTS. (1520, 217).
Organization of American States. (1969). *American convention on human rights*. UNTS. (1144, 123).
Pathal, P. (2016). International environmental crime: Growing concern of international environmental governance. *US-China Law Review*, *13*(5), 382–398.

Paust, J. J. (1995). The complex nature, sources and evidences of customary human rights. *Georgia Journal of International and Comparative Law*, *25*(1), 147–164.

Perepolkin, S. M., Perepolkin, D. S., & Averianova, M. V. (2021). Typology of the fourth generation of human rights. *Journal of International Legal Communication (JILC)*, *1*, 91–101.

Permanent Court of Arbitration (PCA). (2005). Iron Rhine (IJzeren Rijn) railway (Belgium v. Netherlands). *Award*, Para. 223. https://pcacases.com/web/sendAttach/477

Petkis, S. (2016). Rethinking proportionality in the cyber context. *Georgetown Journal of International Law*, *47*(4), 1431–1458.

Piatkowski, M. (2017). The definition of the armed conflict in the conditions of cyber warfare. *Polish Political Science Yearbook*, *46*(1), 271–280.

Prasad, M., & Lochan, R. (2007). Common but differentiated responsibility: A principle to maintain space environment with respect to space debris. *Proceedings on the Law of Outer Space*, *50*, 284–292.

Ramcharan, B. G. (2009). National responsibility to protect human rights. *Hong Kong Law Journal*, *39*(2), 361–400.

Ronen, Y. (2013). Human rights obligations of territorial non-state actors. *Cornell International Law Journal*, *46*(1), 21–50.

Roscini, M. (2014). *Cyber operations and the use of force in international law*. Oxford University Press. https://doi.org/10.1093/acprof:oso/9780199655014.001.0001

Sands, P., Peel, J., Fabra, A., & MacKenzie, R. (2018). *Principles of international environmental law. Cambridge University Press*. https://doi.org/10.1017/9781108355728

Sassòli, M. (2019). *International humanitarian law: Rules, controversies, and solutions to problems arising in warfare*. Edward Elgar Publishing Limited. https://doi.org/10.4337/9781786438553

Sassòli, M., Bouvier, A. A., & Quintin, A. (2011). *How does law protect in war? Cases, documents and teaching materials on contemporary practice*. International Committee of Red Cross.

Saul, M. (2015). Identifying the jus cogens norms: The interaction of scholars and international judges. *Asian Journal of International Law*, *5*(1), 26–54. https://doi.org/10.1017/s2044251314000058

Schmitt, M. (2012). Classification of cyber conflict. *Journal of Conflict and Security Law*, *17*(2), 245–260. https://doi.org/10.1093/jcsl/krs018

Schmitt, M. N. (Ed.). (2013). *Tallinn manual on the international law applicable to cyber warfare*. Cambridge University Press. https://doi.org/10.1017/CBO9781139169288

Schmitt, M. N. (Ed.). (2017). *Tallinn manual 2.0 on the international law applicable to cyber warfare*. Cambridge University Press. https://doi.org/10.1017/9781316822524

Serbanescu, R. (2017). Cyber operations triggering and international armed conflict. *Romanian Journal of International Law*, *17*, 118–128.

Sheer, A., & Li, S. (2019). Space debris: A new broadway to address organizational and operational aspects for removal. *Journal of East Asia and International Law*, *12*(2), 269–282. https://doi.org/10.14330/jeail.2019.12.2.02

Silver, D. B. (2002). Computer network attack as a use of force under article 2(4). In M. N. Schmitt & B. T. O'Donnell (Eds.), *Computer network attack and international law* (pp. 73–97). Naval War College Press.

Simma, B., & Alston, P. (1988–1989). The sources of human rights law: Custom, *jus cogens*, and general principles. *Australian Year Book of International Law*, *12*, 82–108.

Singh, G. (2021). Cyber terrorism: Tool of mass destruction. *International Journal of Law Management & Humanities*, *4*, 979–988.

Solera, O. (2010). The definition of the crime of aggression: Lessons not learned. *Case Western Reserve Journal of International Law*, *42*(3), 801–824

Solis, G. D. (2010). *The law of armed conflict: International humanitarian law in war*. Cambridge University Press. https://doi.org/10.1017/CBO9780511757839

Stahn, C. (2019). *A critical introduction to international criminal law*. Cambridge University Press. https://doi.org/10.1017/9781108399906

Stevens, C. (1994). Interpreting the polluter pays principle in the trade and environment context. *Cornell International Law Journal*, *27*(3), 577–590.

Stromseth, J. E. (2006). New paradigms for the jus ad bellum. *GeorgeWashingtonInternational Law Review*, *38*(3), 561–578.

Stürchler, N. (2007). *The threat of force in international law* (p. 38). Cambridge University Press. https://doi.org/10.1017/CBO9780511494338

Tehrani, P. M., Manap, N. A., & Taji, H. (2013). Cyber terrorism challenges: The need for a global response to a multi-jurisdictional crime. *Computer Law & Security Review*, *29*, 207–215. https://doi.org/10.1016/j.clsr.2013.03.011

Trahan, J. (2012). Meaningful definition of the crime of aggression: Response to Michael Glennon. *University of Pennsylvania Journal of International Law*, *33*(4), 907–970.

UN Commission on Sustainable Development. (1996). *Report of the expert group meeting on identification of principles of international law for sustainable development*. United Nations Press.

UN Conference on Environment and Development. (1992a). *Rio declaration on environment and development*. (UN Doc. A/CONF.125/26 (Vol. I)).

UN Conference on Environment and Development. (1992b). *Agenda 21*. (UN Doc. A/CONF.151.26 (Vol. I) & A/CONF.151.26 (Vol. II)).

UN Conference on Environment and Development. (1992c). *United Nations framework convention on climate change*. UN Treaty Series. (1771, 107).

UN General Assembly (UNGA). (1948). *Universal declaration of human rights*. (UNGA Resolution A/RES/217 A (III)).

UNGA. (1967). *Treaty on principles governing the activities of states in the exploration and use of outer space, including the Moon and the other celestial bodies*. (UNGA Resolution 2222 (XXI). *UNTS*, 610, No. 8843).

UNGA. (1969). *Vienna convention on the law of treaties*. UNTS. (1155, 331).

UNGA. (1970). *Convention for the suppression of unlawful seizure of aircraft*. UNTS. (860, 106).

UNGA. (1971). *Convention for the suppression of unlawful acts against the safety of civil aviation*. UNTS. (974, 178).

UNGA. (1972a). *Declaration of the UN conference on the human environment*. UNTS. (UN Doc. A/CONF.48/14/Rev.1).

UNGA. (1972b). *Request for the inclusion of an additional item in the agenda of the twenty-seventh session*. (UN Doc. A/8791).

UNGA. (1980). *Convention on prohibition on the use of certain conventional weapons which may be deemed to be excessively injurious or to have indiscriminate effects (with Protocols I, II and III)*. UNTS. (1342, 137).

UNGA. (1988). *Protection of global climate for present and future generations of mankind*. (UN Resolution A/RES/43/53).

UNGA. (1995). *Measures to eliminate international terrorism*. (UN Resolution A/RES/49/60).

UNGA. (1997). *International convention for the suppression of terrorist bombings*. UNTS. *(*2149, 256).

UNGA. (1998). *Rome statute of the international criminal court*. UNTS. (2187, pp. 91–152).

UNGA. (1999). *International convention for the suppression of the financing of terrorism*. UNTS. (2178, 197).

UNGA. (2005). *Annex to the letter dated 3 August 2005 from the chairman of the sixth committee addressed to the president of the general assembly*. (UN Doc. A/59/894).

UNGA. (2015). *Transforming our world: The 2030 Agenda for sustainable development*. (UNGA Resolution A/RES/70/1).

UNGA. (2023). *Session Information of the 78th Session of the Six Committee of the UNGA on Measures to Eliminate International Terrorism*. https://www.un.org/en/ga/sixth/78/int_terrorism.shtml

UN Governmental Group of Experts (UNGGE). (2021). *Report of the group of governmental experts on advancing responsible state behaviour in cyberspace in the context of international security*. (UN Doc. A/76/135).
UN Office on Drugs and Crime (UNODC). (2012). *The use of the internet for terrorist purposes*. www.unodc.org/documents/frontpage/Use_of_Internet_for_Terrorist_Purposes.pdf
van Niekerk, B. (1976). Environmental pollution - the new international crime. *South African Law Journal*, *93*(1), 68–80.
Viasat. (2022, March 30). *KA-SAT network cyber attack overview*. https://news.viasat.com/blog/corporate/ka-sat-network-cyber-attack-overview
World Commission on Environment and Development. (1987). *Our common future*. https://sustainabledevelopment.un.org/content/documents/5987our-common-future.pdf

5 The Applicability of General International Law

The *lex specialis derogat legi generali* maxim suggests that 'if a matter is regulated by a general standard as well as by a more specific rule, then the latter should take precedence over the former' (Koskenniemi, 2006). Conversely, general international law shall apply if the matter is not covered by special law. General international law may play a role in special regimes under two circumstances: when the gaps in special laws need to be bridged, in which case general international law may be complementary; and when applying the special law fails to address its objectives (ILC, 2006).

As concluded in previous chapters, regulatory gaps exist in both preventive rules and remedial and punitive rules for coping with malicious cyber activities against space activities (MCASAs). The gaps in the preventive rules, primarily caused by the ambiguous terminology of the rules and the lack of substantive obligations of the principles, could be bridged through interpretation and reification. The complementary role that general international law could play is minimal. However, the loopholes in the remedial and punitive rules are inherent and cannot be countered in the same way. Owing to a lack of initiatives to form new rules in this respect, only general international law may help in terms of the *lex specialis derogat legi generali* maxim. Moreover, there are cases where applying special rules would lead to consequences incongruent with the objectives of the special regimes, for instance, the attribution rule of international space law. A fallback on general international law would be expedient in serving the purposes of the international space law regime better. This chapter examines the applicability issues of general international law to MCASAs, focusing on the international responsibility of the States responsible for space activities involved in MCASAs. It analyses the challenges in applying general international law and concludes that despite the help of general international law, responsibility-related issues for some MCASAs are not addressed by the existing rules.

5.1 Applying General International Law to Hold a State Internationally Responsible

The International Law Commission's (ILC) Articles on Responsibility of States for Internationally Wrongful Acts (ARSIWA) (ILC, 2001a) are considered by courts

DOI: 10.4324/9781003561996-7

and commentators to be 'in whole or in large part an accurate codification of the customary international law of State responsibility' (Crawford, 2013). Moreover, they progressively develop the law (Wittich, 2002). Therefore, without other universal treaties on State responsibility, this sub-section uses the ARSIWA as the general international law rules on State responsibility.

According to Article 2 of the ARSIWA, an internationally wrongful act of a State occurs when a conduct comprising an action or omission is attributable to the State under international law and constitutes a breach of an international obligation of the State. The content of the international obligations, the violation of which gives rise to responsibility, is not defined in the ARSIWA, as it is the function of the primary rules, which involves restating most of substantive international law (ILC, 2001b). The primary rules delineating States' international obligations to prevent the occurrence and the repercussions of the MCASAs having been discussed in previous chapters, this sub-section focuses on the attribution issues.

5.1.1 The Circumstances to Apply the Attribution Rules of International Space Law

As international space law only applies to space activities, whether the attribution rules of international space law or general international law should apply depends on the nature of the MCASAs. Two categories of States may be held responsible for MCASAs: the States relevant to the malicious cyber actors or the act of conducting a malicious cyber activity (MCA), possibly including the State of the nationality of the actor, the State in which the activity is conducted, and the State through the territory of which the MCA is transmitted; and the States responsible for the space activities involved. The first category of States is not subject to international space law as they are irrelevant to the space activities concerned unless the MCA constitutes a space activity per se, leading to the inapplicability of the attribution rules envisioned in Article VI of the Treaty on Principles Governing the Activities of States in the Exploration and Use of Outer Space, including the Moon and the Other Celestial Bodies of 1967 (OST) (UNGA, 1967). Instead, in the absence of specific attribution rules for the cyber context or other relevant branches of international law, the attribution rules of general international law are applicable.

For the second category of States, determining the attribution rules to apply may be challenging. It is noteworthy that if the State responsible for the space activities involved in MCASAs breaches its obligations under international space law while conducting space activities, and the breaching conduct is irrelevant to MCASAs, Article VI of the OST shall decide whether the conduct can be attributed to it unless applying Article VI would lead to consequences incongruent with the objectives of international space law. It is only when their breaches of obligations play a role in MCASAs, such as facilitating the occurrence of the latter, that the attribution dilemma under the present discussion arises. MCASAs are classified into three categories, as mentioned in the Introduction of this study. They can be entirely terrestrial when the locations of conducting the MCA, transmitting unauthorised commands, and the impacted areas are all on Earth. Nonetheless, when the space activities contribute significantly to the occurrence or/and the consequences of MCASAs, Article VI may apply to decide whether the MCASAs could be attributable to the State responsible for the space activities. If the MCA is conducted during space activities, it may also qualify as space activities *per se*. Article VI of the OST shall usually apply unless its application leads to consequences inconsistent with the objectives of international space law. The MCASA cases where the space activities are only manipulated for achieving the purposes pursued by the malicious actor (MCAs manipulating space activities) are the most complex because their nature is challenging to decide, that is, whether they constitute space activities or not.

The role that the 'space' factor plays is decisive in identifying the nature of the last type of MCASAs. It could be minimal, such as in the case where the malicious actor invades the monitoring system of a constellation of communication satellites to disseminate false information on the internet. The effects sought by the malicious actor could be realised completely through terrestrial means, and whether the false information passes through space or terrestrial infrastructure is indifferent to the outcome. The role of the 'space' factor could also be significant. The first hypothesis is that the malicious actor intrudes on a space system to send false radio navigation signals to the aircraft. In a second hypothesis, the malicious cyber actor accesses the monitoring system of a satellite and sends commands that may damage the satellite, just as in the ROSAT X-Ray satellite incident of 1998. A third hypothesis could be the case where the actor intrudes the space system to send orders to a satellite in orbit to deorbit and hit another. In the first hypothesis, the satellite navigation service is unique and could only be provided and not be replaced by terrestrial systems. This is where the significance of the 'space' factor comes into play. In the second hypothesis, the monitoring system of the space object is manipulated to damage the space object, whether to interrupt space services or simply to destroy the space object. Regardless of the ultimate aim of the malicious actor, one consequence of the incident is the damage to the space object, highlighting the importance of the 'space' factor. As the injured party is the State responsible for the space activities itself, the State bears no international responsibility for this incident. Nonetheless, if the destruction of the space object leads to damages to a third party, the case is similar to the situation of the first and third hypotheses, and the State responsible for the space activities may be held accountable when the 'space' factor is significant. In the third hypothesis, the destruction of a satellite can be realised through other ways such as ground-based laser weapons, which could cause power loss in satellites that may amount to damaging the satellites (Boothby, 2017), or direct intrusion into the monitoring system of the targeted satellite. Unlike MCAs, which could be conducted anywhere at almost no cost, anti-satellite weapons and laser weapons are expensive and technically much more complicated than cyber intrusion. It cannot be deemed an appropriate alternative for MCASAs. Manipulating a satellite to destroy another is indispensable for achieving the purpose and could not be replaced by other terrestrial methods. In addition, the satellite manipulated is damaged as well. Therefore, the 'space' factor cannot be ignored in the third hypothesis.

A two-step method could be deduced from the earlier examples when deciding the weight of the 'space' factor in MCAs manipulating space activities. First, whether the purpose could be achieved through other ways. The 'space' factor weighs differently in MCAs interfering with different space activities. When the MCASAs aim to interfere with the services or results that can only be provided by space activities, such as satellite remote sensing, satellite navigation and positioning, and lunar and Martian exploration, the 'space' factor prevails. If the purpose could be achieved using other terrestrial ways, proceeding to the second step, which lies in appraising whether the cost and ease of conducting are comparable to MCASAs, is necessary. When the cost of using the terrestrial methods is similar to or even lower than MCASAs involving the manipulation of space activities, the 'space' factor does not play an essential role in achieving the malicious actor's purpose, and MCASAs could only be considered a random choice by the actor. However, considering the fact that MCASAs could be conducted simply with a computer from anywhere, other terrestrial methods could rarely be considered similar. Furthermore, it is noteworthy that damages to space objects do not necessarily entail the responsibility of a State as the damaged State may well be the space responsible for the space activity.

5.1.2 The Circumstances to Apply the Attribution Rules of General International Law

According to the principle of *lex specialis derogat legi generali*, attribution rules of general international law shall apply to decide whether MCASAs could be attributed to States responsible for space activities involved under two circumstances: when the attribution rules of international space law do not address a specific situation or when applying them would lead to consequences incongruent with the objectives sought by international space law.

5.1.2.1 Applying General International Law to Counter the Loopholes of International Space Law

As concluded in Chapter 2, the attribution rules of international space law do not address the circumstances where several States could be held responsible. In the absence of a universally accepted definition of 'national activities in outer space', the prevailing opinion links 'national activities in outer space' to jurisdiction (Cheng, 1998). In a case where a space tourist of the nationality of State A on a space trip organised by a company under the jurisdiction of State B conducts an MCA on board a spacecraft under the jurisdiction of State C, suppose all three States have carelessly breached their obligations under international space law, and their breach together contributes to the occurrence of the MCASA. According to Cheng's analysis, State C is the responsible State as it exercises quasi-territorial jurisaction, which prevails over personal jurisaction of States A and B. Certainly, the breaching conduct of States A and B could be legally assessed by holding them directly responsible for failing in their duties. However, in the context of the MCASA, this way of assessment, apparently neglecting the liaison between their violation and the MCASA, is incomplete. In contemplating the international responsibility issue of the MCASA, the contributory effects of the breach of the two States should be considered as well. Thus, the failure to provide for such a situation constitutes a loophole in the attribution rules of international space law. It can be partially complemented by general international law.

In cases where one State is implicated in the internationally wrongful act of another, the principle of independent responsibility, that is, 'all States are individually and independently responsible for their own conduct, being conduct that is attributable to them according to attribution rules', shall apply (Crawford, 2013). However, exceptions to the principle exist, which are incorporated in Chapter IV, Part One of the ARSIWA. Applying the principle of independent responsibility in MCASAs may sometimes neglect the relations between the States involved in the internationally wrongful act and the act, thus necessitating referring to the exceptions to the principle.

Articles 16–18 of the ARSIWA embrace three situations of a State's responsibility in connection with the act of another State—aid or assistance in the commission of an internationally wrongful act, direction and control exercised over the commission of an internationally wrongful act, and coercion of another State. These articles are unusual within the ARSIWA in that 'they do not sit comfortably within the dichotomy between primary and secondary rules as they effectively specify certain conduct as internationally wrongful' (Crawford, 2013), such as aiding or assisting in the commission of an internationally wrongful act, dealt with in Article 16. Aid or assistance is the most relevant to MCAs manipulating space activities, as space activities may be considered as providing aid or assistance to achieving the purposes of the malicious actors. According to Article 16 of the ARSIWA,

> [a] State which aids or assists another State in the commission of an internationally wrongful act by the latter is internationally responsible for doing so if: (a) that State does so with knowledge of the circumstances of the internationally wrongful act; and (b) the act would be internationally wrongful if committed by that State.

The status of customary law of Article 16 has been confirmed in the Application of the Convention on the Prevention and Punishment of the Crime of Genocide case (Bosnian Genocide case) (ICJ, 2007). However, applying this article may encounter several difficulties.

The first difficulty lies in defining the term 'aid or assistance'. Aid or assistance arises when a State actively provides military, economic, or technical assistance to another (Lanovoy, 2014). However, uncertainties on what constitutes aid or assistance remain. Two approaches to demarcate the scope of aid or assistance have been suggested. The first approach refers to international practice (Aust, 2011). According to the current international practice, allowing its territory and territorial air space to be used by another State for preparing for or committing unlawful use of force or human rights violations, furnishing logistic support, valuable intelligence, and all forms of assistance, material, technological, or financial to the unlawful conduct of another State, or even providing support to circumvent the requirements of binding United Nations (UN) Security Council resolutions, could all be conceived as aid or assistance (Aust, 2011). Some MCASAs can be similar to the aforementioned situations. For instance, in the case where an MCA is conducted onboard a spacecraft by a space tourist, the State operating the spacecraft is comparable to a State allowing its territory to be used by another State for an internationally wrongful act; if a malicious cyber actor invades a satellite remote sensing system to send wrong information to the receiving stations, it is analogous to the case of furnishing logistic support to the wrongful act of another State. Nonetheless, considering the specific legal status of outer space, a definite conclusion cannot be drawn that space activities provide aid or assistance to malicious cyber actors. In addition, as the circumstances of MCASAs may significantly vary, evaluating the impact of space activities in MCACAs remains a case-specific work.

The second approach is to draw inspiration from primary/special rules on complicity (Aust, 2011). The word 'aid' or 'assistance' appears in several international treaties, such as Article 1(1)(c) of the Convention on the Prohibition of the Use, Stockpiling, Production and Transfer of Anti-Personnel Land Mines and on Their Destruction (UNGA, 1997); Article 1(c) of the Convention on Cluster Munitions (UNGA, 2008); and Article I of Treaty on the Non-Proliferation of Nuclear Weapons (IAEA, 1968). However, this approach is not promising for providing a general definition to 'aid or assistance', as controversies exist regarding the meaning of the word 'assistance' in these treaty regimes, and the meanings of 'assistance' contained only in certain international treaties are insufficient for the formation of a common interpretation of the word, which is of much broader use in international law. 'Aid or assistance' is not mentioned in international space law or the emerging cyber norms, which are most relevant to MCASAs. Thus, the second approach is inappropriate in deciding whether the manipulated space activities constitute aid or assistance to the malicious cyber actor.

In addition, controversies exist in whether omission constitutes aid or assistance. In the Bosnian Genocide case, the court contended that 'positive action has to be taken to furnish aid or assistance to the perpetrators' (ICJ, 2007), implying that aid or assistance through omission is inconceivable. However, an opposite conclusion was reached in the Corfu Channel case, in which the court concluded that Albania incurred responsibility for failing to warn third States of the presence of the mines in its territorial waters (ICJ, 1949a). The premise for qualifying omission as aid or assistance is an obligation to act. Following this logic, in MCASAs, the omission of the State responsible for space activities may constitute aid or assistance if the State should curb the MCAs and the adverse consequences. Several rules in international space law are relevant. Article I of the OST provides for States' freedom to explore and use outer space. Space activities manipulated by malicious cyber actors, threatening other space activities, could be considered as damaging other States' right to free exploration and use of outer space. When space activities are manipulated by malicious cyber actors for military purposes, or the MCASA amounts to the use of force, Article III of the OST and Article 2(4) of the UN Charter may be invoked. According to Article IX of the OST, States Parties 'shall conduct all their activities in outer space . . . with due regard to the corresponding interests of all other States Parties to the Treaty' and to avoid their 'harmful contamination and also adverse changes in the environment of the Earth'. Manipulated space activities may violate these provisions. The States responsible for space activities are under international obligations to act to protect other States' corresponding interests and environmental interests. However, as analysed in Chapters 2 and 4, ambiguities exist in these preventive rules, leading to difficulties in reifying them, and thus, whether the State responsible for the manipulated space activity bears a duty to adopt specific measures remains uncertain. In MCASAs, although omissions can constitute aid or assistance, there are no common criteria for deciding it. Referring to the substantive obligations that the State should bear is indispensable and shall be completed on a case-by-case basis.

The second difficulty resides in applying the guidelines pertinent to the scope of responsibility for aid or assistance prescribed in Article 16 of the ARSIWA. The Article has laid out three guidelines: the assisting State has the knowledge of the circumstances of the internationally wrongful act, the aid or assistance must be provided to facilitate the commission of the wrongful act and must actually do so, and the wrongful act must be such that it would have been wrongful had the assisting State committed it (ILC, 2001b). The last guideline relates more closely to the primary rules. In the context of MCASAs, it can be translated into the following question: whether the State responsible for space activities would be considered to have committed a wrongful act if the State conducted the MCAs. The answer to the question shall be determined by the international obligations bearing on the State, notably those derived from cyber law. The first and second guidelines are vital for deciding whether the State responsible for manipulated space activities provides aid or assistance.

Instead of requiring a more substantial mental element, such as the intent to conduct a wrongful act, the first guideline requires that the assisting State be aware of the circumstances making the act of the assisted State internationally wrongful. Ascertaining the assisting State's knowledge of the circumstances of the international wrongful act is complex, as it depends upon various elements, such as the notoriety of facts, the particular interests of assisting the State in the region, the geographical proximity, and the nature of the aid or assistance and of the wrongful act itself (Lanovoy, 2014). These elements could contribute to deciding whether the State responsible for the manipulated space activities acquires the knowledge of the circumstances; however, they are insufficient. The States operating space systems differ in cyber technology levels. Commercial systems tend to adopt lower cybersecurity standards to save costs. Therefore, without a globally accepted set of minimum cybersecurity standards for space systems, the capabilities to acquire the knowledge of cyber invasions of the space systems involved in MCASA may significantly vary. It would be difficult for outsiders, particularly the victims, to determine whether the State responsible for the manipulated space activities has the capability to acquire or even has acquired the knowledge of the circumstances of the MCASA.

In addition, two situations should be distinguished based on the conditions under which MCAs come to the knowledge of the State responsible for the manipulated space activities. Under the first situation, the State acquires knowledge of the circumstances of the MCA during its performance of duties, or it has performed its duties but acquires the knowledge from other sources; however, it takes no action to prevent the MCA and its aftermath. For instance, it discovers the intrusion of the monitoring system of a space activity through national supervision measures adopted in accordance with Article VI of the OST. If the State is under an international obligation to suppress the MCA or to notify the potential victims under the OST, failure to do so would lead to the State's direct responsibility for breaching its obligations. In the absence of an obligation to take actions to end the MCASA, the State would not be held directly responsible but may be held indirectly responsible for the entire incident for providing aid or assistance. The second situation presupposes that the State fails its duty to supervise and acquires knowledge of the MCA through other sources yet fails to prevent the MCASA and its dire consequences. The State is directly responsible for breaching Article VI of the OST, possibly directly responsible for breaching Articles I and III, and may also bear indirect responsibility for providing aid or assistance. In both situations, the failure of the State responsible for manipulated space activities to prevent the MCASA and its aftermath may incur direct and indirect responsibility. Holding a State directly responsible depends on its obligations under international space law, which should be reified.

The second guideline—the aid or assistance must be provided with a view to facilitating the commission of the wrongful act and must actually do so—only requires that the aid or assistance contribute significantly to the wrongful act (ILC, 2001b), instead of demanding the aid or assistance to be essential for the performance of the wrongful act (Aust, 2011). The fact that the aid or assistance should have made the wrongful act easier to commit suffices. As Article 16 does not reflect the differences in substance and degree of the contribution brought by the aid or assistance (Crawford, 2013), a minimum level of involvement in the wrongful act could be considered as aid or assistance. Similarly, any space activities facilitating MCASAs could be deemed as aid or assistance. Moreover, this guideline contains requirements in subjective aspects: the intent to facilitate the wrongful act. This may wipe out the unreasonableness of considering any space activity involved in MCASAs as aid or assistance. Nonetheless, the subjective aspect is difficult to prove.

5.1.2.2 Applying General International Law to Avoid Unreasonable Consequences of Applying International Space Law

According to the principle of *lex specialis derogat legi generali*, attribution rules of international space law shall apply to MCASAs that could be qualified as space activities. However, a rigid adherence to international space law may lead to consequences incongruent with the objectives of this special law regime. For instance, in the case where a space tourist of the nationality of State A on a space trip organised by a company under the jurisdiction of State B conducts an MCA on board a spacecraft under the jurisdiction of State C, all three States are under the international obligations to ensure that their space activities are carried out 'for the benefit and in the interests of all countries', 'in accordance with international law . . . in the interest of maintaining international peace and security and promoting international cooperation and understanding', as envisioned in Articles I and III of the OST. However, according to the most widely accepted way of interpreting 'national activities in outer space', that is, linking 'national activities in outer space' to jurisdiction (Cheng, 1998), only State C shall be responsible for the MCA, unjustly precluding States A and B from their responsibility for the MCA, despite the malicious actor or the space tourist company exercising elements of governmental authority meeting the attribution requirements of Article 5 of the ARSIWA. Other ways of understanding 'national activities in outer space' may lead to other undesirable consequences. If the nationality standard were adopted in the earlier case, the State of nationality of the space tourism company and the State of nationality of the space tourist would also be held responsible for the MCA. The corollary of this application would be highly stringent restrictions imposed by States on their nationals and companies to participate in or conduct space activities, thus hampering the development of the space tourism economy, which does not align with the objectives of the international space law regime.

On a case-by-case basis, general international law may intervene. The attribution rules of general international law, codified in Articles 4–11 of the ARSIWA, require a link between a State and the actual perpetrators for attributing an internationally wrongful act to the State. In MCASAs, the link between the actual operator of the involved space activities and a State may be challenging to establish, particularly when the space activities are entirely commercial or conducted under a public-private partnership. Article 8 of the ARSIWA provides that

> [t]he conduct of a person or group of persons shall be considered as an act of a State under international law if the person or group of persons is, in fact, acting on the instructions of, or under the direction or control of, that State is carrying out the conduct.

The key to attributing the act of a person or group of persons to a State is to prove the existence of instruction, direction, or control of the State over the person or group of persons.

Although some scholars perceive 'instruction', 'direction', and 'control' as different, their differences are blurred in practice, and most discussions centre on understanding the word 'control'. International judicial decisions have established two control standards. In the Military and Paramilitary Activities in and Against Nicaragua case, the court contended that 'it would in principle have to be proved that that State had effective control of the military or paramilitary operations in the course of which the alleged violations were committed' (ICJ, 1986), establishing the 'effective control' standard. This standard was reaffirmed in the Bosnian Genocide case (ICJ, 2007). However, the appropriateness of applying this standard in the cyber context is questionable. In the cyber realm, technical attribution, that is, technically tracing the actor of MCA, is extremely difficult (Dederer & Singer, 2019). Were the 'effective control' standard to apply, the burden of proof, including technically tracing the originators of malicious activity, would be so high for the victim that a 'free pass' is given to State sponsorship of MCA (Shackelford & Andres, 2011). The International Criminal Tribunal for the Former Yugoslavia (ICTY) established a competing control standard—the 'overall control' standard—in the Tadić case. The Appeals Chamber of the ICTY considered that 'for the attribution to a State of acts of these groups it is sufficient to require that the group as whole be under the overall control of the State', confining the application scope of the overall control standard to organised groups (Appeals Chamber of the ICTY, 1999). It further explained what may constitute the overall control by stating that

> [i]n order to attribute the acts of a military or paramilitary group to a State, it must be proved that the State wields overall control over the group, not only by equipping and financing the group, but also by coordinating or helping in the general planning of its military activity.
>
> (Appeals Chamber of the ICTY, 1999)

The limited application scope of this standard does not pose a real problem for establishing a link between the commercial entities conducting space activities and a State, as these commercial entities can meet the requirements for constituting organised groups. However, other difficulties in applying the 'overall control' standard exist. Although less stringent than the 'effective control' standard, it is still demanding for the victim to prove the technical attribution (Finlay & Payne, 2019; Margulies, 2013). Furthermore, it is not uniformly adopted by international judicial authorities, as the International Court of Justice has rejected its use in the Bosnian Genocide case, contending that the standard has 'the major drawback of broadening the scope of State responsibility well beyond the fundamental principle governing the law of international responsibility: a State is responsible only for its own conduct' (ICJ, 2007). The applicability of the 'overall control' standard to MCASAs is questionable.

Other methods to link non-State actors' (NSAs) acts to States have been proposed. The imputed responsibility approach, discarding the contentions on establishing a viable control standard (Graham, 2010; Sklerov, 2009), seeks to impute responsibility to a State for MCAs originating from its territory (Huang, 2014). Two elements are vital for this approach: (1) the existence of an affirmative duty of States to prevent their territories from being used as launching pads for MCAs, that is, the existence of due diligence obligations bearing upon the States; and (2) the violation of the duty (Graham, 2010). The drawbacks of this approach are evident. The core of the approach lies in determining the obligations bearing on States, whereas, as indicated in Chapter 3 of this study, the content of the due diligence obligation in the cyber context is yet to be determined. Moreover, this approach, which established a presumption of State responsibility for failure to prevent detrimental activities within its borders, is regarded as ill-suited to the cyber context as it would effectively hold the State to an impractically high standard (Payne & Finlay, 2017).

As none of the established tests suit the cyber realm, the importance of introducing a unique attribution standard is highlighted (Schmitt, 2017; Shany & Schmitt, 2020; Tsagourias & Farrell, 2020). State practice since 2014 demonstrates that States have attributed MCAs of NSAs to States even in the absence of evidence of State control, applying a 'control and capabilities' test instead (Stockburger, 2017). According to this approach, several factors should be examined to determine State responsibility, including the relationship between the NSA and the State, the influence of the State over the NSA, the methods used by the NSA, the motivations of the two parties, whether the two parties use similar code, their technical capabilities, and geographic locations (Stockburger, 2017). However, as applying the 'control and capabilities' test may raise similar technical problems to those raised by the 'effective control' standard, and how to perform the test is not entirely clear (Krasikov, 2022), it will still take time for this approach to develop into maturity.

To conquer the common drawback of the 'effective control', 'overall control', and 'control and capabilities' tests, that is, placing an extremely high burden of proof on the victim State, the 'virtual control' test is proposed. This test entails a shift of the burden of proof from the victim State to the accused State when the latter 'funds and equips or knowingly provides sanctuary to NSAs that subsequently engage in malicious cyber activities' (Margulies, 2013). The 'virtual control' test is not appropriate when the victim State acts in self-defence against MCASAs that constitute an armed attack per se or are applied as a military means during an armed attack. It is proposed that if the accused State refuses to prove itself or the information provided proves its responsibility, the victim State may exercise its right to self-defence (Margulies, 2013). Nonetheless, waiting for the accused State to prove its innocence may take some time, which would hinder the victim State from reacting promptly to armed attacks to minimise losses. Moreover, the victim State risks violating the *jus ad bellum* if it takes retaliatory actions before the accused State manages to prove its innocence. Higher attribution standards would better suit this situation.

5.1.3 Sub-Conclusion

Two requirements must be met for holding a State responsible for internationally wrongful act—the act is attributable to the State, and the act breaches the State's international obligations. Whether the attribution rules of international space law, enshrined in Article VI of the OST or the attribution rules of general international law, codified in the ARSIWA, shall apply to determine whether an MCASA is attributable to the State conducting space activities manipulated is dependent on the nature of the MCASA, that is, whether it could be qualified as space activities. Assessing the impact of the 'space' factor in the whole incident could serve this purpose. As Article VI has loopholes in addressing the indirect contributory effects of space activities on MCASAs and applying Article VI may lead to consequences incongruent with the objectives of the international space law regime under certain circumstances, the ARSIWA shall intervene. Nonetheless, even in the cases where applying general international law is more appropriate, attributing an MCASA to the State responsible for the space activity manipulated may still confront difficulties, notably in terms of establishing a link between the NSAs which actually conduct the space activity and the State.

5.2 Applying General International Law to Determine the Content of the International Responsibility

It is noteworthy that two types of international responsibility could arise out of MCASAs. The most severe MCASAs may trigger the application of international criminal law. MCASAs below the threshold of crimes may incur States' international responsibility when the requirements for holding a State internationally responsible are met. The contents of criminal responsibility and normal international responsibility are different. This section focuses on the responsibility of the States conducting space activities in the case of MCASAs below the threshold of international crimes.

Two approaches are provided by international law to victims of MCASAs seeking compensation or other forms of remedies from the State responsible for the space activities involved. International space law only tackles the liability arising out of damages caused by space activities to others, regardless of whether the State responsible for space activities has breached its international obligations under space law. However, as analysed in Chapter 2 of this study, not all damages are covered by the liability regime of international space law, and since proving fault for damages in outer space is challenging, the victims of MCASAs will have to resort to other methods for remedies. In addition to damages, other forms of remedy may also be necessary to rectify the adverse effects of the MCASAs, which are not prescribed by international space law. Thus, the rules of general international law concerning the content of States' international responsibility can thus play a role.

5.2.1 The Legal Consequences of Internationally Wrongful Acts

Two major legal consequences of internationally wrongful acts—cessation and non-repetition, and reparation—are provided in Articles 30 and 31 of the ARSIWA in a general way.

5.2.1.1 Cessation and Non-Repetition

Article 30 deals with two separate but linked issues raised by the breach of an international obligation: the cessation of the wrongful act and the offer of assurances and guarantees of non-repetition by the responsible State if circumstances so require (ILC, 2001b). In the Rainbow Warrior arbitration, the Tribunal highlighted 'two essential conditions intimately linked' for the requirement of cessation of wrongful act to arise, 'namely that the wrongful act has a continuing character and that the violated rule is still in force at the time in which the order is issued' (France-New Zealand Arbitration Tribunal, 1990). In the law of international responsibility, instantaneous breaches and continuing breaches should be distinguished, and Article 30 only applies to continuing breaches. A continuing breach is characterised by 'a course of conduct which extends over a period of time, remaining in breach of international law throughout' (Crawford, 2013). According to Article 14 of the ARSIWA, continuing breaches indicate '[t]he breach of an international obligation by an act of a State having a continuing character extends over the entire period during which the act continues and remains not in conformity with the international obligation', and '[t]he breach of an international obligation requiring a State to prevent a given event occurs when the event occurs and extends over the entire period during which the event continues and remains not in conformity with that obligation' (ILC, 2001a). Thus, according to Article 30, the act to be ceased includes both acts and omissions (ILC, 2001b). However, an act does not have a continuing character merely because its effects or consequences extend in time (ILC, 2001b). Three tools have been proposed for deciding whether a breach is continuing: focusing on the definition of the international obligation breached rather than the consequences, examining the effectiveness of the remedy of cessation after the act first occurs, and assessing whether the act can be repeated in its entirety each day since it has been passed (Pauwelyn, 1996). Assessing by these tools, some MCASAs could be considered as having a continuing character. For instance, the malicious cyber actor illegally accesses the monitoring system of a satellite system and assumes control of the satellites. This invading status may last for a while until the malicious actor ceases this unauthorised access or the intrusion is curbed by others. If the State responsible for the space activities involved is held internationally responsible, it shall adopt measures to cease the intrusion under Article 30 (a). However, to cease an MCASA is not always possible as the State does not always have the technical capability to do so, and failure to cease the act constitutes a new breach of international obligations. Thus, applying Article 30 (a) to the State responsible for the space activities involved in MCASAs should be prudent, or it will create unjust burdens on the State.

Assurances and guarantees against repetition, bearing on future conduct, aim to restore confidence between the parties concerned in fulfilling the obligations (Schmitt, 2017). The specific circumstances of a case, such as the character of the obligation breached and the breach, decide whether assurances and guarantees against repetition are required (ILC, 2001b). Thus, deciding the necessity and appropriateness of this remedy relies on a case-by-case analysis (Crawford, 2013). In practice, assurances and guarantees of non-repetition refer to different acts from the breaching States: 'assurances' are generally provided verbally, such as diplomatic notes or public pronouncement, whereas guarantees of non-repetition entail specific preventive measures (ILC, 2001b). Consider a case in which a State conducting space activity did not consider cyber security issues during the conception and development of its space systems to save costs. Several malicious cyber actors take advantage of this technical loophole and illegally access its systems, causing dire consequences to other States. Assurances from the State responsible for the space activities are insufficient to prevent the advent of similar incidents in the future, thus necessitating the State's guarantees of non-repetition. The State may need to adopt technical, operational, or legislative means to ensure that its space systems will not be exploited by malicious cyber actors. International practice lacks conformity regarding the types of guarantees that may be requested (ILC, 2001b). As the court indicated in the LaGrand case, when an international obligation can be conducted in various ways, the choice of means must be left to the violating State (ICJ, 2001). Thus, the specific measures to be adopted by the States responsible for space activities involved in MCASAs depend on the specific circumstances of each incident and should be determined by this State. Considering the fact that the specific content of the international obligations posed by international space law in the context of MCASAs remains to be determined, the breaching State enjoys the liberty to undertake the measures it considers appropriate for guaranteeing cybersecurity in its space activities. In addition, in the LaGrand case, the court noted that a State may not be in a position to offer a firm guarantee of non-repetition (ICJ, 2001). Whether it could properly do so would depend on the nature of the obligation in question (ILC, 2001b). This is favourable for the States responsible for space activities, notably for those States possessing less technical capabilities and limited budgets for space activities. Consequently, the overall effects of these guarantees for ensuring cybersecurity in space activities are restricted.

5.2.1.2 Reparation

Article 31 of the ARSIWA provides for the general rules on reparation, according to which the responsible State should make full reparation for the injury incurred by the internationally wrongful act, whether material or moral. MCASAs may impact not only States, such as suspending certain governmental services and destroying another State's governmental or military space system, but also individuals and private entities. The losses suffered by individuals and private entities also qualify as injury of the State (Schmitt, 2017) and may be recoverable under the ARSIWA. The ARSIWA does not address the causation issues directly. However, a causal link, reflecting 'directness', 'foreseeability', or 'proximity' between the wrongful act and the damage, is required (ILC, 2001b). In addition, arbitral and judicial practice have introduced other principal standards for establishing a causal link—reasonableness and certainty (Tumonis, 2011). The standard to apply depends on the circumstances of each breach of international obligation (ILC, 2001b). The losses caused by the State responsible for the space activities involved in MCASAs can be direct, foreseeable, and proximate; they can also be indirect, unforeseeable, and remote. Thus, holding this State internationally responsible does not necessarily lead to reparation by the State. The scope of reparation shall also be determined through the causation test.

In cases of concurrent causes, that is, where several factors have jointly caused the damage but only one of them is ascribed to the responsible State, according to international practice and judicial precedents, the reparatory burden should nonetheless be borne by the State in totality, unless in cases of contributory fault (ILC, 2001b). Contributory fault is addressed in Article 39 of the ARSIWA, which articulates that 'account shall be taken of the contribution to the injury by wilful or negligent action or omission of the injured State or any person or entity in relation to whom reparation is sought'. In MCASAs, the State responsible for the space activities involved may bear direct or indirect responsibility for its breaches of international obligations, depending on the circumstances of the specific incident. However, when other concurrent causes are not ascribable to other States, this distinction of direct and indirect responsibility does not impact the 'full reparation' requirements bearing on the State responsible for space activities unless the victim also contributes to the occurrence of the incident and the damage, whether through active actions or negligent actions or omissions. This could be evidenced by the Corfu Channel case (ICJ, 1949b) and the United States Diplomatic and Consular Staff in Tehran case (ICJ, 1980). Moreover, concurrent causes should be distinguished from the case of several responsible States (Crawford, 2013). According to Article 47 of the ARSIWA, each State is separately responsible for the act attributable to it, and that responsibility is not diminished or reduced by the fact that one or more States are also responsible for the same act (ILC, 2001b). The only limitation on reparation in cases of a plurality of responsible States is that the injured party cannot recover, by way of compensation, more than the damage suffered. This Article does not address the situation where only one responsible State is seized and fully compensates for the damage, whereas the other responsible States escape compensation. Whether the State which has compensated is entitled to the right of recourse against the other responsible States is unclear. This problem is of particular significance for MCASAs. In most MCASAs, the most identifiable responsible State is the State responsible for the space activities involved, as the actual malicious cyber actor is usually difficult to trace. Therefore, the State responsible for space activities is likely to be the only party responsible for the compensation. As Article 47 (2) (b) articulates that the right of recourse against the other responsible States shall not be prejudiced, the ARSIWA remains silent concerning the basis of the right to recourse and how to exercise the right. Thus, in MCASAs, although the responsibility of the State of origin of the MCA could be successfully established, it would be practically difficult for the State responsible for the space activities to acquire a refund from the former once it fully compensates the victim State.

According to Article 34 of the ARSIWA, reparation could 'take the form of the restitution, compensation and satisfaction, either singly or in combination'. Adopting only one form of reparation or a combination of several forms depends on the specific circumstances of a case. These forms of reparation are hierarchically structured, with priority accorded to restitution, which is immediately followed by compensation, and then satisfaction where compensation is impossible (Crawford et al., 2010). The primacy of restitution was confirmed by the Permanent Court of International Justice in the Factory at Chorzów case, declaring that '[r]estitution in kind, or, if this is not possible, payment of a sum corresponding to the value which a restitution in kind would bear' (PCIJ, 1928). Aiming to 're-establish the situation which existed before the wrongful act was committed', restitution is nonetheless subject to two limitations—it is not materially impossible and shall conform to the proportionality principle. Among the various consequences that MCASAs could bring about, some could be restored materially, such as destroying a satellite or other properties on Earth; some are not reparable through restitution, such as losses of human lives and disseminating false remote sensing data. Restitution could also be unproportionate, such as in cases where space debris are generated because of MCASAs, notably considering the technical difficulties for specific States, the high cost of removing the space debris, and the legal uncertainties regarding active space debris removal.

Compensation, deemed as a reparative means to complement restitution by Article 36, aims to 'address the actual losses incurred as a result of the internationally wrongful act' and 'corresponds to the financially assessable damage suffered by the injured State or its nationals' (ILC, 2001b), and does not reflect a punitive character. Financially assessable damage includes both the damage suffered by the State and the damage suffered by its nationals within the State's framework of diplomatic protection (ILC, 2001b). Although most consequences of MCASAs are financially measurable, some impacts are challenging to quantify, notably the environmental damage to outer space caused by MCASAs. For instance, in cases where MCASAs lead to the generation of new space debris, the freedom to explore and use outer space enjoyed by all countries, and thus the benefit and interests of all, are impacted. However, as the formulation of injury articulated in Article 31(2) is intended to exclude merely abstract concerns of general interests which are individually unaffected by the breach (ILC, 2001b), States could not qualify as injured States and could not claim for compensation in accordance with Article 36 if they do not suffer from actual material or moral damage. Instead, Article 48 of the ARSIWA could be invoked, according to which any State is entitled to invoke the responsibility of another State and claim from the responsible State the performance of the obligation of reparation if the obligation breached is owed to the international community as a whole. Thus, Article 48 appears to provide a viable way to address the environmental damages caused by MCASAs. However, Article 48 (2) (b) requires that the performance of the obligation of reparation should be claimed 'in the interest of the injured State or of the beneficiaries of the obligation breached'. As in the MCASAs damaging outer space environment cases, the injured States or beneficiaries of the obligation to protect the outer space environment would be challenging to identify, claiming more than a declaratory remedy and cessation would face difficulties, as Article 48 (2) (b) only establishes the general principle (ILC, 2001b).

Satisfaction, crystallised in Article 37, is the remedy for those injuries that are not financially assessable but amount to an affront to the State. It consists of 'an acknowledgement of the breach, an expression of regret, a formal apology or other appropriate modality'. In the cyber context, significant State practice of claims for satisfaction exists, such as insulting a national symbol, violations of sovereignty, and breaches of diplomatic premises (Schmitt, 2017). As MCASAs could produce similar effects as terrestrial MCAs, satisfaction may also be requested by the injured State.

5.2.2 Remedies for Individual Victims

Several scenarios of injury caused to individual victims by MCASAs could be distinguished. In the first scenario, the State of the injured individuals, representing the latter, holds other States responsible for an MCASA and claims compensation covering the damage suffered by the individuals. It is declared in the Mavrommatis Palestine Concessions case that

> [i]t is an elementary principle of international law that a State is entitled to protect its subjects, when injured by acts contrary to international law committed by another State, from whom they have been unable to obtain satisfaction through the ordinary channels.
>
> (PCIJ, 1924)

However, as States enjoy the discretion regarding whether to invoke the responsibility of a State that has allegedly committed a wrongful act in the interest of individuals, they may not always be willing to take action.

The second scenario presupposes that the State of the injured fails to act internationally. Remedies available to individuals at the international level are limited, because international remedies for individuals are seldom provided (Gaja, 2011). In practice, the only remedy available to individual victims is resorting to national courts, except for cases of human rights violations where it is possible for an individual to bring a claim to an international authority (Gaja, 2011). The effects of human rights claims against States on the international level depend on the attitude of the responsible States and the enforcement of judicial decisions by these States (Gaja, 2011). Therefore, when MCASAs impact an individual's human rights, the injured may bring a claim directly against the allegedly responsible States if the State of the individual's nationality decides not to do so in the interest of the individual. For other damages caused by MCASAs, the injured individuals could only resort to national courts for remedies, which can seldom be supported because of the technical difficulties of proof and the immunities that States enjoy.

The third scenario does not entail internationally wrongful acts. There are chances that no State is internationally responsible for an MCASA. Consider a case where a private malicious cyber actor conducts the activity only for his/her own fun without control from any State, and the State responsible for the space activities manipulated has fulfilled its obligations under international space law and other relevant rules yet fails to defend against the cyber intrusion. No State will be held internationally responsible for the MCASA. In such cases, domestic means are perhaps the only viable way for the injured to be compensated, although it will be haunted by technical difficulties of proof.

5.2.3 Sub-Conclusion

The remedial means provided by general international law complement its counterpart in international space law. In addition to compensation, general international law provides more options to compensate various forms of losses that the injured States suffer. Although applying these options may encounter with some difficulties, the remedial effects on the injuries brought about by MCASAs could be magnified to a large extent. As the successful establishment of a State's international responsibility for internationally wrongful acts is a precondition for applying the rules concerning the content of the international responsibility, not all MCASAs are covered. In some MCASAs, no State could be held responsible, and the individual victims could only resort to local remedies for compensation, probably facing extreme technical difficulties in tracing the originator of the losses.

5.3 Conclusion

According to the *lex specialis derogat legi generali* maxim, general international law applies under two circumstances: when special laws do not address the specific issue and when applying special laws leads to consequences incongruent with the objectives of the special regimes. Thus, concerning the attribution issue, in cases where Article VI of the OST has loopholes in attributing MCASAs to States responsible for space activities and where applying Article VI may lead to undesirable consequences, the ARSIWA may apply. Nonetheless, the intrinsic problems of attribution rules of general international law persist. Moreover, general international law helps to counter loopholes of special laws in terms of remedial rules. Rules of general international law on the legal consequences of internationally wrongful acts complement the liability regime of international space law. However, the remedies for individual victims remain limited if the State of their nationality refuses to invoke the responsibility of the allegedly responsible States or when no State could be held responsible for MCASAs.

References

Appeals Chamber of the International Criminal Tribunal for the Former Yugoslavia (ICTY). (1999). *Prosecutor v. Tadić*. Case No. IT-94–1-A.

Aust, H. P. (2011). *Complicity and the law of state responsibility*. Cambridge University Press. https://doi.org/10.1017/CBO9780511862632

Boothby, B. (2017). Space weapons and the law. *International Law Studies*, *93*, 179–214.

Cheng, B. (1998). Article VI of the 1967 space treaty revisited: 'International Responsibility', 'national activities', and 'the appropriate state'. *Journal of Space Law*, *26*, 7–30.

Crawford, J. (2013). *State responsibility: The general part*. Cambridge University Press.

Crawford, J., Pellet, A., Olleson, S., & Parlett, K. (Eds.). (2010). *The law of international responsibility*. Oxford University Press. https://doi.org/10.1093/law/9780199296972.001.0001

Dederer, H., & Singer, T. (2019). Adverse cyber operations: Causality, attribution, evidence, and due diligence. *International Law Studies Series. US Naval War College*, *95*, 430–[i].

Finlay, L., & Payne, C. (2019). The attribution problem and cyber armed attacks. *AJIL Unbound*, *113*, 202–206. https://doi.org/10.1017/aju.2019.35

France-New Zealand Arbitration Tribunal. (1990). *Rainbow warrior (New Zealand v. France). United Nations reports of international arbitral awards*, XX, 215.

Gaja, G. (2011). The protection of general interests in the international community: General course on public international law. *Collected Courses of the Hague Academy of International Law*, *364*. https://doi.org/10.1163/1875-8096_pplrdc_A9789004255579_01.

Graham, D. E. (2010). Cyber threats and the law of war. *Journal of National Security Law & Policy*, *4*, 87–102.

Huang, Z. (2014). Attribution rules in ILC's Articles on state responsibility: Preliminary assessment on their application to cyber operations. *Baltic Yearbook of International Law*, *14*, 41–54.

ICJ. (1949b). Corfu channel (United Kingdom of Great Britain and Northern Ireland v. Albania). Assessment of the amount of compensation due from the people's republic of Albania to the United Kingdom of Great Britain and Northern Ireland. *ICJ Report*, 244.

ICJ. (1980). United States diplomatic and consular staff in Tehran (United States of America v. Iran). Merits judgment. *ICJ Report*, 3.

ICJ. (1986). Military and paramilitary activities in and against Nicaragua (Nicaragua v. United States of America). Merits judgment, *ICJ Report*, 14.

ICJ. (2001). LaGrand (Germany v. United States of America). Merits judgment. *ICJ Report*, 466.

ICJ. (2007). Application of the convention on the prevention and punishment of the crime of genocide (Bosnia and Herzegovina v. Serbia and Montenegro). Merit judgment, *ICJ Report*, 43.

ILC. (2001b). *Commentaries to the draft articles on responsibility of states for internationally wrongful acts.* Report of the ILC. (Supplement No. 10 (A/56/10), chp.IV.E.2).

ILC. (2006). *Conclusions of the work of the study group on the fragmentation of international law: Difficulties arising from the diversification and expansion of international law.* ILC Yearbook, II, Part 2.

International Atomic Energy Agency (IAEA). (1968). *Treaty on the non-proliferation of nuclear weapons.* UNTS. (729, 161–299).

International Court of Justice (ICJ). (1949a). Corfu channel (United Kingdom of Great Britain and Northern Ireland v. Albania). Merits judgment. *ICJ Reports*, 4.

International Law Commission (ILC). (2001a). *Articles on responsibility of states for internationally wrongful acts.* ILC Yearbook, II, Part 2.

Koskenniemi, M. (2006). *Report of the study group of the international law commission: Fragmentation of international law: Difficulties arising from the diversification and expansion of international law.* (UN Doc. A/CN.4/L.682 and Add.1).

Krasikov, D.V. (2022). International responsibility in cyberspace: The problems of attribution of conduct. *European Proceedings of Social and Behavioural Sciences*, 360–365. https://doi.org/10.15405/epsbs.2022.01.58

Lanovoy, V. (2014). Complicity in an internationally wrongful act. In A. Nollkaemper & I. Plakokefalos (Eds.), *Principles of shared responsibility in international law: An appraisal of the state of the art*(pp. 134–168). Cambridge University Press. https://doi.org/10.1017/CBO9781139940009

Margulies, P. (2013). Sovereignty and cyber attacks: Technology's challenge to the law of state responsibility. *Melbourne Journal of International Law*, *14*(2), 496–519.

Pauwelyn, J. (1996). The concept of a 'continuing violation' of an international obligation: Selected problems. *British Yearbook of International Law*, *66*, 415–450.

Payne, C., & Finlay, L. (2017). Addressing obstacles to cyber-attribution: Model based on state response to cyber-attack. *GeorgeWashingtonInternational Law Review*, *49*(3), 535–568.

PCIJ. (1928). Factory at Chorzów (Claim for Indemnity). *Publications of the PCIJ,* Series A, No. 17, 47.

Permanent Court of International Justice (PCIJ). (1924). The Mavrommatis palestine concessions. *Publications of the PCIJ*, Series A, No. 2, 12.

Schmitt, M. N. (Ed.). (2017). *Tallinn manual 2.0 on the international law applicable to cyber warfare.* Cambridge University Press. https://doi.org/10.1017/9781316822524

Shackelford, S. J., & Andres, R. B. (2011). State responsibility for cyber attacks: Competing standards for growing problem. *Georgetown Journal of International Law*, *42*(4), 971–1016.

Shany, Y., & Schmitt, M. N. (2020). An international attribution mechanism for hostile cyber operations. *International Law Studies Series. US Naval War College*, *96*, 196–[i].

Sklerov, M. J. (2009). Solving the dilemma of state responses to cyberattacks: A justification for the use of active defenses against states who neglect their duty to prevent. *Military Law Review*, *201*, 1–85.

Stockburger, P. Z. (2017). Control and capabilities test: Toward a new lex specialis governing state responsibility for third party cyber incidents. *2017 9th International Conference on Cyber Conflict (CyCon).* https://doi.org/10.23919/cycon.2017.8240334

Tsagourias, N., & Farrell, M. (2020). Cyber attribution: Technical and legal approaches and challenges. *European Journal of International Law, 31*(3), 941–967. https://doi.org/10.1093/ejil/chaa057

Tumonis, V. (2011). Complications of conciliatory judicial reasoning: Causation standards and underlying policies of state responsibility. *The Baltic Yearbook of International Law, 11*(1), 135–152. https://doi.org/10.1163/22115897-90000069

UN General Assembly (UNGA). (1967). *Treaty on principles governing the activities of states in the exploration and use of outer space, including the Moon and the other celestial bodies. UNGA Resolution 2222 (XXI)*. United Nations Treaty Series (UNTS). (610, No. 8843).

UNGA. (1997). *Convention on the prohibition of the use, stockpiling, production and transfer of anti-personnel land mines and on their destruction*. UNTS. (2056, 211).

UNGA. (2008). *Convention on cluster munitions*. UNTS. (2688, 39).

Wittich, S. (2002). The international law commission's Articles on the responsibility of states for internationally wrongful acts adopted on second reading. *Leiden Journal of International Law, 15*(4), 891–920.

Part III

Institutional Aspects of the Global Governance of Space Cybersecurity

The concept of international institutions, similar to the notion of international regimes, denotes 'principles, norms, decision rules, and decision-making procedures around which actor expectations converge in a given issue-area', encompassing the processes and actors that shape international politics and comprising three elements: formal structures, international law, and informal groups (Weiss, 2013). These elements coincide with the core functions of effective global governance, including the identification of the problem to be governed, the creation of a forum for negotiations and law-making, a body to implement and interpret the rules, monitoring of compliance with rules, and enforcement (Barnett et al., 2022). Once an issue acquires international awareness and the objective of coping with this issue is determined, the problems to be solved are who are the actors involved in tackling the issue, how to make rules, and how to implement and enforce the rules. The resolution of these problems relies on institutions.

The findings in Part II of this study reveal that as regulatory gaps exist, reification and harmonisation of the existing rules and new law-making are necessary to better combat malicious cyber activities against space activities. Institutions are indispensable for tackling these issues, notably by law-making activities. Several autonomous and uncoordinated branches of international law having differing mandates, principles, and structures are relevant to space cybersecurity, leading to potential normative overlapping and the situation of institutional diversity and pluralism (Young, 2012). Normative conflicts cannot be completely settled according to the general rules of *lex specialis derogate legi generali*, *lex posterior derogate legi priori*, and the principle of harmonisation, according to which several norms bearing on a single issue should be interpreted to provide a single set of compatible obligations (Koskenniemi, 2006). Moreover, even with a perfect regulatory scheme, the purposes of global governance for space cybersecurity cannot be achieved without effective implementation and enforcement of relevant rules. Institutions also play an essential role in coordinating normative conflicts and ensuring compliance with international law. Thus, two major functions of institutions should be highlighted: law-making (Chapter 6) and law implementation and enforcement (Chapter 7).

DOI: 10.4324/9781003561996-8

References

Barnett, M. N., Pevehouse, J. C. W., & Raustiala, K. (2022). Introduction: The modes of global governance. In M. N. Barnett, J. C. W. Pevehouse & K. Raustiala (Eds.), *Global governance in a world of change* (pp. 1–47). Cambridge University Press. https://doi.org/10.1017/9781108915199.001

Koskenniemi, M. (2006). *Report of the study group of the international law commission: Fragmentation of international law: Difficulties arising from the diversification and expansion of international law*. (UN Doc. A/CN.4/L.682 and Add.1).

Weiss, T. G. (2013). *Global governance: Why? What? Whither?* Polity Press.

Young, M. A. (2012). Regime interaction in creating, implementing and enforcing international law. In M. A. Young (Ed.), *Regime interaction in international law: Facing fragmentation* (pp. 85–110). Cambridge University Press. https://doi.org/10.1017/CBO9780511862403

6 Institutional Interaction for Law-Making to Combat MCASAs

A large part of the regulatory problems analysed in Part II could be solved by interpreting and reifying the existing rules. New norms are necessary where regulatory loopholes exist, typically concerning the international criminalisation of certain malicious cyber activities (MCAs). It is incumbent on several types of institutions to tackle the regulatory dilemma through law-making activities, including States, international organisations (IOs), governmental and non-governmental, and industries. As they function in different ways, the norms and standards developed by them differ significantly in terms of forms, binding force, and scope of application. It is noteworthy that the interests pursued and normative preferences of the institutions vary, which may result in normative overlapping and conflicts in issues implying interests of multiple stakeholders and normative vacuums in areas that stakeholders consider inconsequential, thus triggering a normative disequilibrium impacting the effectiveness of global governance. Institutional interactions and coordination could help to alleviate this imbalance.

The global governance of space cybersecurity intersects with the global governance of outer space, cyberspace, and other fields such as international security, human rights, and the environment. In the absence of institutions specifically devoted to law-making for combatting malicious cyber activities against MCASAs, this chapter focuses on the sectoral and trans-sectoral institutional interactions among actors of law-making pertaining to outer space and cyberspace as an illustration and evaluates the status quo of the interplay.

6.1 Institutional Aspects of Law-Making for the Space Sector

Outer space law-making is shifting from the conventional state-centric top-down approach to placing more prospects on the bottom-up approach. A historical review of international law-making for space activities highlights the role of States and the United Nations (UN). Nonetheless, the impact of other stakeholders on the evolution of space law should not be neglected at the moment.

DOI: 10.4324/9781003561996-9

6.1.1 Space Law-Making Under the Auspices of the UN by States

The notion of law-making in international relations implies the cooperation of States, which brought the dawn of the space era (Lachs, 2010). Although specialised IOs are increasingly engaged in specific issues of space activities, such as the UN Educational, Scientific and Cultural Organization (UNESCO), which promotes an exchange of information to assist member States and non-governmental organisations (NGOs) in the training of astronomers and geo-physicists and scientific projects, and the International Telecommunications Union (ITU), which works on the fields of communication with and between space vehicles and the allocation of wavelengths in communication between the Earth and outer space and in outer space, the UN has been the centre for the development of space law, with a well-defined mechanism and procedure (Gorove et al., 1986).

The establishment of the Committee on the Peaceful Uses of Outer Space (COPUOS) marks the beginning of UN's promulgation of space law. Initially gathering only 24 member States, the COPUOS was established as a subsidiary body of the UN General Assembly (UNGA), with one of its missions being to study the nature of legal problems which may arise from the exploration of outer space (UNGA, 1959). The COPUOS adopts the consensus principle for decision-making, implying that every member State had a veto right (Galloway, 1979). Although the consensus technique contributed to the wide acceptance of space treaties (Jasentuliyana, 1986), it is one of the reasons of the extensive and protracted negotiations within the COPUOS. With the assistance of its two sub-committees—the Scientific and Technical Sub-Committee (STSC) and the Legal Sub-committee—and the UN Office for Outer Space Affairs (UNOOSA), drawing from experience of the specialised agencies and other bodies invited to participate in its work, such as the UNESCO, the Food and Agriculture Organization, the ITU, the World Trade Organization, and NGOs, such as the Committee on Space Research (COSPAR), the International Astronautic Federation, the International Institute of Space Law, and the International Law Association (Hobe et al., 2009), the COPUOS finalised its work on a draft treaty, which was submitted to the UNGA. The draft treaty was a compromise among the original 24 member States of the COPUOS, notably between the Soviet Union and the United States (US). It underwent a review process in the UNGA by all member States of the UN, particularly the States that were not members of the COPUOS, before its adoption. The Magna Carta of international space law, the Treaty on Principles Governing the Activities of States in the Exploration and Use of Outer Space, including the Moon and the Other Celestial Bodies (OST) (UNGA, 1967), was finally approved. It was followed by four other treaties: the Agreement on the Rescue of Astronauts, the Return of Astronauts and Return of Objects Launched into Outer Space (UNGA, 1968), the Convention on International Liability for Damage Caused by Space Objects (UNGA, 1972), the Convention on Registration of Objects Launched into Outer Space (UNGA, 1975), and the Agreement Governing the Activities of States on the Moon and Other Celestial Bodies (Moon Agreement) (UNGA, 1979). Although NGOs were involved, their role was secondary during the formulation process of the five binding instruments. They did not impact the final outcome as such, which incarnated a robust political character (Jankowitsch, 2015). In addition, the technical complexity and political importance of the issues related to space activities call for the participation of technical experts, governmental representatives, and lawyers conversant in the field to interact in the law-making process, which the COPUOS has well enabled (Gorove et al., 1986).

After the Moon Agreement, it became increasingly difficult to achieve consensus on new binding instruments inside the COPUOS, owing to various factors. One vital reason for this standstill is the proliferation of the membership of the COPUOS. The membership of the COPUOS has expanded several times to incorporate 102 member States by 2022 (UN COPUOS, n.d.), with the arrival of a significant number of developing States seeking more equitable international economic relations in space law-making (Danilenko, 1989). It implies that the COPUOS has shifted from a forum for appeasing bipolar conflicts of interests to one where the positions of different groups of States are radically opposed (Danilenko, 1989), leading to difficulties in the naissance of new binding instruments and leaving several legal issues unregulated, such as the delimitation of the airspace and outer space and the militarisation of outer space. The consensus principle of the COPUOS only exacerbates this situation. Instead of treaties, non-binding soft law instruments have been adopted, such as declarations, principles, and resolutions of the UNGA.

The role of the UN in law-making is challenged by the emergence of inter-governmental agreements reached outside the UN fora as well, notably the Artemis Accords (AAs). Eager to establish a framework for lunar activities, the National Aeronautics and Space Administration of the US (NASA) released the AAs to establish a 'shared vision for principles, grounded in the Outer Space Treaty of 1967, to create a safe and transparent environment which facilitates exploration, science, and commercial activities for all of humanity to enjoy' (NASA, 2020). The AAs differ significantly from space cooperation agreements. First, space cooperation agreements are based on negotiations and constitute, more or less, a reflection of the interests of all participants, which the Intergovernmental Agreement of the International Space Station program could represent (Agreement Among the Government of Canada, Governments of Member States of the European Space Agency, the Government of Japan, the Government of the Russian Federation, and the Government of the United States of America Concerning Cooperation on the Civil International Space Station, 1998). Although the Artemis programme welcomes other States as partners, the AAs were drafted unilaterally by the US, which, envisioning no scope for negotiations, should be accepted in its entirety by any State willing to join the programme. Second, although space cooperation agreements usually determine the responsibilities and obligations of the participants, the AAs, seeking to establish a common political understanding regarding mutually beneficial practices in the exploration and use of outer space (US Department of State, 2023), is more of a prescriptive nature as the principles articulated in the AAs either consist of the existing norms of the OST or extend beyond the provisions and attempt to establish new norms of behaviour (de Zwart et al., 2023). Typically, the AAs seek to establish a regime for preserving outer space heritage by stipulating that the signatories intend to 'contribute to multilateral efforts to further develop international practices and rules applicable to preserving outer space heritage' (US Department of State, 2023). Signatories are requested to affirm the conformity of the extraction of space resources with Article II of the OST on the non-appropriation principle and to integrate this position into their multilateral efforts in law-making on extraction and use of space resources (US Department of State, 2023). Using this 'accept or decline' approach, the US, attracting not only space-faring nations but also States with limited space capabilities, can successfully sell its political and normative positions to the participants, which would be difficult through a real multilateral way. Russia and China, which do not participate in the Artemis programme for various reasons, are jointly developing the International Lunar Research Station programme, marking their strong initiatives to play an influential role in space law-making (Wu, 2023). The discarding of multilateralism may accelerate and promote new space law-making. In the current climate for space law-making, under which the factors contributing to the emergence of the five space treaties—an urgent need for new rules, a propitious political climate, and deference to space-capable States—are no longer present; States may opt to negotiate agreements with like-minded States rather than compromise via COPUOS (Nelson, 2020). However, the outcome of this shift from multilateralism to unilateralism may lead to the further fragmentation of international space law. The preservation of dialogues among different clubs of like-minded States, parallel club members, and remaining within the UN may help to avoid this situation.

6.1.2 Space-Activities-Related Law-Making by Other IOs and Institutions

In addition to the COPUOS, other institutions of the UN system are involved in space-activities-related law-making as well. Some of them are organs or specialised agencies of the UN system, such as the ITU, which issues regulations pertaining to the management of geostationary orbital positions and spectrum of frequencies, the Conference on Disarmament (CD), which addresses the prevention of an arms race in outer space, and the World Meteorological Organization, which also works on satellite remote sensing. The scope of their work sometimes overlaps with that of the COPUOS. For instance, UNESCO adopted a Declaration of Guiding Principles on the Use of Satellite Broadcasting for the Free Flow of Information, the Spread of Education and Greater Cultural Exchange in 1972, confirming that satellite broadcasting shall be conducted in conformity with international law and be made available to all countries, and emphasising the purposes of satellite broadcasting for educational and cultural exchanges (UNESCO, 1972). The UNGA adopted the Principles Governing the Use by States of Artificial Earth Satellites for International Direct Television Broadcasting (UNGA, 1982), reiterating the principles in the Declaration of the UNESCO and further addressing issues on State responsibility, the duty and right to consult, copyright and neighbouring rights, and so forth. The ITU worked from a technical perspective and adopted effective space plans for satellite connectivity and broadcasting (ITU, 2023).

Despite the overlapping, coordination and harmonisation among these institutions in the framework of the UN are not burdensome. First, the delimitation of their responsibilities is relatively clear. As the COPUOS works on strengthening the international legal regime governing outer space, resulting in improved conditions for expanding international cooperation in the peaceful uses of outer space, other institutions focus on certain specific areas of outer space and space activities, whether technical or of their application. The relations between the UN and its specialised agencies are normally defined by institutional arrangements, which not only determine the division of responsibilities between them, but also contain articles on reciprocal representation providing for the rights of attending meetings of the other, on the exchange of information and documents, and other issues pertaining to institutional interactions (Agreement Between the United Nations and the United Nations Educational, Scientific and Cultural Organization, 1949; Agreement Between the United Nations and International Telecommunications Union, 1952; Agreement Between the United Nations and the World Meteorological Organization, 1956). Second, parallel membership exists. For instance, the ITU had 193 member States, the UNESCO 194 member States, the International Maritime Organization (IMO) 175 member States and Associate members and the CD 65 members by 2023. All member States of the CD and the COPUOS are member States of the ITU, the UNESCO, and the IMO. The States, when participating in the law-making activity of one institution, are expected to consider their standpoints in others to ensure coherence, which could be guaranteed through national coordination (Danilenko, 1989).

IOs outside the UN system are also concerned with space law-making. The International Atomic Energy Agency (IAEA) adopted the Convention on Early Notification of a Nuclear Accident (Convention on Early Notification) and the Convention on Assistance in the Case of a Nuclear Accident or Radiological Emergency (Convention on Assistance) in 1986. Both of them are applicable to outer space: Article 1 of the Convention on Early Notification expressly delimits their scope of application to include any accident involving facilities or activities of a State party or persons or legal entities under its jurisdiction or control, including 'any nuclear reactor wherever located' (IAEA, 1986a); and the Convention on Assistance does not exclude its application to accidents occurring in outer space or caused by space activities (IAEA, 1986b). The COPUOS is specifically tasked with developing the Principles Relevant to the Use of Nuclear Power Sources in Outer Space (Principles of NPS) (UN COPUOS, 1992) and drafting the Safety Framework for Nuclear Power Source Applications in Outer Space (Safety Framework). The provisions contained in Principle 5 on the Notification of re-entry of the Principles of NPS overlap with those in the Convention on Early Notification, with diversifications in terms of the circumstances to provide notification, the subjects to whom the notification should be addressed, the scope of information to be provided, and the updating and frequency of provision of information (Terekhov, 1987). The STSC initiated a partnership in 2007 with the IAEA to develop safety standards for the launch, operation, and end-of-service mission phases of space NPS applications, and the work was surprisingly rapidly finalised in 2009 (Venturini, 2020). The Safety Framework, prepared by the COPUOS jointly with the IAEA, is a product of institutional cooperation without further needs to address normative conflicts.

Gathering thirteen national or regional space agencies of major space-faring nations, notably including China National Space Administration, European Space Agency, Japan Aerospace Exploration Agency, NASA, and State Space Corporation of Russia, and with the primary purposes to 'exchange information on space debris research activities between member space agencies, to facilitate opportunities for cooperation in space debris research, to review the progress of ongoing cooperative activities and to identify debris mitigation options' (IADC, n.d.), the Inter-Agency Space Debris Coordination Committee (IADC) has contributed to mitigating space debris through adopting the IADC Space Debris Mitigation Guidelines (IADC Guidelines) (IADC, 2002) based on consensus among members. Although the number of participants in the decision-making is fairly small, the IADC Guidelines are the result of a qualitative agreement (Danilenko, 1989), as the participants are the most influenced by the rules. The IADC Guidelines proved to be a significant success not only inside the IADC but also in the UN, as it was based on this document that the STSC of the latter adopted its space debris mitigation guidelines (STSC, 2007), which were endorsed by the COPUOS (UN COPUOS, 2007) and the UNGA (UNGA, 2007). Space debris mitigation measures, originating from State practice, have received international recognition through the IADC Guidelines and the UN Guidelines, and are now adopted by numerous States and IOs (Li, 2015; UNOOSA, n.d.).

The experiences of the IAEA and the IADC represent different ways of interaction among IOs from the perspective of harmonising international rules. Without cooperation, the rules made by the IAEA and the COPUOS vary, leading to possible normative conflicts. As the legal nature of the Convention on Early Notification and the Convention on Assistance made by the IAEA and the Principles of NPS of the COPUOS diverge, State parties to the Conventions are presumed to abide by the binding provisions of the Conventions rather than the non-binding Principles in the case of normative conflicts, as breaching the former may lead to international responsibility with less doubt. For forming harmonised rules, the COPUOS has cooperated directly with the IAEA in drafting the Safety Framework. Contrarily, the IADC has elaborated the IADC Guidelines independently. As the IADC has normally provided a special technical presentation before the annual meeting of the STSC since 1997 (Johnson, n.d.), it had the opportunity to review and discuss the IADC Guidelines at the STSC in 2003 and 2004, leading to the adoption of a similar set of space debris mitigation Guidelines by the latter (Bacon, 2019). It is an exemplary case where the decision made by a few space powers on a small platform reserved for a small number of States impacts international space law-making.

6.1.3 The Bottom-Up Law-Making by Other Stakeholders

Boosted by the needs to govern the soaring space activities and the difficulties of law-making through the traditional top-down method, non-State entities are increasingly participating in the law-making process, not only as observer institutions or advisors but as active and substantial contributors to the evolution of international space law. Thus, the bottom-up approach has begun to play a part in space law-making. First, the role that NGOs are playing is receiving increasing importance. In addition to the first few NGOs pertaining to space law, such as the International Institute of Space Law and the International Law Association, which are the major forums for space lawyers and have been continuously contributing to the development of space law through colloquiums, research reports, and so on (Lyall & Larsen, 2009), new NGOs are ambitious about participating in the formation of new space norms. For example, the Moon Village Association (MVA), established in 2017, 'provides a platform and takes actions supporting communications and cooperation among all elements of human society vis-à-vis the Moon Village, including both space-faring and not space-faring countries and offers them the opportunity to play a role in its realization' (MVA, n.d.). Among the several objectives of the MVA, acting 'as a representative of the civil society and international space community in the decision-making process which is assessing or related to the Moon Village concept' is included (MVA, n.d.), implying that the MVA aims to play a significant role in the law-making process for human activities on the Moon. In addition to actively participating in COPUOS sessions by submitting reports of its work, the MVA intends to contribute substantially to the formation of a legal framework for lunar activities. It developed a neutral forum for multistakeholder discussions on lunar exploration in 2021, the Global Expert Group on Sustainable Lunar Activities (GEGSLA), with the goal of preparing materials that will be submitted to the COPUOS to support the discussions and deliberations on critical issues surrounding increased lunar activity in the COPUOS (MVA, 2021). The GEGSLA comprises major stakeholders in lunar activities, including representatives from space agencies/government, industry, IOs, academia, and civil society. These participants are divided into Members, who have the right to participate in all major activities of the GEGSLA, notably decision-making; observers, who could participate actively in discussions and express their views at the meetings of the GEGSLA; and sponsors, individuals, or organisations that financially contribute to the activities of the GEGSLA (MVA, 2021). GEGSLA finalised its Recommended Framework and Key Elements for Peaceful and Sustainable Lunar Activities in 2022 (MVA, 2022), which has been submitted to the COPUOS in 2023 (UN COPUOS, 2023).

Second, new forums for negotiating space law issues have been established, highlighting multistakeholder efforts through informal institutions. Facing the strong tendency of space mining, addressing legal issues concerning space resources became inevitable. Without consensus in the COPUOS to establish a working group for this matter until 2021 (UN COPUOS Legal Subcommittee, 2021), non-governmental initiatives took the first step by establishing the Hague Space Resources Working Group (Hague Working Group) in 2016, following a round table in 2014 attended by industrial leaders, scientists, diplomats, and political and legal experts from worldwide to discuss and propose solutions for the lack of a legal framework for the use of space resources (UN COPUOS, 2018). The Hague Working Group 'promoted international cooperation and multistakeholder dialogue between members and observers . . . , including representatives of the United Nations Office of Outer Space Affairs' (De O. Bittencourt Neto et al., 2020).

Participants are divided into three categories: (1) members, the number of which is limited to a total of 35, as major stakeholders from government, industry, universities, civil society, and research centres, are responsible for making decisions; (2) observers, who are professionals directly involved in space resources issues, may speak at face-to-face meetings upon invitation by the chair and receive all final documentation distributed within the Hague Working Group; and (3) external persons who are only informed of the progress of the work (International Institute of Air and Space Law, n.d.). After four years of work, the Hague Working Group adopted and released the Building Blocks for the Development of an International Framework on Space Resources Activities (BBs) in 2019, which were submitted to the Legal Subcommittee of the COPUOS (UN COPUOS, 2020). It is expected that the BBs may considerably impact space resource activities (Hofmann & Bergamasco, 2020). As the BBs are favourable for developing a space mining industry, they may also be preferred by States with corresponding capacities (Xu & Su, 2020). Although the space-faring nations capable of conducting space resources activities are the minority and will remain the minority for a long time, international law on space resources cannot be effective without their support (Danilenko, 2016). The BBs' influence over the work of the Working Group on Legal Aspects of Space Resources remains to be observed. However, it is promising as a starting point for a legal framework for space-resources-related activities that are currently unregulated. The international consortium of the Hague Working Group gathered multiple stakeholders, governmental and non-governmental, public and private, as decision-makers, rendering it a unique hybrid forum for negotiating legal issues about space resources. In addition, unlike the COPUOS, which reflects a traditional hierarchical mode of governance where NGOs could not participate in decision-making, in the forum provided by the Hague Working Group, States, NGOs, experts from academia, and the industry are all equal and independent decision-makers.

Third, industrial efforts to standardise space activities from a technical perspective can be witnessed. The industries have been participating in IOs, NGOs, and informal forums for negotiations, and they used to play a secondary role in space law-making instead of directly participating in decision-making. As the commercialisation of space activities progresses, industrial actors emerge as new players in the law-making game, typically for framing technical standards. The Hague Working Group is but one example. The International Organization for Standardization (ISO) could be another. Although the ISO only accepts national standard bodies as members, the groups of experts—technical committees—that are proposed by the ISO's national members are the actual standards designers (ISO, n.d.a). The P-member (ISO, n.d.b)[1] of ISO working groups should organise consultations among its national stakeholders to develop national positions on draft ISO standards and present them to the relevant ISO technical committees (ISO, n.d.c), reflecting a collective view on the issue in question, including undoubtedly the industrial perspective. The Orbital Debris Coordination Working Group (ODCWG) under the Sub-Committee 'Space Systems and Operations' of the Technical Committee 'Aircraft and Space Vehicles' (Davey & Taylor, 2005) is concerned with the development of technical standards on space debris mitigation and issued its first set of international standards in 2011 (Davey & Taylor, 2005). The ISO standards, normally more detailed and targeted, remain industrial standards of a non-binding nature (Garber, 2017). Nonetheless, they have been introduced into national legislation as it is required that ISO members adopt the standards nationally, and they have become market requirements (Mejía–Kaiser, 2009).

It is expected that the industrial operators' role as standard developers will become increasingly significant as soft law instruments, particularly technical standards, are considered most promising for settling technical issues (Aoki, 2012). This role has been confirmed and encouraged by some States. For instance, the US has been including fostering 'fair and open global trade and commerce through the promotion of suitable standards and regulations that have been developed with input from US industry' into its National Space Policy since 2010 (US, 2010, 2020). In this way, space powers can sell not only space products or services but also technical standards through the industrial sector. Exporting US standards could be realised not only through the participation of industrial entities in various standard-developing activities but also by including the standards in contracts concluded between US entities and foreign contracting parties. It helps the US commercial space sector to preserve its competitiveness and dominance. From the perspective of law-making, it can effectively promote the industry's participation in framing universally accepted technical standards. It is noteworthy that different space powers may develop different technical standards to sell on the international market, leading to competition not only among space products and services but also among technical standards. Without international harmonisation of these standards, the transaction costs in the space sector will increase in the long run, which will eventually affect the end-users.

6.1.4 Sub-Conclusion

The increasing participation by various stakeholders in space law-making reveals the tendency towards multistakeholderism and the adoption of a bottom-up approach in space law-making. However, the central role of States and the COPUOS remains undeniable. Considering the strong political and military implications of the space sector, whether the transformation from multilateralism to complete multistakeholderism would be completed is questionable. The norms and standards elaborated by NGOs and other informal forums seldom contradict the fundamental principles of space law, as NGOs and the informal forums usually submit the norms and standards to the COPUOS with an intention to expand their acceptance scope through this multilateral platform. The standards developed by the industry are essentially technical, constituting reification of and supplement to the ambiguous space law rules.

Nonetheless, the fragmentation of international space law cannot be avoided entirely. First, even the rules adopted through the COPUOS mechanism may sometimes be incoherent, which could be illustrated by the diverging dispositions concerning the exploration of the Moon contained in the OST and the Moon

Agreement (Danilenko, 1989). Second, other IOs are also working on some specific legal aspects related to space activities, framing legal documents that may differ significantly from those adopted by the UN and possibly leading to normative conflicts. The issue could be attenuated in cases of parallel membership with national coordination as a prerequisite. Institutional cooperation, particularly the joint development of new rules, is the most promising approach for tackling this situation. Third, a shift from multilateral platforms to small clubs of like-minded States is an emerging tendency in space law-making. It could break the deadlock of forming new space law rules, notably binding rules. However, it may aggravate the dilemma of fragmentation. Thus, staying with multilateral platforms, such as the COPUOS, is necessary.

6.2 Institutional Aspects of Cyberspace Law-Making

The global governance of cyberspace began with the distributed governance of the Internet, which was limited, unorganised, and restricted within online communities that asserted that information had to be free and uncontrolled (Liaropoulos, 2016). This approach was appropriate when the online communities were 'small, homogeneous and self-regulatable based on consensus-building and net neutrality' (Liaropoulos, 2016). It was even widely assumed that the distributed and highly decentralised technology would make public regulation difficult or even impossible (Deibert & Crete-Nishihata, 2012). However, with the development of the Internet and the meteoric growth of its users, the distributed approach is no longer suitable for the governance of the Internet, let alone the global governance of cyberspace, which is a broader notion than the Internet.

There are different views towards the most appropriate governance approach for cyberspace. Multilateralism, implying a hierarchical mode of governance, was supported by States attaching more importance to the need for governments to exercise sovereignty in cyberspace (Liaropoulos, 2016). Although multistakeholders are involved in policy framing and law-making, it is contended that 'the adjustment pressures rooted in inconsistent regulatory and normative frameworks would lead to calls for orchestration over the long-term', and the shifting of relevant negotiations to the multilateral platforms of the UN can be expected (Hofmann & Pawlak, 2023). The multistakeholder governance model, regarded as a form of participatory democracy that aims to bring together all stakeholders in a new form of communication to legitimise decision-making at the international level (Glen, 2014), is widely considered to be the most effective model for cyberspace. Although it suffers from a legitimacy gap (Carr, 2015), multistakeholderism is indispensable. First, from the beginning, non-State actors (NSAs) have been active participants in the global governance of cyberspace. The transnational networks of engineers, primarily based in Western countries, have been the original founders of cyberspace governance, with the users and private sector shaping cyberspace itself (Deibert & Crete-Nishihata, 2012). The end-to-end argument formulated in 1984, which organises the placement of functions in a distributed computing network sharing a basic common protocol, the TCP/IP, could be one illustration (Deibert & Crete-Nishihata, 2012). The Internet

Corporation for Assigned Names and Numbers (ICANN), an internationally organised not-for-profit company incorporated in California in 1997,[2] is responsible for the Internet Assigned Numbers Authority functions, such as Internet Protocol space allocations, the Domain Name System management, and root server system management (Liaropoulos, 2016), and formulating policies in the sovereign domains of nations (Bajaj, 2014) could be another example. Although the US government was in a position to influence the ICANN (Liaropoulos, 2016), it cannot directly control Internet governance, which is partly reflected in the Memorandum of Understanding concluded between the ICANN and the US Department of Commerce, establishing the operating parameters for the ICANN to privatise and internationalise Internet governance (Cogburn, 2016). Today, governance by private entities has not vanished in cyberspace. Instead, the private sector continues to dedicate itself to establishing new standards. Second, cyberspace is a multi-faceted domain with various implications. It is relevant to areas such as crime, international security, trade and economy, development, and human rights (Hofmann & Pawlak, 2023). This nature of cyberspace determines that it is not a domain that could be regulated with only one specific legal regime. Rather, it will be subjected to an assortment of different regimes, some private, public, international, and national or local (Perritt, 2000), necessitating the participation of multistakeholders. Multilateralism does not preclude the participation of public entities such as IOs and States. These subjects work together while performing different functions: private entities work to develop globally applicable codes of conduct regarding privacy, data, and cybersecurity and to set general technical standards for cyberspace; national authorities promote best practices and legislation, establish relevant institutions, and develop international cooperation with other public authorities within IOs and through international treaties; IOs, NGOs, and other informal platforms provide forums for cooperation and negotiations (Pernice, 2018).

Unlike space law-making, which is experiencing the transformation from multilateralism towards multistakeholderism, the multistakeholderism of cyberspace law-making has already been founded from the beginning, which is recognised by the UN (UNGA, 2002a).[3] States and the IOs are latecomers in law-making for cyberspace, and other forms of institutions are also joining the private entities to exert their efforts.

6.2.1 The Continuing Impact of the NSAs Over Cyberspace Norm-Developing

The early reluctance of IOs and States to regulate the Internet has led to the establishment of Internet self-regulatory, community-driven supranational bodies, such as the World Wide Web Consortium (W3C), the Internet Engineering Task Force (IETF), and the ICANN, which oversee the functioning and further development of technical standards (Polanski, 2017). They have been the initial actors in cyberspace norm-developing. Although there is a tendency to increase States' participation in the cyber law-making process, their impact cannot be neglected. In addition, other NSAs, such as legal scholars, are deeply involved.

6.2.1.1 Continuing Efforts From the Private Sectors

Unlike the ICANN, which is a US-based corporation, the W3C and the IETF are multistakeholder standard-setting entities. The W3C is an international public-interest non-profit organisation founded in 1994 that creates standards for the World Wide Web. Organisations of all sizes and types, for-profit or not-for-profit, including commercial, educational, and governmental entities, could all join the W3C as members. Individuals are not qualified to become members; they may only participate in the W3C's activities if they are employed by a W3C member or if they participate in a Working or Interest Group as 'invited experts' with the approval of the group Chair and Team contact (W3C, n.d.a). Among the 383 members by the end of 2023, there are private companies, universities, research institutions, and a few governmental entities from worldwide (W3C, n.d.b). Following a consensus-based approach (W3C, n.d.c), the W3C is 'designed to bring interested parties together to work on developing web standards, and protocols and guidelines to help to ensure the growth and longevity of the web' (Gillis, n.d). The W3C web standards only describe the best practices of web development and are not legally binding. The IETF, founded in 1986, is a similar organisation that aims to 'produce high quality, relevant technical and engineering documents that influence the way people design, use and manage the Internet in such a way as to make the Internet work better', including 'protocol standards, best current practices, and informational documents of various kinds' (Alvestrand, 2004). Unlike the W3C, there is no membership in the IETF. Any interested individuals can participate by signing up to a working group mailing list or registering for an IETF meeting, and thus play a role in the decision-making process as decisions are made within working groups by rough consensus. All the technical standards, recommendations, protocols, best practices, and so forth formed in these multistakeholder platforms contribute to the smooth working of the Internet, representing a high level of self-regulation. Nonetheless, from the perspective of preventing MCAs, the effects of these technical norms are limited.

The private sector has begun to be concerned with cybersecurity as well. Microsoft's proposals are appropriate illustrations in this regard. In 2014, Microsoft published its white paper titled 'International Cybersecurity Norms: Reducing Conflict in an Internet-Dependent World', highlighting six cybersecurity norms: States should have a clear principle-based policy for handling product and service vulnerabilities or take actions that would otherwise undermine public trust in products and services; States should have a clear principle-based policy for handling product and service vulnerabilities; States should exercise restraint in developing cyber weapons; States should commit to non-proliferation activities related to cyber weapons; States should limit their engagement in cyber offensive operations to avoid creating a mass event; and States should assist private sector efforts to detect, contain, respond to, and recover from events in cyberspace (Mckay et al., 2014). It is the first comprehensive proposal from the private sector on norms purporting to regulate the conduct of States to ensure cybersecurity (Mckay et al., 2014). Concerned with the fact that norms for States alone could not protect global trust in technology and information and communications technology (ICT) users and realising that norms for the industry are indispensable, Microsoft published another white paper titled 'From Articulation to Implementation: Enabling Progress on Cybersecurity Norms' (Charney et al., 2016), which also addressed the challenges in implementing cybersecurity norms. Against the backdrop that governments continue to invest in greater capabilities in cyberspace, and nation-State attacks on civilians are on the rise, Microsoft, believing that the world needs new international rules to protect the public from nation-State threats in cyberspace and eager to transform its proposed six norms for nation-States into a Treaty, called for the adoption of a Digital Geneva Convention to protect cyberspace in times of peace (Digital Geneva Convention) in 2017. It is submitted that the Digital Geneva Convention should notably include key clauses through which States commit to refrain from attacking cyber systems, exercise restraint in developing cyber weapons, limit the proliferation of cyber weapons, limit engagement in cyber offensive operations, and so on (Microsoft, 2017). The Microsoft proposal was supported by a Tech Accord to protect people in cyberspace (Cybersecurity Tech Accord), which demonstrates the industry's commitment to a set of common principles and behaviours to protect civilians in cyberspace (Microsoft, 2018a), and the proposal to establish an 'Attribution Organization' to receive and analyse the evidence related to a suspected State-sponsored cyberattack, and then credibly and publicly identify perpetrators (Microsoft, 2018b). Microsoft's initiative of a Digital Geneva Convention has not received much attention (Pernice, 2018). The call for establishing an international attribution organisation presupposes that attribution is possible, which is without any signs in practice (Pernice, 2018) and is criticised for overlooking the existing legal mechanisms (Jeutner, 2019). Nonetheless, the work of the Cybersecurity Tech Accord is progressing. It has already gathered 90 signatories covering North America, Latin America, Europe, and Asia-Pacific (Cybersecurity Tech Accord, 2018). Moreover, it also works closely with leading civil society groups[4] and participates actively in relevant work that is progressing in IOs such as the UN and the ITU. As a private entity, Microsoft has been exemplary in pushing forward the adoption of internationally binding rules governing States' activities to ensure cybersecurity. It unified the voice of the industry and made it heard. Considering that the ability of private entities to drive meaningful behavioural change by governments is limited and that the public-private partnership also has inherent limitations, Microsoft also suggested that victimised companies refuse to engage in economic activity with the offending countries, thus 'retaliating' for any improper conduct (Charney, 2014). Nonetheless, owing to a continuing lack of consensus among key State players such as the US, China, Russia, and the European Union (EU) (Kelesza & Weber, 2021), the possibility of adopting an effective and enforceable treaty concerning cyberspace is unlikely for the moment and for the several years to come.

In summary, the private sector remains the chief actor in cyberspace self-regulation. Private entities of different legal statuses, NGOs, corporations, and so on, continue to play a pivotal role in establishing technical standards to ensure the smooth functioning of the Internet. Furthermore, they provide essential grassroots, transparent, inclusive, and multistakeholder platforms for different NSAs to voice their concerns and allow them to contribute substantively to standards-setting. However, their overall impact on law-making to prevent the occurrence of MCAs is trivial. In addition, although the private sector, being aware of the significance of cybersecurity and the responsibility that States should bear in this regard, has made efforts to promote the adoption of internationally binding rules, the effect of their initiatives is minimal without the intent of States. It remains incumbent on States to play the essential role.

6.2.1.2 Efforts From the Legal Scholars

According to Article 38 (1) (d) of the Statute of the International Court of Justice (ICJ) (ICJ, 1946), the teachings of the most highly qualified publicists of the various nations can be used as subsidiary means for the determination of rules of law. It is suggested that this type of subsidiary source of international law would only carry weight in so far as they referred back to one of the principal sources, treaties, customs, and general principles of law (Thirlway, 2019). Their primary value rests on thorough research into what the law is said to be, that is, the *lex lata* (Aust, 2005). In addition, it is considered that scholarly opinions influence the process of law-making by States, which is particularly visible when a general law law-making convention is elaborated (Thirlway, 2019). The provision of the Statute of the ICJ serves as a solid justification and foundation for participation of legal scholars in the law-making process concerning cyberspace, which could be best represented by the Tallinn Manual drafted by an International Group of Experts at the invitation of the NATO (North Atlantic Treaty Organisation) Cooperative Cyber Defense Centre of Excellence (CCDCoE), intending to be a non-legally-binding scholarly work that provides an objective restatement of international law as applied in the cyber context.

The Tallinn Manual 1.0 (Schmitt, 2013) was completed by a group of 23 experts in military affairs and conflict and security law, with M. N. Schmitt, a professor from the US Naval College, as the Chair, reviewed by another group of 13 experts, and has been claimed to reflect the teachings of the most highly qualified publicists (Boer, 2013). The International Committee of the Red Cross (ICRC) and other States and organisations were invited to send observers to the group (Jensen, 2017). The authority of the Tallinn Manual 1.0 has been widely criticised. It is asserted that the experts who drafted and reviewed the Manual were from only a few Western States, who addressed the cyber issues in their professional positions (Fleck, 2013). Direct references have been made to the national military manuals on the law of armed conflict of Western countries, such as Canada, Germany, the United Kingdom (UK), and the US (Fleck, 2013). Moreover, the scope of the Tallinn Manual 1.0 is limited in that it focuses on those areas of law that are of specific interest to NATO (Kessler & Werner, 2013), although CCDCoE is not a part of NATO's overarching command structure and receives no funding from NATO (Check, 2015). All these factors have led to the overreliance on Western legal sources, which may hamper its acceptance in other countries (Eichensehr, 2014).

The drafting of the Tallinn Manual 2.0 has responded to these criticisms through a more diverse International Group of Experts and the expansion of the scope of the content. The second group of experts was broader in both origin (including not only experts from Western countries but also four members respectively from Thailand, Japan, China, and Belarus) and substantive expertise (including experts in human rights, space law, and international telecommunication law) (Jensen, 2017). The drafting process reflected a higher degree of multistakeholderism. With 'the Hague Process' launched jointly by the Dutch government and the CCDCoE, several meetings with States were organised during which they could review and comment on the substance of the draft Manual 2.0 before it was finalised (Jensen, 2017). This process has had more than 50 States as participants, including all the permanent members of the UN Security Council (Jensen, 2017). The scope of the Manual has been largely extended to cover not only the legal issues related to 'above-threshold cyber activities', which amount to prohibited uses of force in terms of their scale and effect or which are executed in the context of armed conflicts, but also those regarding the 'below-threshold cyber activities' violating other international norms (Efrony & Shany, 2018). It proposes a comprehensive regulatory scheme of 154 rules dedicated to regulating MCAs, integrating general international rules and specialised international law rules, such as human rights, diplomatic, space, and telecommunication laws (Schmitt, 2017). The publication of Tallinn Manual 2.0 marked significant progress compared with its precedent; however, it has encountered similar criticisms. In the drafting process, although the situation of absolute Western dominance has been overturned, the disparity of countries where the experts came from persists, and the selection process of the experts, which was claimed to be based on two factors, that is, an impersonal validity claim and the experience and position of the expert, lacked transparency (Tanodomdej, 2019). In addition, although some States' views towards the rules in the second version of the manual have been considered before the finalisation of the work, the empirical study demonstrates that it is unclear whether States are ready to accept the rules and that States show uneven interest in promoting legal certainty in cyberspace (Efrony & Shany, 2018).

In 2021, the CCDCoE launched the five-year project of Tallinn Manual 3.0, involving the updating of all chapters of the Tallinn Manual 2.0 to address the evolving nature of cyber operations and State responses and adding new topics of importance to States (CCDCoE, 2021). The new project maintains the working approach of the previous projects for elaborating the Manual in that an International Group of Experts comprising renowned international scholars is responsible for developing and approving the Manual, and States are invited to provide input and communicate their national viewpoints (CCDCoE, 2021). The disparity of the nationalities of the experts would be attenuated by the efforts of the project to engage a broader community of international law specialists as researchers and peer reviewers. Inputs are also expected from individuals and entities worldwide.

The Tallinn Manuals, an aggregation of scholarly restatement of international law as applied in the cyber context, much commented and cited, could serve as a subsidiary means to determine the rule of law. However, the impact of the Manuals on the law-making for cyberspace is compromised by their contested authority owing to the development process. An apparent Western-centric disparity of experts' nationalities was the major cause of criticism. Although the projects to develop the Manuals provided opportunities for States to communicate their views on the *lex lata* applicable to cyberspace and contributed to raising States' awareness in this respect, they failed to reconcile States' conflicting views, which is a significant step for international law-making. Moreover, they disregarded the generality of State practice, a decisive factor in the formation of customary international law (Tanodomdej, 2019). Nonetheless, unifying States' views and forming coherent State practice do not depend on the academia but on the States themselves.

6.2.2 States' Participation in Law-Making

The private entities took the task of overseeing the functioning and further development of technical standards, leaving the transmission of digital content uncontrolled (Polanski, 2017). It is the latter which often constitutes the major threats to cybersecurity. States have taken the initiative to cope with this issue in two ways: national legislation and the promotion of relevant international norm-developing through IOs.

National cyber legislation differs significantly from one another. Take cybercrime law, for example: not every country has enacted relevant laws, and those countries with specific laws may have differing elements and focuses (Podgor, 2004). Regional conventions and norms play a significant role in harmonising national legislation in this respect. European States tend to follow the guidelines established in the Convention on Cybercrime adopted by the Council of Europe (Budapest Convention) (Council of Europe, 2001), and the EU Directives on Attacks against Information Systems (EU, 2013; Mihai, 2016; Rashkovski et al., 2016), African countries have learnt from the African Union Convention on Cyber Security and Personal Data Protection (African Union, 2014) when elaborating national rules countering cybercrimes (Yilma, 2016), and Southeast Asian countries harmonise their national legislation based on the Declaration to Prevent and Combat Cybercrime (ASEAN, 2017) signed at the 31st Summit of the Association of Southeast Asian Nations (ASEAN) (Smith, 2020). Nevertheless, differences in national legislation persist even in this most harmonised aspect of cybersecurity, let alone other domains touching upon more politically sensitive aspects such as sovereignty issues and human rights. The incoherent State practice cannot justify the emergence of customary rules.

At the international level, States have begun to explore the approaches to regulating cyberspace as well. Technical governance forums for cyberspace, initially unpoliticised or mostly technical, are becoming the objects of intense political competition and are considered seriously as vectors of policy formation (Deibert & Crete-Nishihata, 2012). It is contended that the reluctance of States to engage in relevant law-making has left a power vacuum, testifying to the assertion that international law fails to address modern challenges posed by technological development (Macak, 2017). Thus, the politicisation of the technical forums is a welcomed trend, as it implies that States have begun to take law-making initiatives. States participate in cyber law-making through international forums, particularly universal IOs such as the UN. Additionally, regional IOs have made more effective contributions to law-making for cyberspace, as several binding instruments have been adopted at the regional level.

6.2.2.1 Participation Through the UNGA

There is a split in States' views towards the approaches to coping with cyber issues. Although Russia and China favour policy tools such as a new treaty or code of conduct, the US and the EU have long resisted attempts to advance a State-centric and central governance approach at the UN (Hofmann & Pawlak, 2023). However, regulatory and legal uncertainties owing to inter-organisational competition and growing inequalities resulting from States' limited capacities to participate in multiple concurrent cyber processes have pushed many States to resort to the UN, rendering the UN's role in governing cyberspace indispensable (Hofmann & Pawlak, 2023). Moreover, the split in perspectives is haunting the UN, which has transformed into a procedural division. The US-sponsored Global Group of Experts on Cybersecurity (GGE) and the Russia-sponsored Open-ended Working Group on Developments in the Field of Information and Telecommunications in the Context of International Security (OEWG) were both established and worked in parallel during 2019–2021. The First GGE was established in 2004, gathering experts from 15 States (UNGA, 2005). However, before 2007, which featured low levels of cyber threat awareness among State decision-makers, there was a lack of international interest in cyber stability issues, and the willingness of the UN Security Council's permanent members to agree on the direction of a GGE report was low (Tiirmaa-Klaar, 2021). It was not until several cyber incidents occurred during 2006–2008 that policymakers became aware of the need to address the issue by establishing commonly accepted rules limiting State activities in cyberspace (Tiirmaa-Klaar, 2021). The GGE has adopted four reports incorporating essential observations on the risks and recent ICT developments. Nonetheless, the guidelines established in the reports remain general and have been criticised for their poor real-world impact (Pernice, 2018). The work of the GGE has been contested by some States as the membership of the GGEs is too limited to justify its legitimacy to develop norms and rules for the entire UN membership (Hofmann & Pawlak, 2023). The OEWG, open to all member States, was established in 2019 (UNGA, 2018). It gathered experts from approximately 140 States to participate in substantive sessions (UNGA, 2019, 2020, 2021a) and has received contributions from multiple IOs and NGOs (UNODA, n.d.). The final report of the OEWG has replicated many GGE conclusions but also included new proposals, notably recommending that States participate in the regular institutional dialogue under the auspices of the United Nations (UNGA, 2021b), including the OEWG 2021–2025. However, the US has reservations about the need for the new OEWG (UNGA, 2021c). Instead, the significance of a multistakeholder approach has been highlighted by several other States (UNGA, 2021c). Furthermore, the US has explicitly expressed its opposition to the calls for new legal obligations and the development of new treaties or customs in cyberspace, proclaiming that spending a decade or more negotiating a new legally binding instrument would be 'futile' and 'a tremendous distraction' (UNGA, 2021c). This view is shared by several other States, such as Australia, Belgium, Canada, and so on (UNGA, 2021c).

Both the work of the GGE and the OEWG continue to advance, signifying the persistence of the procedural division. The UNGA established a new five-year OEWG on security of and in the use of ICTs (OEWG 2021–2025), tasked to 'further develop the rules, norms and principles of responsible behaviour of States and the ways for their implementation and if necessary, to introduce changes to them or elaborate additional rules of behaviour', 'to establish, under the auspices of the United Nations, regular institutional dialogue with the broad participation of States', and so forth (UNGA, 2021b). The OEWG 2021–2025 has issued two progress reports (UNGA, 2022a; UNGA, 2023a), generating statements of explanation of position from several States (UNGA, 2022b, 2023b). Although States such as Russia, China, Iran, and Nicaragua continue to prioritise the task of the OEWG 2021–2025 to develop relevant norms and highlight the intergovernmental nature of the OEWG (UNGA, 2023b), the US emphasises the importance of effectively implementing the existing norms and reaffirms the importance of a multistakeholder approach, stressing that the UN 'can play an important role in coordinating with and highlighting this wide range of actors actively engaged in capacity building on relevant cyber issues, as well as implementing specific capacity building programs as directed by Member States' (US, 2023). On the other hand, although the mandate of the GGE ended in 2021, its supporting States, to minimise the concerns that OEWG would become the sole venue to orchestrate how to govern cyberspace and sovereignty would become the dominant policy frame, pushed the UNGA to adopt a resolution establishing a new regulatory dialogue (Hofmann & Pawlak, 2023)—the Programme of action to advance responsible State behaviour in the use of information and communications technologies in the context of international security (Programme of Action, POA) (UNGA, 2022c). It is asserted that the POA was established as a 'permanent, inclusive, action-oriented mechanism to discuss the existing and potential threats, to support States' capacities and efforts to implement and advance commitments to be guided by the framework for responsible State behaviour' (UNGA, 2022c). However, vehement opposition to the concept of the POA has been received from Russia, which asserted that the OEWG 2021–2025 is 'the first and only inclusive, open, transparent and truly democratic negotiating mechanism on international information security at the United Nations', required the POA not to 'prejudge the decision on a future negotiating mechanism on international information security at the United Nations', and reaffirmed its intention to develop a UN convention on ensuring international information security (UNGA, 2023c). Some other States, such as Cuba, supported the Russian assertion and contended that the POA would 'have harmful effect of further reducing the likelihood of adopting legally binding obligations' (UNGA, 2023c).

The cyberspace law-making arena offers almost every State the opportunity to express their views on governing cyberspace. Nonetheless, as it is deeply politicised and both the POA and the OEWG adopt a consensus approach, it would be unlikely that any substantial improvements will be made, particularly concerning the much-debated issue of developing new binding international instruments. Even if a new binding instrument is formed, it is doubtful that the US and its allies will ratify it, reducing its effectiveness significantly. Nonetheless, the work on explaining how to apply the current international law and norms to cyberspace will continue. The UNGA is undoubtedly only one of many occasions for law-making. From a practical perspective, it constitutes a constituent part of the multistakeholder law-making process.

6.2.2.2 Participation Through the ITU

The ITU plays a role in building confidence and security in the use of ICTs through the World Summit on Information Society (WSIS) and the ITU Plenipotentiary Conference (ITU, n.d.a).

Upon the proposal of the Secretary-General of the ITU, the UNGA endorsed holding the WSIS (UNGA, 2002b) to develop and foster a clear statement of political will and take concrete steps to establish the foundations for an information society for all (ITU, n.d.b). The ITU was tasked with the leading managerial role in the executive secretariat of the Summit and its preparatory process (UNGA, 2002b). Governments, relevant UN bodies, other IOs, NGOs, civil society, and the private sector were all encouraged to actively participate in the preparatory process of the WSIS and the WSIS itself (UNGA, 2002b). In response to the fact of being entrusted as Facilitator of Action Line C5, 'Building confidence and security in the use of ICTs', by Heads of States and world leaders at the WSIS, the ITU launched the Global Cybersecurity Agenda (GCA) in 2007 as a framework for international cooperation to promote cybersecurity and enhance confidence and security in the information society (Schjølberg, 2008). The GCA is built upon five strategic pillars, including 'Legal Measures' as the first pillar, seeking to develop advice on how criminal activities committed over ICTs could be dealt with through legislation in an internationally compatible manner, and 'International cooperation' as the fifth pillar, aiming to develop a strategy for international cooperation, dialogue, and coordination in dealing with cyber threats (Schjølberg, 2008). To strengthen its role in building confidence and security in the use of ICTs, the ITU began developing the Guidelines for utilisation of the GCA in 2020 and submitted the revised Draft Guidelines to the ITU Council in 2022, which was approved and transmitted to the ITU Plenipotentiary Conference of the same year (ITU, 2022). Concerning legal measures, the Guidelines articulate that 'ITU should continue its efforts to facilitate multistakeholder discussions and collaboration for addressing the challenges associated with cybersecurity', 'continue to work with relevant partners for foster development and maintenance of resources on cybersecurity and cybercrime legislation to help Member States to understand the legal aspects of cybersecurity', and so forth (ITU, 2022). In terms of international cooperation, the Guidelines highlight the unique role of the UN in fostering cooperation, dialogue, and coordination on global cybersecurity matters among all nations, and with the private sector and other stakeholders, and requires the ITU to continue its efforts in promoting relevant international cooperation. Based on the five strategic pillars, the ITU began releasing the Global Cybersecurity Index (GCI) in 2015, a trusted reference that measures the commitment of countries to cybersecurity at a global level to raise awareness of the importance and different dimensions of the issue (ITU, 2019).

The WSIS and one of its follow-ons, the Internet Governance Forum (IGF), were seen as a way for the ITU to re-leverage some legitimacy in Internet governance after being marginalised in the 1990s (Deibert & Rohozinski, 2017). Today, through these programmes, the ITU represents a space for different stakeholders, including civil society and others, to discuss Internet governance issues in ways they are otherwise precluded from doing (Deibert & Rohozinski, 2017). However, the current and prospective law-making role of the ITU in this respect remains minimal. It cannot adopt binding regulations on technology or the use of the Internet as this is not within its powers (Pernice, 2018). Additionally, it is noteworthy that although in relevant ITU documents the multistakeholder approach has been underscored and ITU lists several hundreds of NSAs among its membership, only its member States have the right to participate and vote in the Plenipotentiary Conference to decide the future policies of the ITU (Liaropoulos, 2016). After all, the ITU is only a multilateral platform for States.

6.2.3 Sub-Conclusion

The law-making mode for cyberspace is shifting from self-regulation to multistakeholderism, with increasing participation of States. The private sector, through NGOs and other multistakeholder platforms, continues to play an essential role in developing technical standards for the smooth and sustainable functioning of the Internet. Private entities and legal scholars are attempting to influence the international law-making process for cyberspace; nonetheless, it still depends on States' will to make new rules to govern cyberspace or apply the existing international law to cyberspace. States participate in the law-making for cyberspace through national legislation or activities of IOs. As national legislation differs significantly and international and regional attempts to harmonise national laws remain at an early stage, State practice could barely be considered evidence of the existence of customary law. The UNGA and the ITU constitute the major platforms for States to negotiate cyberspace law-making issues. Different types of stakeholders may join as observers or in other capacities, whereas States are the only qualified subjects to participate in the decision-making process. As splits exist among States on the approach to govern cyberspace, that is, through the current international law, or through the adoption of new binding rules, and on specific matters, such as the sovereignty and human rights issues, the negotiations will continue for a while. Considering the fact that there is limited doubt on the applicability of the existing international law to cyberspace, despite legal gaps and divergences concerning how to apply the existing international law, cyberspace is not a chaotic space without legal orders.

6.3 Guaranteeing Institutional Interactions

The interplay between the institutions for space law-making and those for cyber law-making is limited, although both reflect a certain degree of multistakeholderism. First, the law-making mechanisms for outer space and cyberspace are both in the process of transformation but in different stages. Space law-making is shifting from a complete top-down approach to a hybrid way involving both the top-down and the bottom-up approaches, whereas the law-making for cyberspace is heading the opposite, from the bottom-up approach, which is reflective of self-regulation, to a hybrid way with an increasing involvement of States and IOs. The space sector remains deeply marked by State-centralism. For cyberspace, the private sector's role in norm-developing is nonnegligible, and the reluctance of many States towards making new internationally binding rules renders the role of States controversial. Second, the possibilities of forming new binding norms are different. States' will to make new rules on space activities is relatively strong, particularly compared with the situation in cyber law-making, where States share different views pertaining to the necessity of new internationally binding rules. Third, the two sectors' chief law-making institutions are different. In one State, different institutions and personnel are responsible for space activities and cyberspace issues. They are unable to consider other sectors' interests in international negotiations without sufficient national coordination. Although the UN and the ITU are essential in providing multilateral platforms, the specific organs responsible for the two sectors differ. All these factors have resulted in the difficulties of formal interactions between the two mechanisms for coordination purposes. However, the lack of trans-sectoral institutional interaction would lead to the incoherence of international rules and cause conflicts of laws, rendering their implementation more complex. Institutional interactions are indispensable.

Several issues should be resolved to promote trans-sectoral institutional interaction. As the possibilities of developing new rules and norms for space activities and cyberspace differ, the first issue is determining the appropriate field for law-making to tackle the legal challenges raised by MCASAs. The second is to decide the participants in the law-making process, as in both fields, various stakeholders are involved and play different roles in pushing forward the law-making process. The third issue lies in the approaches to ensure a certain degree of interaction among institutions of different fields to avoid future conflicts of law.

6.3.1 Determining the Sector to Develop the Law Combatting MCASAs

Limiting or reducing the role of some regimes, whereas prioritising the role of others by carving up international governance into set functional areas would impede institutional interactions (Young, 2012) and thus weaken the effects of the rules and norms made, the ideal way for developing rules and norms combatting MCASAs is that all relevant institutions, including those related to law-making for space activities, cyberspace, and even environmental protection and other branches of international law, work collaboratively. Nonetheless, for the time being, this is unrealistic, as it demands a mechanism to hold all relevant stakeholders and endow all of them with decision-making rights, the establishment of which appears to be unpromising. Even if such a mechanism were established, its work would be likely to be fruitless, considering the abundant interests valued by various stakeholders. Thus, to begin with, it would be better to develop relevant rules in some specific fields and then expand the impact of the rules to raise the overall awareness of the importance of ensuring space cybersecurity.

The institutions of the space field are the most appropriate institutions for bridging the regulatory gaps to promote the preventive effects of international law over MCASAs. First, some branches of international law apply only in certain specific circumstances: international environmental law is applicable only when MCASAs produce adverse impacts on the environment, whether on Earth or in outer space; *jus ad bellum* applies when MCASAs are above the threshold of threat or use of force; international humanitarian law governs the situation where MCASAs are used in armed conflicts; and so forth. The law-making institutions of these branches are not suitable for comprehensively formulating rules to ensure space cybersecurity. Second, compared with the institutions for cyberspace law-making, the institutions of the space field prove to be a better choice. The international law-making for cyberspace is politicised such that consensus on adopting new binding instruments is difficult for the time being. What exacerbates the situation is that several Western States object to the idea of elaborating new binding agreements and consider that international law in the status quo suffices to regulate cybersecurity issues. Moreover, soft law instruments for regulating cyberspace, notably UNGA resolutions with prescriptive implications, are uncommon. In addition, NSAs' efforts to regulate cybersecurity issues are not much valued. In brief, there is less chance of making new instruments for cybersecurity, whether binding or non-binding. Concerning international law-making for space activities, although there is a standstill in achieving new binding agreements, States' will to address space issues is nonnegligible, which could be evidenced by the continuously submitted proposals related to the prevention of an arms race in outer space (Su, 2017; UNGA, 2023d)[5] and the efforts to develop norms for activities on the Moon. Third, although space cybersecurity issues relate to general cybersecurity, it is cybersecurity for the smooth conduct of space activities and the well-functioning of space systems, reflecting the characteristics of space activities, which distinguish it from other entirely terrestrial cybersecurity issues. Space cybersecurity constitutes an integral part of the overall outer space security. Therefore, the space institutions are more suitable for law-making activities for ensuring space cybersecurity. However, this is only the first step towards a comprehensive regulatory scheme to ensure space cybersecurity. With the promotion of space law and relevant technical standards and the enhancement of inter-sectorial communication and coordination, other institutions may also be obligated to adjust relevant rules so that a comprehensive legal regime be formed.

Although space law includes some dispositions with compensatory effects, the punitive rules are not incorporated. There is no tendency in space institutions to make special rules to punish those posing threats to space security. Thus, the space institutions may play a role in perfecting its compensatory rules while leaving the work to develop relevant punitive rules to other institutions. The regional conventions and initiatives to harmonise national legislation on cybercrimes can be a suitable starting point. Regional initiatives, notably the Budapest Convention, have gathered State members from outside the region.[6] Some States, when elaborating relevant national rules, may refer not only to the conventions on cybercrimes of the region where they are located but also to conventions or initiatives of other regions.

For instance, Article 32(2) of the Ethiopian Computer Crime Proclamation is borrowed from the Budapest Convention and the African Union Cybercrime Convention, although Ethiopia is not a State Party to the Budapest Convention (Yilma, 2016). Nonetheless, as previously highlighted, all these efforts aim to harmonise national legislation on cybercrime; they do not entail international criminalisation of the most severe cybercrimes. The task of demarcating the threshold of international crimes in the cyber sphere should be left to the institutions responsible for international criminal law-making.

6.3.2 Determining the Institutions to Make Rules?

As analysed earlier, both the top-down and bottom-up approaches have been adopted for space law-making. However, they are used for the formulation of different rules and norms. The top-down approach, which is applied notably by States through multilateral platforms or by coalition among several States, has contributed to developing binding and non-binding prescriptive rules and norms bearing on States. They establish the basic principles that States should abide by when conducting their space activities. Thus, most of them are rather general in nature and need further interpretation. Although the law-making activities were conducted in the UN system and other IOs, a US-led model of law-making is emerging, represented by the AAs. This model, which may facilitate and accelerate the development of rules among like-minded States, is not appropriate for dealing with issues that have an international impact, such as space cybersecurity. All States have legitimate interests in outer space. With the interconnection of satellite systems, MCASAs may produce large-scale effects that influence not only space powers and any group of like-minded States but also the States using services supplied by space systems. Thus, international platforms allowing all States to express their concerns, notably the UN, would be the most appropriate choice for developing the principles of guiding States to ensure space cybersecurity. First, the most significant part of international space law has been developed under the auspices of the UN, which has proved the feasibility of making space law on this platform. Second, the UN is the largest and most represented IO worldwide, allowing most States to make their voice heard. The voting mechanism of the UNGA, where many soft law instruments, such as resolutions and declarations, and binding instruments, such as conventions and treaties, have been approved, reflects the interests valued by States, because each member State of the UNGA has one vote, regardless of their population, size, level of development, and so on. Third, within the UN, although several institutions and organs are involved in space law-making, the coordination and harmonisation among them are not so burdensome, owing to the relatively clear delimitation of the functions of each, parallel membership, and the internal coordination mechanism of the UN.

The bottom-up approach functions as an excellent complement to the top-down approach. The more detailed and precise a draft instrument is, the less likely States would approve it. This explains why, using the top-down approach, most rules adopted are rules of principle that are not ready for direct application. Some terms are ambiguous to such an extent that they may even arouse controversies in their interpretations. Using the bottom-up approach, the industry and experts may be directly involved in technical standards development, which may help to clarify the substantive implications of the rules of principle. Their participation may be realised through various multistakeholder forums, or platforms or even IOs, although they usually have no decision-making power in the IOs.

State practice is essential for forming international customary rules for combatting and punishing cybercrimes. Increasingly more States have enacted national rules in this respect. Although harmonising efforts on the regional level may boost the formation of regional customs, they will not help to cope with the most severe MCAs, as the latter always present an international feature, assessed whether by the territorial scope of their impacts or the States involved in their conduct. Furthermore, according to the current status of national legislation, the level of international harmonisation remains relatively low. Thus, an international harmonising instrument is a prerequisite. Although the formation of such an instrument would involve various difficulties, its promotion on the UN platform is worthy of effort and time.

There is an increasing appeal to include the most devastating MCAs as international crimes, notably by classifying them as the crime of aggression (Ambos, 2016; Miller, 2014; Ogbe, 2023; Ophardt, 2010–2011). Thus, the need to strengthen relevant international rules, envisioned in Articles 2 (4) of the UN Charter and the Kampala Agreement on the Crime of Aggression (Kampala Agreement) (ICC, 2010), which became Articles 8*bis* and 15*ter* of the Rome Statute on the International Criminal Court (ICC) (UNGA, 1998), is highlighted (Ogbe, 2022). The negotiation history of the Kampala Agreement reveals that this instrument reflects significant compromises but also marks a significant step to advance international criminal law (Wenaweser, 2010; Kreß & von Holtzendorff, 2010). After the approval of the Kampala Agreement, there were worries about its ratification and implementation, as the Agreement was the work outcome of a small group comprising some sincerely committed decision-makers (Weisbord, 2013). These worries somewhat vanished with 45 States' acceptance or ratification of the Kampala Agreement by the end of 2023 and the activation of the ICC's jurisdiction over the crime of aggression in 2017 (ICC, 2017). All these facts demonstrate that the ICC can work as an international platform to develop international criminal law and is promising in addressing cyber threats by classifying some cybercrimes as aggression (Ogbe, 2023; Ophardt, 2010–2011). However, according to Article 8*bis* of the Rome Statute, criminal responsibility for aggression only arises when 'the planning, preparation, initiation or execution, by a person in a position effectively to exercise control over or direct the political or military action of a State, of an act of aggression', precluding the individuals that are not in such a position from any criminal responsibility under this article and leaving a large impunity gap (Ambos, 2016). The provisions on the crime of aggression in its status quo are inappropriate to cope with cybercrimes amounting to aggression. Clearly, the sole efforts from the ICC do not suffice, necessitating an 'intersecting web of organizations and collaborative efforts' (Ophardt, 2010–2011). First, not all States are parties to the Rome Statute. The absence of some major powers, such as China, India, Russia, and the US, may undermine the effectiveness of the Rome Statute, particularly because several of these States are also cyber powers. Second, the UN Security Council also plays a significant role in addressing the crime of aggression. According to Article 39 of the UN Charter, '[t]he Security Council shall determine the existence of . . . or act of aggression and shall make recommendations, or decide what measures shall be taken'. The decisions and actions of the Security Council in this regard constitute an essential source of international practice in deciding what act may amount to aggression. What is more important is that individual crime of aggression, addressed by the Rome Statute, is the last act punished considering the jurisdictional restraints of the ICC and political concerns *vis à vis* the Security Council; thus, developments in *jus ad bellum* may have a greater impact on curbing cyber-aggression than the ICC crime of aggression (Miller, 2014), which calls for joint efforts of the Security Council, the ICC, and States.

6.3.3 Towards a High Degree of Interaction

Both the interaction among law-making institutions of different fields (horizontal interaction) and the interaction among the stakeholders of the same field (vertical interaction) are indispensable for law-making to ensure space cybersecurity and combat MCASAs.

Parallel membership, mutual agreements, and institutional agreements are the major legal bases for regime interaction (Young, 2012). Mutual agreement helps to reduce difficulties in implementing overlapping rules of different regimes, and parallel membership and institutional agreements contribute towards facilitating horizontal interaction. Concerning formal institutions, the UN is the most promising IO for law-making for both the cyber and space fields. Considerable overlap exists among the States participants in the negotiations of the two fields, although their degrees of concern and attitudes towards the two fields differ. The coherence of the attitude and performance of each State in the different sub-platforms on space activities and cyber issues offered by the UN should be guaranteed by national coordination, which is essential for avoiding conflicts of future rules. However, the stakeholders participating in informal institutions to develop norms and standards pertinent to space activities and cyber issues significantly vary, with slight overlap. For instance, few private operators of space activities joined the Microsoft initiatives, and almost no cyber industry became involved in the activities of the multi-stakeholder platforms concerning the space sector. The cross-participation of the informal institutions from different sectors is the key to alleviating the plight. Similarly, internal coordination in relevant NGOs, large trans-sectoral corporations, and other stakeholders participating in the law-making of different fields is indispensable for the coherence of new rules and norms. The success of the Safety Framework prepared jointly by the COPUOS and the IAEA demonstrates that agreements and partnerships among institutions centring on different fields may avoid conflicts of law at the source. Institutional agreements and different forms of cooperation, including attending the sessions of one another as observers, would be essential for harmonising the concerns and interests of different sectors.

Compared with horizontal interaction, vertical interaction is relatively easy to realise, as in many relevant fields, multistakeholderism has already become a fact. There are several multistakeholder platforms for institutions of different natures to participate in law-making activities. States continue to be the only subjects entitled to make internationally legally binding rules. Although other stakeholders have made various efforts to influence States' decisions, such as participating in the activities of formal institutions and submitting proposals, exerting pressure on governments through different channels, gathering like-minded stakeholders to expand influence, making international or regional initiatives, establishing different platforms, and so forth, the final result continues to rely on States' collective will. States have left space for other stakeholders to develop non-binding norms, particularly technical standards, while keeping their control and supervision on the norm-developing activities to guarantee the conformity of the latter with the internationally binding rules or other non-binding rules that States consider more important.

6.3.4 Sub-Conclusion

Considering the current status and tendency of space and cyber law-making, initiating law-making activities in space institutions would be more appropriate. By raising awareness of the importance of space cybersecurity in other fields, institutions of relevant fields may begin formulating rules to tackle some specific aspects, circumstances, or effects of MCASAs. Concerning space institutions, the UN should remain the essential platform for the negotiations and formulation of new rules as it could best serve the interests of most States. The bottom-up approach, where other informal stakeholders play a central role, could be applied to remedy the defects of the traditional State-centric approach that prevailed in the first several decades of space law-making. However, the law-making task of the punitive rules in the case of MCASAs should be reserved for the States, the Security Council, and the ICC. To prevent potential conflict of laws, both horizontal and vertical institutional interactions are indispensable. Vertical interactions are relatively straightforward and spontaneous, whereas horizontal interactions should be guaranteed through parallel membership and institutional agreements and partnerships.

6.4 Conclusion

An appropriate regulatory scheme is a prerequisite to ensure space cybersecurity better. As the existing rules and norms are significantly obscure and fragmented, requiring reification and interpretation or leaving regulatory gaps and overlapping, developing new rules and norms is necessary to improve the global governance of space cybersecurity. Space cybersecurity concerns several fields, notably the space and cyber fields. Although both law-making institutions of the two fields reflect a certain degree of multistakeholderism, their features and development direction significantly differ. From a realistic perspective, the space law-making institutions would be the most appropriate to take the first steps. The traditional top-down approach would continue to be essential in establishing the principles and norms to combat MCASAs. Nonetheless, NSAs are expected to contribute more to developing technical standards, best practices, and other soft law rules. Further, other fields will also take the initiative to make relevant rules to tackle some specific aspects, circumstances, or effects of MCASAs. To avoid further fragmentation and conflicts of law, intersectoral institutional interaction, both horizontal and vertical, is indispensable for law-making in response to the drawbacks of the existing rules combatting MCASAs. Particularly, horizontal interactions can be better realised through parallel membership and institutional agreements and partnerships.

Notes

1 ISO members can select whether to be part of a particular Technical Committee and their level of involvement. O-members can observe the standards that are being development, offering comments, and advice; whereas P-members actively participate by voting on the standards.

2 ICANN now has offices in Los Angeles, Istanbul, Singapore, Montevideo, Brussels, Beijing, Geneva, Nairobi, and Washington, DC.

3 It is articulated that '[g]overnments, businesses, other organizations and individual users' are all participants to the global culture of cybersecurity, who 'should review their own policies, practices, measures and procedures regularly, and should assess whether they are appropriate to their environment'.

4 Several results of the cooperation between the Cybersecurity Tech Accord have been produced, such as the Joint civil society statement on cyber peace and human security, delivered to the UN General Assembly First Committee on Disarmament and International Security on October 8, 2021, https://cybertechaccord.org/joint-civil-society-statement-on-cyber-peace-and-human-security-at-the-2021-un-general-assembly-first-committee-on-disarmament-and-international-security/; the Joint statement of support on consumer IoT device security of February 15, 2022 https://cybertechaccord.org/industry-hackers-and-consumers-for-a-global-baseline-for-consumer-iot-security/; and so forth.

5 Concerning space arms prevention, three proposals have been the most active: the Draft Treaty on the Prevention of Placement of Weapons in Outer Space and the Threat or Use of Force against Outer Space Objects proposed by China and Russia at the Conference on Disarmament, the Draft International Code of Conduct for Outer Space Activities promoted by the EU, and the initiative of unilateral commitment of no first placement of weapons in outer space raised by Russia. Recently, more proposals have been submitted to the UN for approval, such as the UK-sponsored draft resolution titled 'Reducing space threats through norms, rules and principles of responsible behaviours', the Russian-led 'Further practical measures for the prevention of an arms race in outer space', and so forth.

6 Up to the end of 2023, among the 69 Parties to the Budapest Convention, other than European States, there are States from Africa, such as Cameroon and Nigeria; from Asia, such as Azerbaijan and Japan; from North America, such as Canada and the Dominican Republic; from South America, such as Chile and Colombia; and the Oceania, such as Australia. Observer counties are from all the aforementioned continents. In addition, several regional and international organisations are invited as observer organisations to the Budapest Convention, including the African Union Commission, the Organization of American States, the Commonwealth Secretariat, the ITU, the Organization for Economic Cooperation and Development, the UN Office on Drugs and Crime, and so on.

References

African Union. (2014). *African Union convention on cyber security and personal data protection.* https://au.int/sites/default/files/treaties/29560-treaty-0048_-_african_union_convention_on_cyber_security_and_personal_data_protection_e.pdf

Agreement Among the Government of Canada, Governments of Member States of the European Space Agency, the Government of Japan, the Government of the Russian Federation, and the Government of the United States of America Concerning Cooperation on the Civil International Space Station. (1998). https://aerospace.org/sites/default/files/policy_archives/Space%20Station%20Intergovernmental%20Agreement%20Jan98.pdf

Agreement Between the United Nations and International Telecommunications Union. (1952). UNTS. (30, 316).

Agreement Between the United Nations and the United Nations Educational, Scientific and Cultural Organization. (1949). UNTS. (1, 233).

Agreement Between the United Nations and the World Meteorological Organization. (1956). UNTS. (123, 245).

Alvestrand, H. (2004). *A mission statement for the IETF.* www.rfc-editor.org/rfc/pdfrfc/rfc3935.txt.pdf

Ambos, K. (2016). Individual criminal responsibility for cyber aggression. *Journal of Conflict and Security Law, 21*(3), 495–504. https://doi.org/10.1093/jcsl/krw010

Aoki, S. (2012). The function of 'soft law' in the development of international space law. In I. Marboe (Ed.), *Soft law in outer space: The function of non-binding norms in international space law* (pp. 57–86). Böhlau Verlag Ges.m.b.H. und Co.KG.

Association of Southeast Asian Nations (ASEAN). (2017). *The ASEAN declaration to prevent and combat cybercrime.* https://asean.org/wp-content/uploads/2017/11/ASEAN-Declaration-to-Combat-Cybercrime.pdf

Aust, A. (2005). *Handbook of international law.* Cambridge University Press. https://doi.org/10.1017/CBO9780511494123

Bacon, J. (2019, December 23–24). NASA & US government orbital debris mitigation policies. *Speech made at the 8th Range Safety Conference in Tel Aviv*, Israel. https://ntrs.nasa.gov/api/citations/20200002258/downloads/20200002258.pdf

Bajaj, K. (2014). Cyberspace: Post-Snowden. *Strategic Analysis, 38*(4), 582–587. https://doi.org/10.1080/09700161.2014.918448

Boer, L. J. M. (2013). Restating the law as it is: On the Tallinn manual and the use of force in cyberspace. *Amsterdam Law Forum, 5*(3), 4–18. https://doi.org/10.37974/alf.257

Carr, M. (2015). Power plays in global internet governance. *Millennium: Journal of International Studies, 43*(2), 640–659. https://doi.org/10.1177/0305829814562655

Charney, S. (2014). Governments and APTs: The need for norms. *Microsoft white paper.* https://query.prod.cms.rt.microsoft.com/cms/api/am/binary/REXXtU

Charney, S., English, E., Kleiner, A., Malisevic, N., McKay, A., Neutze, J., & Nicholas, P. (2016). *From articulation to implementation: Enabling progress on cybersecurity norms.* https://query.prod.cms.rt.microsoft.com/cms/api/am/binary/REVmc8

Check, T. (2015). Analyzing the effectiveness of the Tallinn manual's jus ad bellum doctrine on cyberconflict, NATO-centric approach. *Cleveland State Law Review, 63*(2), 495–514.

Cogburn, D. L. (2016). Cyber space and social media. In A. Acharya (Ed.), *Why govern? Rethinking demand and progress in global governance*(pp. 252–271). Cambridge University Press. https://doi.org/10.1017/CBO9781316756829.013

Cooperative Cyber Defense Centre of Excellence (CCDCoE). (2021). *CCDCOE to host the Tallinn manual 3.0 process.* https://ccdcoe.org/news/2020/ccdcoe-to-host-the-tallinn-manual-3-0-process/

Council of Europe. (2001). *Convention on cybercrime.* European Treaty Series. (No.185).

Cybersecurity Tech Accord. (2018). 2018 in Review. https://cybertechaccord.org/uploads/prod/2019/03/2018report.pdf

Danilenko, G. M. (1989). Outer space and the multilateral treaty-making process. *High Technology Law Journal, 4*(2), 217–248. https://doi.org/10.15779/z38kh3t

Danilenko, G. M. (2016). International law-making for outer space. *Space Policy, 37*, 179–183. https://doi.org/10.1016/j.spacepol.2016.12.002

Davey, J., &Taylor, E. A. (2005). Development of ISO standards addressing mitigation of orbital debris. *Proceedings of the Fourth European Conference on Space Debris*, ESA SP-587. https://conference.sdo.esoc.esa.int/proceedings/sdc4/paper/40/SDC4-paper40.pdf.

De O. Bittencourt Neto, O., Hofmann, M., Masson-Zwaan, T., & Stefoudi, D. (Eds.). (2020).*Building blocks for the development of an international framework for the governance of space resource activities: A commentary*. Eleven International Publishing.

de Zwart, M., Henderson, S., & Neumann, M. (2023). Space resource activities and the evolution of international space law. *Acta Astronautica, 211*, 155–162. https://doi.org/10.1016/j.actaastro.2023.06.009

Deibert, R. J., & Crete-Nishihata, M. (2012). Global governance and the spread of cyberspace controls. *Global Governance: A Review of Multilateralism and International Organizations, 18*(3), 339–361. https://doi.org/10.1163/19426720-01803006

Deibert, R., & Rohozinski, R. (2017). International organization and cyber governance. *Oxford Research Encyclopedia of International Studies*. https://oxfordre.com/internationalstudies/view/10.1093/acrefore/9780190846626.001.0001/acrefore-9780190846626-e-69. https://doi.org/10.1093/acrefore/9780190846626.013.69

Efrony, D., & Shany, Y. (2018). A rule book on the shelf? Tallinn manual 2.0 on cyberoperations and subsequent state practice. *American Journal of International Law, 112*(4), 583–657. https://doi.org/10.1017/ajil.2018.86

Eichensehr, K. E. (2014). Tallinn manual on the international law applicable to cyber warfare; Edited by Michael N. Schmitt. *American Journal of International Law, 108*(3), 585–589.

European Union (EU). (2013). Directive 2013/40/EU of the European parliament and of the council of 12 August 2013 on attacks against information systems and replacing council framework decision 2005/222/JHA. *OJL, 218*, 8–14.

Fleck, D. (2013). Searching for international rules applicable to cyber warfare—a critical first assessment of the new Tallinn manual. *Journal of Conflict and Security Law, 18*(2), 331–351. https://doi.org/10.1093/jcsl/krt011

Galloway, E. M. (1979). Consensus decision-making by the United Nations committee on the peaceful uses of outer space. *Journal of Space Law, 7*, 3–13.

Garber, S. J. (2017). Incentives for keeping space clean: Orbital debris and mitigation waivers. *Journal of Space Law, 41*(2), 179–202.

Gillis, A. S. (n.d). *W3C (World Wide Web Consortium)*. www.techtarget.com/whatis/definition/W3C-World-Wide-Web-Consortium

Glen, C. (2014). Internet governance: Territorializing cyberspace? *Politics & Policy, 42*(5), 635–657. https://doi.org/10.1111/polp.12093

Gorove, S., Jasentuliyana, N., Schachter, O., Dembling, P. G., O'Brien, J. E., Nanda, V. P., & Szasz, P. C. (1986). Treaty law and outer space: The role of the United Nations. *Proceedings of the Annual Meeting (American Society of International Law), 80*, 368–385.

Hobe, S., Schmidt-Tedd, B., & Schrogl, K. (Eds.). (2009). *Cologne commentary on space law, Vol. I, outer space treaty*. Carl Heymanns Verlag.

Hofmann, M., & Bergamasco, F. (2020). Space resources activities from the perspective of sustainability: Legal aspects. *Global Sustainability, 3*(4), 1–7. https://doi.org/10.1017/sus.2019.27

Hofmann, S. C., & Pawlak, P. (2023). Governing cyberspace: Policy boundary politics across organizations. *Review of International Political Economy, 30*(6), 2178–2205. https://doi.org/10.1080/09692290.2023.2249002

IADC. (2002). *IADC space debris mitigation guidelines (last revision in 2021)*. IADC-02-1. www.iadc-home.org/documents_public/

IAEA. (1986b). *Convention on assistance in the case of a nuclear accident or radiological emergency*. UNTS. (1457, 133).

ICC. (2017). Activation of the jurisdiction of the court over the crime of aggression. *Resolution ICC-ASP/16/Res.5, § 1.* https://asp.icc-cpi.int/sites/asp/files/asp_docs/ASP16/ICC-ASP-16-20-vol-I-ENG.pdf

Inter-Agency Space Debris Coordination Committee (IADC). (n.d.). *What's IADC.* www.iadc-home.org/what_iadc

International Atomic Energy Agency (IAEA). (1986a). *Convention on early notification of a nuclear accident.* UNTS. (1439, 275).

International Court of Justice (ICJ). (1946). *Statute of the international court of justice.* UNTS. (XV, 355).

International Criminal Court (ICC). (2010). Amendments to the Rome statute of the international criminal court. *Resolution RC/Res.6 of the Review Conference of the Rome Statute.* https://treaties.un.org/doc/Treaties/2010/06/20100611%2005–56%20PM/CN.651.2010.pdf

International Institute of Air and Space Law. (n.d.). *The Hague international space resources governance working group.* www.universiteitleiden.nl/en/law/institute-of-public-law/institute-of-air-space-law/the-hague-space-resources-governance-working-group

International Organization for Standardization (ISO). (n.d.a). *Get involved.* www.iso.org/get-involved.html

ISO. (n.d.b). *Who develops standards.* www.iso.org/who-develops-standards.html

ISO. (n.d.c). *ISO membership manual.* www.iso.org/files/live/sites/isoorg/files/store/en/PUB100399.pdf

ITU. (n.d.a). *ITU cybersecurity activities.* www.itu.int/en/action/cybersecurity/Pages/default.aspx

ITU. (n.d.b). *Basic information: About WSIS.* www.itu.int/net/wsis/basic/about.html

International Telecommunications Union (ITU). (2019). *ITU/BDT cyber security programme global cybersecurity index (GCI) guidelines for member states.* www.itu.int/en/ITU-D/Cybersecurity/Documents/GCIv4/GCI_V4_Guidelines_for_Member%20States.pdf

ITU. (2022). *Draft guidelines for utilization of the global cybersecurity agenda by the ITU.* Revision 2 to Document C22/32-E. www.itu.int/md/S22-CL-C-0032/en

ITU. (2023, October 17). Effective space plans for satellite connectivity and broadcasting. www.itu.int/hub/2023/10/effective-space-plans-for-satellite-connectivity-and-broadcasting/

Jankowitsch, P. (2015). The background and history of space law. In F. G. von der Dunk & F. Tronchetti (Eds.), *Handbook of space law*(pp. 1–28). Edward Elgar Publishing.

Jasentuliyana, N. (1986). Treaty law and outer space: Can the united nations play an effective role. *Annals of Air and Space Law, 11*, 219–228.

Jensen, E. T. (2017). The Tallinn manual 2.0: Highlights and insights. *Georgetown Journal of International Law, 48*(3), 735–778.

Jeutner, V. (2019). The digital Geneva convention: A critical appraisal of Microsoft's proposal. *Journal of International Humanitarian Legal Studies, 10*, 158–170. https://doi.org/10.1163/18781527-01001009

Johnson, N. (n.d.). *Origin of the inter-agency space debris coordination committee.* https://ntrs.nasa.gov/api/citations/20150003818/downloads/20150003818.pdf

Kelesza, J., & Weber, R. H. (2021). Protecting the internet with internet law. *Computer Law & Security Review, 40*, 105531. https://doi.org/10.1016/j.clsr.2021.105531

Kessler, O., & Werner, W. (2013). Expertise, uncertainty, and international law: Study of the Tallinn manual on cyberwarfare. *Leiden Journal of International Law, 26*(4), 793–810. https://doi.org/10.1017/s0922156513000411

Kreß, C., & von Holtzendorff, L. (2010). The Kampala compromise on the crime of aggression. *Journal of International Criminal Justice, 8*, 1179–1217. https://doi.org/10.1093/jicj/mqq069

Lachs, M. (2010). *The law of outer space: An experience in contemporary law-making.* Martinus Nijhoff Publishers.

Li, L. (2015). Space debris mitigation as an international law obligation. I*nternational Community Law Review, 17*(3), 297–335. https://doi.org/10.1163/18719732-12341307

Liaropoulos, A. (2016). Exploring the complexity of cyberspace governance: State sovereignty, multistakeholderism, and power politics. *Journal of Information Warfare, 15*(4), 14–26.

Lyall, F., & Larsen, P. B. (2009). *Space law: A treatise*. Ashgate Publishing Company.
Macak, K. (2017). From cyber norms to cyber rules: Re-engaging states as law-makers. *Leiden Journal of International Law*, *30*(4), 877–899. https://doi.org/10.1017/s0922156517000358
Mckay, A., Neutze, J., Nicholas, P., & Sullivan, K. (2014). *International cybersecurity norms: Reducing conflict in an internet-dependent world*. https://query.prod.cms.rt.microsoft.com/cms/api/am/binary/REVroA
Mejía-Kaiser, M. (2009). Informal regulations and practices in the field of space debris mitigation. *Air and Space Law*, *34*(1), 21–34.
Microsoft. (2017). A digital Geneva convention to protect cyberspace. *Microsoft Policy Papers*. https://query.prod.cms.rt.microsoft.com/cms/api/am/binary/RW67QH
Microsoft. (2018a). A tech accord to protect people in cyberspace. *Microsoft Policy Papers*. https://dig.watch/wp-content/uploads/2021/12/Policy-Paper-Industry-Accord.pdf
Microsoft. (2018b). An attribution organization to strengthen trust online. *Microsoft Policy Papers*. https://query.prod.cms.rt.microsoft.com/cms/api/am/binary/RW67QI
Mihai, I. (2016). Romanian legislation on cybercrime. *International Journal of Information Security and Cybercrime*, *5*(2), 25–30. https://doi.org/10.19107/ijisc.2016.02.03
Miller, K. L. (2014). The Kampala compromise and cyberattacks: Can there be an international crime of cyber-aggression. *Southern California Interdisciplinary Law Journal*, *23*(2), 217–260.
Moon Village Association (MVA). (n.d.). *About the association*. https://moonvillageassociation.org/about/
MVA. (2021). *Global expert group on sustainable lunar activities (GEGSLA)*. https://moonvillageassociation.org/global-expert-group-on-sustainable-lunar-activities-gegsla/
MVA. (2022). *Recommended framework and key elements for peaceful and sustainable lunar activities*. https://moonvillageassociation.org/gegsla/documents/gegsla-recommended-framework/
National Aeronautics and Space Administration of the United States (NASA). (2020). *The Artemis accords: Principles for cooperation in the civil exploration and use of the Moon,Mars, Comets and Asteroids for peaceful purpose*. www.nasa.gov/wp-content/uploads/2022/11/Artemis-Accords-signed-13Oct2020.pdf
Nelson, J. W. (2020). The Artemis accords and the future of international space law. *ASIL Insights*, *24*(31), 1–7.
Ogbe, R. (2022). The legal justification of cyber crime as crime of aggression in international law. *International Review of Law and Jurisprudence*, *4*(2), 145–150.
Ogbe, R. (2023). International law, cyber crime and crime of aggression. *African Journal of Criminal Law and Jurisprudence*, *8*, 24–29.
Ophardt, J. A. (2010–2011). Cyber warfare and the crime of aggression: The need for individual accountability on tomorrow's battlefield. *Duke Law & Technology Review*, *9*, 1–27.
Pernice, I. (2018). Global cybersecurity governance: A constitutionalist analysis. *Global Constitutionalism*, *7*(1), 112–141. https://doi.org/10.1017/s2045381718000023
Perritt, H. (2000). Klaus w. Grewlich, governance in cyberspace: Access and public interest in global communications. *EDI Law Review*, *7*(2&3), 195–198.
Podgor, E. S. (2004). Cybercrime: National, transnational, or international. *Wayne Law Review*, *50*(1), 97–108.
Polanski, P. P. (2017). Cyberspace: A new branch of international customary law? *Computer Law & Security Review*, *33*, 371–381. https://doi.org/10.1016/j.clsr.2017.03.007
Rashkovski, D., Naumovski, V., & Naumovski, G. (2016). Cybercrime tendencies and legislation in the republic of Macedonia. *European Journal on Criminal Policy and Research*, *22*(1), 127–151. https://doi.org/10.1007/s10610-015-9277-7
Schjølberg, S. (2008). *Report of the chairman of the HLEG (High-Level Experts Group) to ITU secretary-general*. www.itu.int/en/action/cybersecurity/Documents/gca-chairman-report.pdf

Schmitt, M. N. (Ed.). (2013). *Tallinn manual on the international law applicable to cyber warfare*. Cambridge University Press. https://doi.org/10.1017/CBO9781139169288

Schmitt, M. N. (Ed.). (2017). *Tallinn manual 2.0 on the international law applicable to cyber warfare*. Cambridge University Press. https://doi.org/10.1017/9781316822524

Smith, R. B. (2020). Cybercrime in ASEAN: Anti-child pornography legislation. *Journal of Indonesian Legal Studies*, *5*(2), 277–294. https://doi.org/10.15294/jils.v5i2.37931

Su, J. (2017). Space arms control: Lex lata and currently active proposals. *Asian Journal of International Law*, *7*(1), 61–93. https://doi.org/10.1017/s2044251315000223

Tanodomdej, P. (2019). The Tallinn manuals and the making of the international law on cyber operations. *Masaryk University Journal of Law and Technology*, *13*(1), 67–86. https://doi.org/10.5817/mujlt2019-1-4

Terekhov, A. D. (1987). 1986 IAEA conventions on nuclear accidents and the consideration of the use of nuclear power sources in outer space in the legal sub-committee of COPUOS. *The. Proceedings on the Law of Outer Space*, *30*, 403–410.

Thirlway, H. (2019). *The sources of international law*. Oxford University Press. https://doi.org/10.1093/law/9780198841814.001.0001

Tiirmaa-Klaar, H. (2021). The evolution of the UN group of governmental experts on cyber issues: From a marginal group to a major international security norm-setting body. *Cyberstability Paper Series: New Conditions and Constellations in Cyber*. https://hcss.nl/wp-content/uploads/2021/12/Klaar.pdf

UN COPUOS. (n.d.). Committee on the peaceful uses of outer space: Membership evolution. www.unoosa.org/oosa/en/ourwork/copuos/members/evolution.html

UN Committee on the Peaceful Uses of Outer Space (UN COPUOS). (1966). *Report of the committee on the peaceful uses of outer space*. (UN Doc. A/6431).

UN COPUOS. (1992). *Principles relevant to the use of nuclear power sources in outer space*. (UNGA Resolution 47/68).

UN COPUOS. (2007). *Space debris mitigation guidelines of the committee on the peaceful uses of outer space*. (UN doc. A/62/20).

UN COPUOS. (2018). *The Hague space resources governance working group: Information provided by the Netherlands*. (UN Doc. A/AC.105/C.2/2018/CRP.18).

UN COPUOS. (2020). *Building blocks for the development of an international framework on space resource activities: Working paper submitted by Luxembourg and the Netherlands*. (UN Doc. A/AC.105/C.2/L.315).

UN COPUOS. (2023). *Report of the Moon village association on the global expert group on sustainable lunar activities- status/deliverables/plan*. (UN Doc. A/AC.105/C.1/2023/CRP.20).

UN COPUOS Legal Subcommittee. (2021). *Third revised Co-moderators' proposal (9 June 2021-Final Consultations)*. www.unoosa.org/oosa/en/ourwork/copuos/lsc/space-resources/index.html

UN COPUOS Scientific and Technical Sub-Committee (STSC). (2007). *Report of the scientific and technical subcommittee on its forty-fourth session, held in Vienna from 12 to 23 February 2007*. (UN Doc. A/AC.105/890).

UN Educational, Scientific and Cultural Organization (UNESCO). (1972). *Declaration of guiding principles on the use of satellite broadcasting for the free flow of information, the spread of education and greater cultural exchange*. https://en.unesco.org/about-us/legal-affairs/declaration-guiding-principles-use-satellite-broadcasting-free-flow

UN General Assembly (UNGA). (1959). *International cooperation in the peaceful uses of outer space*. (UNGA Resolution 1472 (XIV)).

UN Office for Disarmament Affairs (UNODA). (n.d.). Open-ended working group. https://disarmament.unoda.org/open-ended-working-group/

UN Office for Outer Space Affairs (UNOOSA). (n.d.). Compendium of space debris mitigation standards adopted by states and international organizations. www.unoosa.org/oosa/en/ourwork/topics/space-debris/compendium.html

UNGA. (1967). *Treaty on principles governing the activities of states in the exploration and use of outer space, including the Moon and the other celestial bodies.* (UNGA Resolution 2222 (XXI)). United Nations Treaty Series (UNTS). (610, No. 8843).
UNGA. (1968). *Agreement on the rescue of astronauts, the return of astronauts and return of objects launched into outer space.* (UNGA Resolution 2345 (XXII)). UNTS. (672, No. 9574).
UNGA. (1972). *Convention on international liability for damage caused by space objects.* (UNGA Resolution 2777 (XXVI)). UNTS. (961, No. 13810).
UNGA. (1975). *Convention on registration of objects launched into outer space.* (UNGA Resolution 3235 (XXIX)). UNTS. (1023, No. 15020).
UNGA. (1979). *Agreement governing the activities of states on the Moon and other celestial bodies.* (UNGA Resolution 34/68). UNTS. (1363, No. 23002).
UNGA. (1982). *Principles governing the use by states of artificial earth satellites for international direct television broadcasting.*(UNGA Resolution 37/92).
UNGA. (1998). *Rome statute of the international criminal court.* UNTS. (2187, pp. 91–152).
UNGA. (2002a). *Creation of A global culture of cybersecurity.* (UNGA Resolution 57/239).
UNGA. (2002b). *World summit on the information society.* (UNGA Resolution A/RES/56/183).
UNGA. (2005). *Group of governmental experts on developments in the field of information and telecommunications in the context of international security.* (UN Doc. A/60/202).
UNGA. (2007). *GA resolution on the report of the special political and decolonization committee* (A/62/403). (UNGA Resolution A/RES/62/217).
UNGA. (2018). *Developments in the field of information and telecommunications in the context of international security.* (UNGA Resolution A/RES/73/27).
UNGA. (2019). *List of participants.* (UN Doc. A/AC.290/2019/INF/1).
UNGA. (2020). *List of Participants.* (UN Doc. A/AC.290/2020/INF/1).
UNGA. (2021a). *List of participants.* (UN Doc. A/AC.290/2021/INF/1).
UNGA. (2021b). *Open-ended working group on development in the field of information and telecommunications in the context of international security: Final substantive report.* (UN Doc. A/AC.290/2021/CRP.2).
UNGA. (2021c). *Compendium of statement in explanation of position in the final report.* (UN Doc. A/AC.290/2021/INF.2).
UNGA. (2022a). *Report of the open-ended working group on security of and in the use of information and communications technologies 2021–2025.* (UN Doc. A/77/275).
UNGA. (2022b). *Compendium of statements in explanation of position on the adoption of the progress report of the open-ended working group as contained in A/77/275, annex.* (UN Doc. A/AC.292/2022/INF/4.)
UNGA. (2022c). *Programme of action to advance responsible state behaviour in the use of information and communications technologies in the context of international security.* (UN Resolution A/RES/77/37.)
UNGA. (2023a). *Report of the open-ended working group on security of and in the use of information and communications technologies 2021–2025.* (UN Doc. A/78/265).
UNGA. (2023b). *Compendium of statements in explanation of position on the adoption of the progress report of the open-ended working group as contained in A/78/265, annex.* (UN Doc. A/AC.292/2023/INF/5).
UNGA. (2023c). *Programme of action to advance responsible state behaviour in the use of information and communications technologies in the context of international security: Report of the secretary-general.* (UN Doc. A78/76).
UNGA. (2023d). *Consensus scuttled in first committee over two competing draft resolutions on space security, creating parallel processes, polarization, say speakers.* (UN Doc. GA/DIS/3730).
United States (US). (2010). National space policy of the United States of America. https://obamawhitehouse.archives.gov/sites/default/files/national_space_policy_6–28–10.pdf

US Department of State. (2023, May 5). *Artemis accords*. www.state.gov/artemis-accords/
US. (2020). National space policy of the United States of America. https://trumpwhitehouse.archives.gov/wp-content/uploads/2020/12/National-Space-Policy.pdf
US. (2023). United States response to UNODA's request for views of the landscape of information and communications technology capacity-building programs and initiatives within and outside the United Nations at the global and regional levels. *Working Papers: Input to Mapping Exercise on Capacity-Building by United States*. https://docs-library.unoda.org/Open-Ended_Working_Group_on_Information_and_Communication_Technologies_-_(2021)/US_Response_to_UNODA_Capacity_Building_Mapping_Exercise_(final).pdf
Venturini, G. (2020). The legal regime of the use of nuclear power sources in space missions. In J. L. Black-Branch & D. Fleck (Eds.), *Nuclear non-proliferation in international law—volume V*(pp. 73–91). T.M.C. Asser Press. https://doi.org/10.1007/978-94-6265-347-4_5
World Wide Web Consortium (W3C). (n.d.a). *Why join W3C*. www.w3.org/membership/
W3C. (n.d.b). *Current members & testimonials*. www.w3.org/membership/list/
W3C. (n.d.c). *About W3C web standards*. www.w3.org/standards/about/
Weisbord, N. (2013). Bargaining practices: Negotiating the Kampala compromise for the international criminal court. *Law and Contemporary Problems*, *76*(3–4), 85–117.
Wenaweser, C. (2010). Reaching the Kampala compromise on aggression: The chair's perspective. *Leiden Journal of International Law*, *23*, 883–887. https://doi.org/10.1017/S0922156510000439
Wu, X. (2023). The international lunar research station: China's new era of space cooperation and its new role in the space legal order. *Space Policy*, *65*, 101537. https://doi.org/10.1016/j.spacepol.2022.101537
Xu, F., & Su, J. (2020). New elements in the Hague space resources governance working group's building blocks. *Space Policy*, *53*, 101386. https://doi.org/10.1016/j.spacepol.2020.101386
Yilma, K. M. (2016). Some remarks on Ethiopia's new cybercrime legislation. *Mizan Law Review*, *10*(2), 448–458.
Young, M. A. (2012). Regime interaction in creating, implementing and enforcing international law. In M. A. Young (Ed.), *Regime interaction in international law: Facing fragmentation* (pp. 85–110). Cambridge University Press. https://doi.org/10.1017/CBO9780511862403

7 Promoting the Implementation and Enforcement of the Law Pertinent to Space Cybersecurity

Even with a perfect regulatory scheme, global governance goals of space cybersecurity cannot be achieved without the effective implementation and enforcement of the rules. Implementation and enforcement, although often used together, have different meanings, implying that the subjects empowered to implement and enforce rules are different. Implementation means 'to fulfil or perform a contract' (Sloan, 1968) and relates to the behaviour that should be performed in conformity with the law, whereas enforcement indicates '[t]he act or process of compelling compliance with a law, mandate, command, decree, or agreement' (Black, 2009) and deals with non-compliance or violation of international law. Both implementation and enforcement are crucial for ensuring compliance with international law. In the context of space cybersecurity, implementing and enforcing relevant rules may trigger different challenges.

7.1 Harmonising the Implementation of International Law

In the context of international law, implementation 'refers to the further steps States must take as required by a convention' (O'Connell, 1994), and subjects of international law are the implementors. States are naturally subjects of international law as they 'pre-eminently' possess 'international rights and obligations' and have the capacity to 'maintain [their] rights by bringing international claims' and 'to be responsible for [their] breaches of obligation by being subjected to such claims' (Crawford, 2019). International organisations (IOs) with such capacities can also be considered to possess legal personality under specific conditions (Crawford, 2019). These two types of normal subjects of international law, which should bear corresponding international obligations, are the major subjects to implement international law.

In the absence of international rules and norms specifically dedicated to ensuring space cybersecurity and considering the fact that their development may take quite a long time, the implementation of the existing rules is crucial for the effective global governance of space cybersecurity. The coherent implementation of international law can guarantee that the existing international rules are observed in a harmonised manner and help to alleviate the problems resting with the current regulatory regime of space cybersecurity. Convergence of States' implementing

DOI: 10.4324/9781003561996-10

actions implies the formation of universally accepted interpretations of the obscure provisions. The coherent implementation may advance the international law-making process as well, as it represents that States are already practising in the same way, despite the existing law not being sufficiently substantive or the lack of international law on certain aspects. Thus, involving the States in a new internationally binding instrument when a coherent State implementation exists would be much easier than when States' practices diverge significantly. However, the current State implementation of the rules relevant to combatting malicious cyber activities against space activities (MCASAs) is far from harmonised. Even if some States adopt national measures to combat MCASAs in conformity with the existing international law, the effects of such measures would be limited if other States fail to act similarly, particularly under the circumstances that space systems are becoming increasingly globally interconnected. Once the space systems of the States implementing anti-MCASA measures are connected with other space systems without similar measures, an MCASA against the latter would continue to affect the former. Thus, coherence in States' implementation of the existing rules is necessary to enhance the effectiveness of the global governance of space cybersecurity.

However, the coherent implementation of international law by States cannot be easily realised. There are several reasons. First, not all States abide by the same international rules. Statistics of the signatories of the different international agreements relevant to space cybersecurity can illustrate this point. Furthermore, States and IOs may select to follow, entirely or partially, or not to follow the many non-binding soft law rules contributing to combatting MCASAs.

Second, despite States implementing the same provisions, their understanding of the provisions, their methods of implementation, and the measures adopted may vary significantly. Several factors result in this situation. In the first place, States' ways of implementing international law are different (Crawford, 2019), which are usually regulated by their Constitutions (Graefrath, 1984–1985). In the second place, the actual measures that States adopt to implement the law sometimes depend on the content of treaties, which provides various degrees of freedom to States as to their choice of implementing methods (Bodansky, 2011). Some provisions of treaties establish specific actions to be taken by signatories. For instance, Article II of the Convention on Registration of Objects Launched into Outer Space (UNGA, 1975) demands State Parties to maintain an appropriate national registry of space objects and inform the Secretary-General of the United Nations (UN) of its establishment, and Article VIII requires the State of registry to furnish to the Secretary-General of the UN certain specified information concerning the space object carried on its registry. When the provisions are not self-executing (Sloss, 2020; Vázquez, 1995)[1] or are not directly applicable, States' actions to comply with the treaties tend to diverge. This is the case with most existing rules relevant to space cybersecurity. Most space law rules are general principles that need clarification, leading to many controversies on their interpretation. The international rules on cybersecurity are yet to be formulated. The difficulties in developing international cyber law testify to the differences in States' understandings of their international obligations to ensure cybersecurity. At present, many States have adopted national laws concerning cybersecurity; however, their content differs significantly.

Third, implementation concerns not only the States and IOs but also involves the participation of the industry and other relevant organisations (Bodansky, 2011). The industry may contribute to implementing international laws by providing expertise in establishing domestic technical standards and measures (Bodansky, 2011). The United States (US) Memorandum on Cybersecurity Principles for Space Systems (Administration of Donald J. Trump, 2020) articulates expressly that '[s]pace system owners and operators should collaborate to promote the development of best practices'. However, there is a wide gap in the development level of the space and cyber industries among States. Moreover, the values prioritised by relevant national industries differ. An interest-driven industry may sacrifice other aspects, such as security and environmental protection concerns, for commercial interests, and an industry eager for development and expansion may concentrate on technological advancements, subordinating other aspects to some extent. Thus, the industry-proposed technical standards and measures vary from State to State, further diverging States' implementation of legislation.

IOs and the industry could contribute towards harmonising States' implementation. IOs normally do not implement international law themselves unless they are bound to do so by international treaties (Ramcharan, 1983). They help to promote the implementation through various ways, including encouraging and inducing States to implement international law, assisting States in overcoming difficulties in implementation, such as by providing financial and technical assistance and clarifying the content of international obligations, mobilising and empowering domestic constituencies by requesting States to submit reports and prepare national implementation plans, entering into dialogue with governments on implementation, and so forth (Bodansky, 2011). States may encounter difficulties in implementing international law, particularly when international law is so fragmented that State officials often find it challenging to learn and understand (Young, 2023). In response to this situation, IOs could provide training to State officials as part of the capacity-building programmes (Young, 2023). The importance of building 'indigenous capacity in space law and policy' was recognised by the third UN Conference on the Exploration and Peaceful Uses of Outer Space (UN, 2014), in accordance with which the UN Office for Outer Space Affairs (UNOOSA) has taken the initiative to include education and training in space law in its capacity-building projects. In addition to workshops on space law, the UNOOSA launched the Education Curriculum on Space Law for educational institutions and training initiatives to use as teaching tools (UN, 2014). Further, it established a directory on education opportunities in space law (UN COPUOS, 2023). Some regional organisations also launched similar capacity-building programmes. The Asia-Pacific Space Cooperation Organization offers training and education in space law open to students, junior engineers, and researchers for 'strengthening the space law education at the regional and global level', 'developing the skills and knowledge of participants', 'providing information related to national space legislation and policy for the participants', and so forth (Seyedavadi, 2019). The European Space Agency (ESA) provides various education opportunities to different groups of audiences, including students, teachers from primary and secondary teachers, and young professionals (ESA, n.d.a). Particularly, the ESA/ECSL (European Centre for Space Law) Executive Course on Space Law and Regulations is destined for government representatives and industry professionals (ESA, n.d.b). Moreover, some IOs provide multilateral platforms for States to exchange their interpretations and opinions concerning the existing international law, allowing States to understand how other States implement international law and then draw lessons therefrom. The UNOOSA maintains an online collection of national space laws and regulations based on submissions made by States (UNOOSA, n.d.). Nonetheless, for the time being, no compliance monitoring mechanism has been established which requires States to submit national reports on implementing space law.

Every sword has two blades: the industry could be a factor that aggravates the incoherence of States' implementation of international law; however, it also contributes to harmonising the substantial implementing measures in return, notably in highly technical areas such as the space and cyber areas. As explained in Chapter 6, the industry participates in international technical standard development in various ways. The technical standards, although non-binding on States, can be widely adopted by the industry. They clarify the meaning of some binding rules and thus facilitate States' implementing activities. When international standards established by the industry are adopted at a large scale, the domestic technical standards and norms based on industrial expertise would be influenced and tend to assimilate the international ones, rendering national standards and norms internationally harmonised to some extent. Furthermore, competent governmental officials may acquire awareness of international standards and consider them during legislation. Unfortunately, as the depth and breadth of industrial involvement in international standard-developing activities differ from field to field, the industry can only play a subsidiary role in promoting States' implementation.

7.2 Towards Effective Enforcement of International Law

International institutions and States are the major subjects in enforcing international law. In the sphere of space cybersecurity, the roles and means of international law enforcement by these subjects are different. Their enforcement effects differ as well. Unfortunately, none of these subjects can guarantee complete compliance with relevant international rules. From a realistic perspective, enhancing the enforcement effect is challenging.

7.2.1 International Institutions

There are two types of international institutions which are involved in international law enforcement: authorities established by specific treaty regimes to enforce the treaty and judicial authorities for coping with non-compliance situations in a more general way, such as the International Court of Justice (ICJ) and the International Criminal Court (ICC). They work as lubricants for promoting cooperation and law enforcement (Kantorowicz-Reznichenko, 2020).

7.2.1.1 *Authorities Established by Treaties*

No authorities have been specifically established to ensure the enforcement of the international rules combatting MCASAs, necessitating a review of the treaty-established authorities of relevant branches of international law. Neither space law nor cyber law has instituted such authorities. Some of the other branches of international law relevant to space cybersecurity have founded authorities to enforce the law, such as international environmental law and the law of armed conflict; however, as their relevance with space cybersecurity is limited, the impact on the overall enforcement of pertinent international rules is restricted.

International institutional machinery to develop the law, supervise the implementation, and resolve conflicts has been particularly effective in coping with global environmental risks (Boyle, 1991). Some international environmental treaties have established their own compliance and enforcement mechanisms. The Montreal Protocol for the Protection of the Ozone Layer (The Conference of Plenipotentiaries on the Protocol on Chlorofluorocarbons to the Vienna Convention for the Protection of the Ozone Layer, 1987) and the compliance systems of the climate regime based on the Kyoto Protocol (UN, 1997) and the 2015 Paris Agreement (UN, 2015) offer suitable examples (Doelle, 2021). It is generally considered that international environmental regimes somewhat deviate from the traditional enforcement mechanisms and focus more on encouraging and facilitating compliance (Bodansky, 2011; Rajamani & Peel, 2021). For instance, the authority to address non-compliance with the Kyoto Protocol—the Compliance Committee—comprises a Facilitative Branch and an Enforcement Branch, responsible respectively for providing assistance to State Parties to promote compliance and dealing with the cases where State Parties fail to meet their commitments (Sands et al., 2018). Nonetheless, none of these treaties expressly extend their scope of application to outer space. It is rather dubious whether these institutional mechanisms would function when MCASAs threaten the outer space environment. Furthermore, as denoted in Chapter 4, international environmental law could only apply to the MSACAs causing environmental harm. Thus, the role of the existing enforcement authorities established by international environmental treaties is trivial in the holistic enforcement of the international rules pertinent to space cybersecurity.

International institutions are indispensable in enforcing the law of armed conflict. In addition to the UN system and the judicial enforcement mechanism, best represented by that of the International Criminal Court, four enforcement mechanisms have been established by the treaties on the law of armed conflict–the Protecting Powers, the International Committee of the Red Cross (ICRC), the ad hoc fact-finding commissions, and International Humanitarian Fact-finding Commission (IHFFC)—vesting them with the authority to enforce the treaties (Zyberi,

2018). According to Article 2 of the Protocol additional to the Geneva Conventions of 12 August 1949, and relating to the protection of victims of international armed conflicts (Protocol I), a 'Protecting Power' is

> a neutral State or other State not a Party to the conflict which has been designated by a Party to the conflict and accepted by the adverse Party and has agreed to carry out the functions assigned to a Protecting Power under the Conventions and this Protocol.
>
> (DCG, 1977)

The ICRC or other impartial humanitarian organisation shall be designated as a substitute in case of failure to appoint a Protecting Power (DCG, 1977). More than 80 provisions of the treaties on the law of armed conflict entrust Protecting Powers with various tasks, which overlap significantly with those of the ICRC (Sassòli, 2019). The ad hoc fact-finding commissions could be established following the dispositions on the enquiry procedure of the four Geneva Conventions, which are prescribed in Article 52 of the Convention (I) for the Amelioration of the Condition of the Wounded and Sick in Armed Forces in the Field (DCG, 1949a); Article 53 of the Convention (II) for the Amelioration of the Condition of Wounded, Sick, and Shipwrecked Members of Armed Forces at Sea (DCG, 1949b); Article 132 of the Convention (III) relative to the Treatment of Prisoners of War (DCG, 1949c); and Article 149 of the Convention (IV) relative to the Protection of Civilian Persons in Time of War (DCG, 1949d). The enquiry procedure allows the institution of an enquiry upon the request of one Party to the conflict and the agreement between the interested Parties. ICRC's role in enforcing the law of armed conflict is diverse, as it is articulated in the Statutes of the ICRC that it is tasked to 'work for the faithful application of international humanitarian law applicable in armed conflicts and to take cognizance of any complaints based on alleged breaches of that law' (ICRC, 2017). It works as a 'neutral intermediary between Parties in conflict and between Parties and the victims' (Chan, 2000). The IHFFC was constituted in 1991 in accordance with Protocol I (DCG, 1977). It is competent to 'enquire into any facts alleged to be a grave breach or other serious violation of the Geneva Conventions or Protocol I' and to 'facilitate, through its good offices, the restoration of an attitude of respect for the Geneva Conventions and Protocol I' (ICRC, 2021). These authorities pressure State Parties to promote their compliance with the law of armed conflict through supervision and help to identify whether non-conformity occurs through activities such as fact-findings. However, unlike the Dispute Settlement Body of the WTO or the Enforcement Branch of the Compliance Committee of the Kyoto Protocol, they cannot directly address the situation where a breach of the law of armed conflict occurs. Applying the law of armed conflict to space cybersecurity is possible only in specific conditions. Hence, the overall enforcement effect of these institutions in combatting the MCASAs is minimal.

The Security Council responsible for enforcing the law of the peace may intervene in the circumstances where MCASAs constitute threats to the peace, breaches of the peace, and acts of aggression. The enforcement competence is vested in the

Security Council by Chapter VII of the UN Charter, which concerns the Security Council's enforcement action in case of violation the law of the peace. Nonetheless, several challenges exist in the Security Council countering MCASAs through international law enforcement. First, the Security Council can take action only when MCASAs constitute a violation of the law of the peace. Some MCASAs are trivial or even unnoticeable, with minimal negative effects. For instance, a malicious actor can invade a satellite remote sensing system and monitor it without authorisation for a moment to access the remote sensing data that the actor requires for his own research. Such incidents can barely be considered of much relevance to world peace. Only those MCASAs that cause the most devastating aftermath may be addressed by the Security Council. Second, what constitutes threats to the peace, breaches of the peace, and acts of aggression is unclear. According to Article 39 of the UN Charter,

> [t]he Security Council shall determine the existence of any threat to the peace, breach of the peace, or act of aggression and shall make recommendations, or decide what measures shall be taken in accordance with Articles 41 and 42, to maintain or restore international peace and security.

The Security Council is granted significant discretion to decide whether to take enforcement actions and the actions to take, which is much criticised (Aitken, 2017). Combined with the controversies over the term 'threat or use of force' contained in Article 2(4) and 'armed attack' in Article 51, the political nature of the Security Council owing to 'its selective and opportunistic approach' (Krisch, 2012; Roscini, 2010) further blurs the threshold for it to take actions. Even for the most severe MCASAs, the Security Council may decide not to initiate its international law enforcement mechanism. Third, the veto right enjoyed by the five permanent members could easily preclude any action from the Security Council against them. It can be evidenced by recent failures of the Security Council to adopt its first and second draft resolutions on preventing arms races in outer space owing to negative votes.[2]

No international authority is instituted by treaties to enforce international rules relevant to ensuring space cybersecurity. Other than space law and cyber law, the link between other branches of international law and space cybersecurity is somewhat limited. Some of these regimes have established specific institutions to enforce the law; however, their effect in enhancing the overall enforcement of space cybersecurity-related international rules is trivial.

7.2.1.2 Judicial Authorities

Relying on judicial institutions to enforce the international rules relevant to space cybersecurity appears more reasonable compared with other mechanisms of dispute resolution. Dispute resolution undoubtedly contributes to promoting compliance, although they are not technically enforcement techniques (Roscini, 2010). In addition to the informal methods of dispute settlement, particularly negotiation, good offices, mediation, and the semi-judicial method of conciliation (Crawford, 2019), dispute resolution includes the arbitral and judicial process, which is a more formal way. Compared with adjudication, arbitration offers more confidentiality, the preclusion of third parties' intervention, and more flexibility on 'the issues to be resolved, the applicable law, the composition of the panel, and other procedural aspects' (Vidmar, 2002). The flexibility of arbitration makes it suitable for resolving territorial or quasi-territorial disputes (Vidmar, 2002). Thus, it has been essentially used to settle this type of interstate dispute for centuries since the dawn of statehood. Nonetheless, arbitration is not appropriate for all interstate disputes, as it has proved 'most productive in relatively apolitical disputes where the parties' claims to the land are based on historical arguments and documentary evidence', and States are more willing to enter into a judicial process if the issue in question is highly political and contentious (Copeland, 1999). The mixed nature of most space cybersecurity issues–they are technical, legal, and often highly political—accords priority to judicial proceedings over other dispute settlement techniques when relevant disputes arise.

The ICC judges the cases of international crimes contained in the Rome Statute of the ICC (UNGA, 1998), and according to the analysis in Chapter 4, only a few MCASAs may fall under the application scope of the Rome Statute, making the role of the ICC to enforce the international rules relevant to ensuring space cybersecurity insignificant. The ICJ is the most critical international judicial authority in enforcing these rules. The ICJ's role in enforcing international law 'derives from its adjudication in contentious cases and its advisory opinions to UN organs upon request' (Kantorowicz-Reznichenko, 2020). This role is subject to certain limitations. First, the ICJ 'can only exercise jurisdiction over a State with its consent', which is 'a well-established principle of international law embodied in the Court's Statute' (ICJ, 1954). The consent could take various forms. States may submit disputes to the ICJ based on special agreements or *compromis*, conferring on the court voluntary jurisdiction (ICJ, 1946). The consent can be provided in treaties and conventions in force (ICJ, 1946). It can take the form of a State's explicit or implicit intention to accept the ICJ's jurisdiction (*forum prorogatum*) as well. Further, States could also opt to accept the ICJ's compulsory jurisdiction through Declarations Recognizing the Jurisdiction of the Court as Compulsory (Declarations) over legal disputes concerning

> (a) the interpretation of a treaty; (b) any question of international law; (c) the existence of any fact which, if established, would constitute a breach of an international obligation; (d) the nature or extent of the reparation to be made for the breach of international obligation,

as prescribed in Article 36(2) (Optional Clause) of the Statute of the ICJ (ICJ, 1946). The ICJ can help to clarify the meanings and content of the international rules relevant to space cybersecurity and decide whether a breach of the rules exists and the consequences of such breaches, thus contributing to promoting both the implementation and the enforcement of relevant international rules. Nonetheless, the ICJ cannot play its enforcement role voluntarily but on the premise of States' consent and submission of the case to the Court. The consent is not always easy to establish, particularly when compulsory jurisdiction is sought. The compulsory jurisdiction is not so compulsory as optional in nature (Alexandrov, 2006). The effectiveness of the provision on compulsory jurisdiction depends on the number of States adhering to it and the terms of their Declarations (Merrills, 2016). States can opt to accept the Optional Clause by making Declarations or not to adhere to it. They are also 'free either to do so unconditionally and without limit of time for its duration, or to qualify it with conditions or reservations' (ICJ, 1984). Among the 193 State Parties to the Statute of the ICJ, only 74 States have accepted to be bound by the Optional Clause.[3] The expression 'accepting the same obligation' of Article 36(2) suggests that 'there shall be complete reciprocity in the operation of compulsory jurisdiction under the Optional Clause as between two States which have accepted the obligation in different terms' (Waldock, 2003). Thus, in practice, the reservations made by States in the Declaration determine, to a large extent, the scope of the ICJ's compulsory jurisdiction (Lamm, 2003). Although scholars have been optimistic towards the future of compulsory jurisdiction (Llamzon, 2008; Merrills, 2016), the limitations of the Optional Clause are non-negligible. It can be concluded that the international law enforcement role of the ICJ depends essentially on the will of the States. However, as States are not always willing to bring legal disputes to the ICJ and may resolve contentious matters through other approaches to dispute settlement, the ICJ's role in enforcing the international rules related to space cybersecurity can be somewhat limited in terms of its jurisdiction. Many major space powers, such as China, France, Russia, and the USA, are absent from the States whose Declarations have been made and continue to be in force. The States responsible for the space activities involved in MCASAs may bear a heavy responsibility to prevent the occurrence of MCASAs according to international law. The non-adherence of these space powers to the Optional Clause implies that in case of one of these States' alleged non-compliance with international law, the ICJ is incompetent to render judgements unless they enter into special agreements with the claimant State, accept the ICJ's jurisdiction through express acts or implicit intention to do so, or the non-compliance concerns a treaty containing the provisions admitting the ICJ's jurisdiction over dispute pertinent to the treaty.

Second, the implementation of ICJ judgements faces challenges at the domestic level. It is stipulated in Article 92 of the UN Charter that '[e]ach Member of the United Nations undertakes to comply with the decision of the International Court of Justice in any case to which it is a party'. The States submitting a dispute to the ICJ would usually comply with the Court's judgement. Nonetheless, the addressee of the ICJ decision may refuse to implement it. The USA's refusal to be bound by the ICJ judgement in favour of Nicaragua in the Case Concerning the Military and Paramilitary Activities in and against Nicaragua (Military and Paramilitary Activities) (ICJ, 1986), which ignited much concern over the ICJ's capability to enforce international law (Scott & Carr, 1987), serves as an illustration. In cases of non-compliance with the ICJ's judgements, there are several approaches for the other State in favour of which the judgement was delivered to enforce it: the State could take countermeasures, submit the case to the domestic court of the non-compliant State, or have recourse to the Security Council or the General Assembly, or in a few cases, to another international organisation than the UN system (Brown, 1987; Couzigou, 2017). Among these approaches, although countermeasures should be undertaken in conformity with the obscure proportionality principle, it may be the most reliable way to guarantee the implementation of ICJ judgements. Several hurdles exist to hamper the favoured State's attempt to execute the ICJ's decision through domestic judicial proceedings: the standing of the State before a domestic court, political considerations on the virtue of which domestic courts may refuse to become involved, State immunity issues, and so forth (Brown, 1987; Couzigou, 2017). Article 94(2) of the UN Charter provides for the situation of non-compliance with ICJ judgements, stipulating that 'the other party [of the judgement] may have recourse to the Security Council, which may, if it deems necessary, make recommendations or decide upon measures to be taken to give effect to the judgement'. Nevertheless, the discretionary power of the Security Council to decide whether to act and what measures to take adds a strong political tone to this approach of enforcing ICJ judgements, leaving it unreliable (Couzigou, 2017). Nicaragua took recourse to Article 94(2) after the ICJ delivered its judgement on the Military and Paramilitary Activities case, seeking help from the Security Council without success, simply because the US exercised its veto power; this case could well demonstrate the shortcomings of the Article 94(2) mechanism to ensure compliance with ICJ judgements (Oellers-Frahm, 2017). When those major space powers, which are also permanent members of the Security Council, fail to comply with the ICJ judgements delivered against them in a dispute concerning space cybersecurity, the possibility of compelling compliance through the Security Council is low. According to Article 10 of the UN Charter,

> the General Assembly may discuss any questions or any matters within the scope of the present Charter or relating to the powers and functions of any organs provided for in the present charter, and . . . may make recommendations to the Members of the United Nations or to the Security Council or both on any such questions or matters;

thus, the General Assembly could also take actions for enforcing ICJ judgements as it falls under the scope of the General Assembly's competence. The General Assembly can exert political pressure on the non-compliant State through recommendations (Oellers-Frahm, 2017). However, the General Assembly's enforcing power is also subject to limitations. Decisions of the General Assembly shall be made by a two-thirds majority or a majority of the members present and voting, depending on the questions to decide. As the General Assembly is a highly political organ, deciding whether to enforce a judgement in case of non-compliance proves to be a political game, the result of which is difficult to predict. Other international or regional organisations could also help to enforce ICJ judgement based on their fundamental instruments, such as the International Civil Aviation Organization

(Convention on International Civil Aviation, 1944)[4] and the International Labour Organization.[5] However, their scope of competence is rather limited and of low relevance to space cybersecurity.

7.2.2 Individual States

Reciprocity, which could be conceived as 'the status of a relationship between two or more States in which the conduct of one is in some way or other juridically dependent upon the conduct of the other party, in most instances but not all amounting to equivalent treatment' (Simma, 2012), is considered the underlying principle of international law enforcement (Paris & Ghei, 2003; Whelan, 2023). The self-help measures by which States enforce international law—rewards and sanctions—correspond to this principle. Rewards may be accorded to States to induce their compliance, whereas sanctions would be imposed in case of non-compliance to urge the States to abide by the law. Rewards can take various forms, such as loans, cash transfers, investments, debt forgiveness programs, reducing the existing barriers to trade and investment, transferring technology, military aid and other security guarantees, diplomatic recognition, the granting of access to an IO, the promise of cooperation, and so forth (Bradford & Ben-Shahar, 2012). Rewards are not always effective or appropriate in enforcing international law owing to the complicated political and economic relations between States (Bradford & Ben-Shahar, 2012).

The word 'sanction' is sometimes used interchangeably with 'countermeasures', with the latter preferred (ILC, 2001b). Countermeasures is 'a measure legitimate under international law against that other State, in consequence of an internationally wrongful act of that other State' (Noortmann, 2005). However, their implementation is subject to conditions and limitations. First, countermeasures shall not affect the obligations deriving from the law of the peace, for the protection of fundamental human rights, or of a humanitarian character prohibiting reprisals and other international peremptory norms (ILC, 2001a). Nonetheless, a State should fulfil its obligations under any dispute settlement procedure which is in force between it and the responsible State and the injured State and respect the diplomatic or consular inviolability (ILC, 2001a). Second, countermeasures must be taken with a prior demand by the injured State that the violating State fulfils its international obligations and the notification of any decision to take countermeasures (ILC, 2001a). Third, the countermeasures should conform to the proportionality principle (ILC, 2001a), which is essential for determining the threshold between a lawful countermeasure and an illegal response (Franck, 2008). Finally, countermeasures shall terminate upon the violating State's compliance with its obligations (ILC, 2001a). Among these conditions and limitations, applying the proportionality standard could be a sophisticated task (Cannizzaro, 2001; ILC, 2001b). It has been confirmed in the Case concerning the Air Service Agreement of 27 March 1946 between the United States of America and France that 'judging the "proportionality" of countermeasures is not an easy task and can at best be accomplished by approximation' (case concerning the Air Service Agreement of 27 March 1946 between the United States of America and France, 1978).

It implies that the proportionality principle should be applied 'with a certain flexibility' (Lahmann, 2020); however, the criteria for determining proportionality and the extent of the flexibility are unclear. In addition to the obscure implications of the proportionality principle, taking countermeasures based on self-judging constitutes a drawback of this enforcement method (O'Connell, 1994). Notably, in the sphere of space cybersecurity, considering the controversies in interpreting several provisions, it may happen that the act or omission of a State is considered as having fulfilled its duties under international rule by some States, but not by others. Despite the damaged State demanding that the allegedly violating State act in conformity with the law, it is unlikely that the latter will change its idea and behave as required when it deems its duties fulfilled. In this case, the damaged State, with a notification of the decision to launch countermeasures addressed to the allegedly violating State, would take countermeasures on its own judgement, possibly leading to the escalation of conflicts.

Third States other than the injured States could take actions to ensure compliance as well. It is articulated in Article 48 of the ARSIWA that if '[t]he obligation breached is owed to a group of States including that State and is established for the protection of a collective interest of the group', or it is 'owed to the international community as a whole', third States could invoke the international responsibility of the breaching State. They may act unilaterally, such as instituting legal claims in judicial authorities. However, whether third States are entitled to take countermeasures remains debatable (Proukaki, 2010). States could also act collectively as a whole—the international community—to enforce the obligations *erga omnes partes* or obligations *erga omnes*. One weakness of collective actions is that in the cases where only some States participate in the collective actions to pressurise the breaching State, the enforcement effect would be undermined, as the breaching State can obtain resources from the non-participating States.

The shortcomings of international law enforcement by States are apparent. States are not always willing to take countermeasures or bring legal disputes to judicial authorities. From a realistic perspective, several factors other than legal considerations contribute to deciding whether to take action towards other States' non-compliance: political considerations, State interest, the costs to enforce, and so on (Muhammadin, 2014). The effectiveness of States' enforcement of international law is significantly diminished.

7.2.3 ***Promoting Enforcement Effects***

International institutions and States are no doubt the major actors in enforcing international law; however, their approaches to ensuring compliance with international law differ, each with non-negligible shortcomings. Thus, the enforcing effects are far from satisfying. Decisions rendered by international judicial bodies, particularly the ICJ, are not always implemented by the addressees and do not directly impact States' compliance with international law. Instead, the decisions could lead to reputational losses of the losing State. Reputation 'refers to other States' beliefs about the likelihood that the State in question will comply with a treaty' (Scott &

Stephan, 2006). Theoretically, reputational losses may lead to other States' refraining from cooperating and entering into future commitments with the losing State. As long as a State expects beneficial cooperation, it will cherish its reputation by conforming to treaties. Nonetheless, reputation is not the only decisive element for deciding whether to enter into commitments with a certain State. Political, technical, and other concerns may be more important. In addition, whether the decision by a judicial body impacts the reputation of the losing State and the extent of the impact would be complex to determine, as they depend on the reputations of both the judicial bodies and the affected State, which are subject to update and discontinuities (Scott & Stephan, 2006). Therefore, the overall enforcement effect through international judicial bodies is dependent on a complex of factors.

In addition to reputational considerations, self-help measures by States, particularly countermeasures, could trigger the breaching State's fear of retaliation. States may undertake countermeasures individually or collectively with other States, depending on the circumstances of the breaching. As denoted earlier, countermeasures are undertaken based on self-judging. States may interpret an international rule differently, leading to different judgements on whether an act or omission of a State breaches the rule. The effect of retaliation relies on 'mutuality and anticipated future benefits from the reciprocal relationship', meaning that if the breaching State exploits an 'end game' situation, the enforcement effect of retaliation disappears (Scott & Stephan, 2006). Therefore, the enforcement effect of retaliation is affected by several factors as well. The reputational and retaliatory impacts of countermeasures on the allegedly breaching State remain uncertain.

Although full enforcement of pertinent international law cannot completely guarantee space cybersecurity, it helps to enhance the effectiveness of global governance. Thus, promoting the enforcement effectiveness of relevant rules is vital. Compared with other special regimes, such as the law of armed conflict and the trade law, which have established ad hoc institutions for supervising States' implementation of the rules, the lack of a supervisory mechanism for ensuring space cybersecurity is self-evident. The establishment of an international supervision mechanism with ad hoc institutions would undoubtedly help. Through such institutions, by requesting States to submit reports and prepare national implementation plans, actively collecting implementation information, holding periodic meetings to review the implementation of the rules at the national level, and so forth, pressure would be exerted on States so that they conform to the international rules. Nevertheless, considering the fragmentation of the rules relevant to space cybersecurity and the hardship of concluding an internationally binding instrument to cope with MCASAs, the possibility of establishing such institutions is low. Vesting the existing international bodies, such as the UN Committee on the Peaceful Uses of Outer Space, the UN Office for Disarmament Affairs, and the International Telecommunications Union, with supervisory functions would be more feasible. They could form a relatively complete supervisory system by exercising their functions separately.

The will of the States is decisive for enforcement effects. As countermeasures, which are initiated based on States' self-judgement of whether there is a violation of international law, could be easily abused, it was proposed that countermeasures should not be resorted to prior to 'the exhaustion of all the amicable settlement procedures available under general international law, the United Nations Charter or any other dispute settlement instrument to which it is a party' (Arangio-Ruiz, 1992). However, the existing evidence is insufficient to prove the existence or the emergence of such a rule (Noortmann, 2005). Although it is declared in Article 52 of the ARSIWA that countermeasures cannot be taken if 'the dispute is pending before a court or tribunal which has the authority to make decisions binding on the parties', submitting the dispute to a judicial authority cannot be perceived as a peremptory step before taking any countermeasures. Thus, States could liberally opt to submit the dispute to the competent judicial authority or directly take countermeasures, except under circumstances where special treaty regimes include compulsory dispute resolution clauses. What expands States' freedom in this respect is the fact that States are often reluctant to include compulsory dispute resolution clauses in the treaties that they conclude and that only a minority of the existing treaties include such clauses (Guzman, 2002). Further, States may ignore other States' breaching of obligations without taking any actions, even when they suffer from such breaches. In MCASAs, victims include not only States but also private entities and individuals; however, access to compensation for private entities and individuals is often absent. In such cases, private entities and individuals are the most motivated to investigate the responsibility of the responsible subjects, which may include malicious cyber actors, the State of origin of the malicious cyber activity, and the States conducting space activities. Moreover, individuals do not face direct diplomatic pressure that often deters States from calling other States to account (Helfer & Slaughter, 1997). The promotion of enforcement effect can also be realised by pursuing the responsible subjects for compensation by private entities and individuals. If the malicious cyber actors could be identified and it can be established that the actors violate domestic laws, private entities and individuals may resort to local judicial authorities for compensation. Thus, at the domestic level, promoting national legislation to prevent and punish malicious cyber activities is essential. In the circumstances where the malicious cyber actor cannot be identified but other States' responsibility for breaching their obligations can be proved, private entities and individuals, as victims, are virtually denied access to compensation in most cases if their national States decide not to take any actions against the responsible States, either through submitting the dispute to a third judicial body or countermeasures. When MCASAs have infringed on the victims' human rights, they may pursue the responsibility of the responsible States through the petition system of the UN Human Rights Committee when the complaint is within the authorised scope of the Optional Protocol to the International Covenant on Civil and Political Rights (Helfer & Slaughter, 1997; Optional Protocol to the International Covenant on Civil and Political Rights, 1966). In other circumstances, private claims can barely be accepted by international judicial bodies. It has been proposed that the WTO system be opened to private claims following a precedent; nonetheless, the current international practice demonstrates limited possibility of adopting such a proposition (Stephan, 2017). Opening the ICJ to claims of private entities or individuals is even more difficult.

7.2.4 Sub-Conclusion

International institutions enforce international law by supervising States' implementation or as 'supranational' judicial bodies, whereas States adopt self-help measures. Although the inherent mechanisms to compel compliance with international law may differ, the approaches adopted by States and international institutions share a similarity in that they depend significantly on the will of States. There is no treaty-established mechanism to supervise States' implementation of the rules relevant to ensuring space cybersecurity, and thus, the international pressure to compel compliance is trivial. These factors render the overall enforcement effects of the rules unwarranted. The lack of supervision mechanisms could be rectified by empowering certain existing international institutions with the capacity to supervise States' implementation. In many MCASAs, private entities and individuals are the most impacted; nevertheless, they are often barred from remedies unless their States, representing the private victims, take actions to hold another State accountable. Guaranteeing private victims access to remedies would help to enforce relevant international law. However, from a realistic perspective, opening the ICJ to claims submitted by private entities or individuals is almost impossible. As relying on local remedies appears to be the only choice left to private victims, promoting national legislation and improving the domestic judicial system are indispensable.

7.3 Conclusion

The implementation and enforcement of the international rules for ensuring space cybersecurity partially decide the effectiveness of the global governance of space cybersecurity. Although the coherent implementation of international law by States is challenging to realise, IOs and the industry could contribute towards alleviating the difficulties. IOs, both international and regional, can help to promote the implementation in various ways, notably by assisting states in overcoming the difficulties in implementation through capacity-building programmes. The industry may assist States in reifying the obscure international rules by establishing technical standards. When the standards are adopted at the international level at a large scale, they become international standards facilitating the implementation of the international rules in return. From a realistic perspective, enhancing the enforcement effectiveness of the existing rules relevant to space cybersecurity takes work. Empowering the existing institutions with supervising functions could be one way. Promoting national legislation and improving the domestic judicial system to open access to private victims is another.

Notes

1 Some monist States (States in which some treaties have the status of law in the domestic legal system, even in the absence of implementing legislation), such as the United States, distinguish between self-executing, which may be enforced in the courts without prior implementing legislation, and non-self-executing treaties, which may not be enforced in the courts without prior legislation.

2 The first draft resolution introduced by Japan and the United States, allegedly aiming at keeping weapons out of outer space, calls on 'all States, in particular those with major space capabilities, to contribute actively to the objective of the peaceful use of outer space and of the prevention of an armed race in outer space' and 'to refrain from acting contrary to that objective and to the relevant existing treaties in the interest of maintaining international peace and security and promoting international cooperation'. It failed in April 2024 due to Russia's veto. See *UN News*. (2024, April 24). Russia vetoes security council draft resolution on a weapon-free outer space. https://news.un.org/en/story/2024/04/1148951. Following this failure, the second draft resolution sponsored by Russia also failed in May 2024, as it received seven vetoes. See *UN News*. (2024, May 20). Second draft resolution on weapons-free outer space fails in security council. https://news.un.org/en/story/2024/05/1150126
3 By the end of 2023, there are 74 declarations in force. See ICJ (2023). *Declarations recognizing the jurisdiction of the court as compulsory*. www.icj-cij.org/declarations
4 Article 88 of the Convention on International Civil Aviation provides for penalty in case of non-conformity of States with ICJ decisions as suspension of the non-compliant State's voting power in the Assembly and in the Council of the International Civil Aviation Organization.
5 Article 33 of the International Labour Organization Constitution provides that in case of non-compliance with ICJ judgements, 'the Governing Body may recommend to the Conference such action as it may deem wise and expedient to secure compliance therewith'. Retrieved from www.ilo.ch/dyn/normlex/en/f?p=1000:62:0::NO:62:P62_LIST_ENTRIE_ID:2453907:NO

References

Administration of Donald J. Trump. (2020). Memorandum on cybersecurity principles for space systems. *Daily Compilation of Presidential Documents,* 1–4.

Aitken, H. (2017). The security council and international law enforcement: A Kelsenian perspective on civilian protection peacekeeping mandates. *Journal of Conflict and Security Law*, *22*(3), 395–432. https://doi.org/10.1093/jcsl/krx010

Alexandrov, S. A. (2006). The compulsory jurisdiction of the international court of justice: How compulsory is it? *Chinese Journal of International Law*, *5*(1), 29–38. DO: 10.1093/chinesejil/jml008

Arangio-Ruiz, G. (1992). Fourth report on state responsibility, by Mr. Gaetano Arangio-Ruiz. *Special Rapporteur*. UN Doc. A/CN.4/444, Add.1, Corr.1 and Add.2–3. *ILC Report*, A/47/10, Chap. III (B) (3).

Black, H. (Ed.) (2009). *Black's law dictionary* (10th ed.). Thomson Reuters.

Bodansky, D. (2011). Implementation of international environmental law. *Japanese Yearbook of International Law*, *54*, 62–96.

Boyle, A. E. (1991). Saving the world implementation and enforcement of international environmental law through international institutions. *Journal of Environmental Law*, *3*(2), 229–246. https://doi.org/10.1093/jel/3.2.229

Bradford, A., & Ben-Shahar, O. (2012). Efficient enforcement in international law. *Chicago Journal of International Law*, *12*(2), 375–432. https://doi.org/10.2139/ssrn.1558493

Brown, C. (1987). Enforcement of ICJ decisions in United States courts. *Maryland Journal of International Law*, *11*(1), 73–92.

Cannizzaro, E. (2001). The role of proportionality in the law of international countermeasures. *European Journal of International Law*, *12*(5), 889–916. https://doi.org/10.1093/ejil/12.5.889

Case concerning the Air Service Agreement of 27 March 1946 between the United States of America and France. (1978). *Reports of international arbitral awards,*XVIII, 417–493. https://legal.un.org/riaa/vol_18.shtml

Chan, J. (2000). Implementation of international humanitarian law. *Asia Pacific Law Review, 8*(2), 211–228. https://doi.org/10.1023/a:1009041318371

The Conference of Plenipotentiaries on the Protocol on Chlorofluorocarbons to the Vienna Convention for the Protection of the Ozone Layer. (1987). *Montreal protocol on substances that deplete the ozone layer*. UNTS. (1522, 28).

Convention on International Civil Aviation. (1944). UNTS. (15, 295).

Copeland, C. S. (1999). The use of arbitration to settle territorial disputes. *Fordham Law Review, 67*(6), 3073–3108.

Couzigou, I. (2017). Enforcement of UN security council resolutions and of ICJ judgements: The reliability of political enforcement mechanisms. In A. Jakab, & D. Kochenov (Eds.), *The enforcement of EU law and values: Ensuring member states' compliance*(pp. 363–378). Oxford University Press. https://doi.org/10.1093/acprof:oso/9780198746560.001.0001

Crawford, J. (2019). *Brownlie's principles of public international law*. Oxford University Press. https://doi.org/10.1093/he/9780198737445.001.0001

Diplomatic Conference of Geneva (DCG). (1949a). *Convention (I) for the amelioration of the condition of the wounded and sick in armed forces in the field*. UNTS. (75, 31).

DCG. (1949b). *Convention (II) for the amelioration of the condition of wounded, sick and shipwrecked members of armed forces at sea*. UNTS. (75, 86).

DCG. (1949c). *Convention (III) relative to the treatment of prisoners of war*. UNTS. (75, 135).

DCG. (1949d). *Convention (IV) relative to the protection of civilian persons in time of war*. UNTS. (75, 287).

DCG. (1977). *Protocol additional to the Geneva conventions of 12 August 1949, and relating to the protection of victims of international armed conflicts*. UNTS. (1125, 3).

Doelle, M. (2021). Non-compliance procedures. In L. Rajamani & J. Peel (Eds.), *The Oxford handbook of international environmental law* (pp. 972–987). Oxford University Press. https://doi.org/10.1093/law/9780198849155.001.0001

European Space Agency (ESA). (n.d.a). *Education*. www.esa.int/Education

ESA. (n.d.b). *ESA/ECSL executive course on space law and regulations*. www.esa.int/About_Us/ECSL_-_European_Centre_for_Space_Law/ESA_ECSL_Executive_Course_on_Space_Law_and_Regulations

Franck, T. M. (2008). On proportionality of countermeasures in international law. *American Journal of International Law, 102*(4), 715. https://doi.org/10.2307/20456680

Graefrath, B. B. (1984–1985). How different countries implement international standards on human rights. *Canadian Human Rights Yearbook, 1984*, 3–30.

Guzman, A. T. (2002). The cost of credibility: Explaining resistance to interstate dispute resolution mechanisms. *Journal of Legal Studies, 31*(2), 303–326. https://doi.org/10.1086/340811

Helfer, L. R., & Slaughter, A.-M. (1997). Toward a theory of effective supranational adjudication. *The Yale Law Journal, 107*(2), 273. https://doi.org/10.2307/797259

International Court of Justice (ICJ). (1946). *Statute of the international court of justice*. UNTS. (XV, 355).

ICJ. (1954). Case of the monetary gold removed from Rome in 1943 (Italy v. France, United Kingdom of Great Britain and Northern Ireland and United States of America). preliminary question, *ICJ Report*, 19.

ICJ. (1984). Military and Paramilitary Activities In And Against Nicaragua (Nicaragua v. United States of America). jurisdiction and admissibility, judgement, *ICJ Report*, 392.

ICJ. (1986). Nicaragua v. United States of America. Merits judgement, *ICJ Report*, 14.

ICJ. (2023). *Declarations recognizing the jurisdiction of the court as compulsory*. www.icj-cij.org/declarations

International Committee of the Red Cross (ICRC). (2017). *Statutes of the international committee of the red cross*. www.icrc.org/en/document/statutes-international-committee-red-cross-0

ICRC. (2021). *The international humanitarian fact-finding commission (IHFFC)*. www.icrc.org/en/document/international-humanitarian-fact-finding-commission-facsheet
International Law Commission (ILC). (2001a). *Articles on responsibility of states for internationally wrongful acts*. ILC Yearbook, II, Part 2.
ILC. (2001b). *Commentaries to the draft articles on responsibility of states for internationally wrongful acts*. Report of the ILC. (Supplement No. 10 (A/56/10), chp.IV.E.2).
Kantorowicz-Reznichenko, E. (2020). The enforcement of international law. In M. O. Hosli & J. Selleslaghs (Eds.), *The changing global order: Challenges and prospects* (pp. 361–384). Springer. https://doi.org/10.1007/978-3-030-21603-0_18
Krisch, N. (2012). Chapter VII. In B. Simma, D-E. Khan, G. Nolte, A. Paulus & N. Wessendorf (Eds.), *The charter of the United Nations: A commentary, volume II* (pp. 1237–1427). Oxford University Press. https://doi.org/10.1093/law/9780199639779.001.0001
Lahmann, H. (2020). *Unilateral remedies to cyber operations: Self-defence, countermeasures, necessity, and the question of attribution*. Cambridge University Press. https://doi.org/10.1017/9781108807050
Lamm, V. (2003). Reciprocity and the compulsory jurisdiction of the international court of justice. *Acta Juridica Hungarica*, *44*(1–2), 45–66. https://doi.org/10.1556/ajur.44.2003.1-2.3
Llamzon, A. P. (2008). Jurisdiction and compliance in recent decisions of the international court of justice. *The European Journal of International Law*, *18*(5), 815–852. https://doi.org/10.1093/ejil/chm047
Merrills, J. G. (2016). Recent practice with regard to the optional clause: An assessment. In G. Z. Capaldo (Ed.), *The global community yearbook of international law and jurisprudence 2015* (pp. 903–916). Oxford University Press. https://doi.org/10.1093/acprof:oso/9780190647759.001.0001
Muhammadin, F. M. (2014). Can international law be enforced towards its subjects within the international legal order? *Jurnal Hukum Ius Quia Iustum*, *21*(2), 175–202. https://doi.org/10.20885/iustum.vol21.iss2.art2
Noortmann, M. (2005). *Enforcing international law: From self-help to self-contained regimes*. Ashgate. https://doi.org/10.4324/97813155796100
O'Connell, M. E. (1994). Using trade to enforce international environmental law: Implications for United States law. *Indiana Journal of Global Legal Studies*, *1*(2), 273–292.
Oellers-Frahm, K. (2017). Enforcement of the international court of justice decisions. In P. W. Almeida & J. Sorel (Eds.), *Latin America and the international court of justice* (pp. 131–141). Routledge. https://doi.org/10.4324/9781315717890
Optional Protocol to the International Covenant on Civil and Political Rights. (1966). UNTS. (999, 172).
Paris, F., & Ghei, N. (2003). The role of reciprocity in international law. *Connell International Law Journal*, *36*(1), 93–123.
Proukaki, E. K. (2010). *The problem of enforcement in international law: Countermeasures, the non-injured state and the idea of international community*. Routledge. https://doi.org/10.4324/9780203865569
Rajamani, L., & Peel, J. (2021). International environmental law: Changing context, emerging trends, and expanding frontiers. In L. Rajamani & J. Peel (Eds.), *The Oxford handbook of international environmental law*(pp. 1–30). Oxford University Press. https://doi.org/10.1093/law/9780198849155.001.0001
Ramcharan, B. G. (1983). The role of international bodies in the implementation and enforcement of humanitarian law and human rights law in non-international armed conflicts. *American University Law Review*, *33*(1), 99–116.
Roscini, M. (2010). The United Nations security council and the enforcement of international humanitarian law. *IsraelLaw Review*, *43*(2), 330–359.
Sands, P., Peel, J., Fabra, A., & MacKenzie, R. (2018). *Principles of international environmental law*. Cambridge University Press. https://doi.org/10.1017/9781108355728

Sassòli, M. (2019). *International humanitarian law: Rules, controversies, and solutions to problems arising in warfare*. Edward Elgar Publishing Limited. https//doi.org/10.4337/9781786438553

Scott, G. L., & Carr, C. L. (1987). The ICJ and compulsory jurisdiction: The case for closing the clause. *American Journal of International Law, 81*(1), 57–76. https://doi.org/10.2307/2202131

Scott, R. E., & Stephan, P. B. (2006). *The limits of leviathan: Contract theory and the enforcement of international law*. Cambridge University Press. https://doi.org/10.1017/CBO9780511511370

Seyedavadi, M. E. (2019, September 23–26). APSCO's approach to capacity-building in space law and policy. *Presented at UN/Turkey/APSCO Conference On Space Law and Policy, Held in Istanbul*. www.unoosa.org/documents/pdf/spacelaw/activities/2019/T5–4-MES_APSCOs_Approach_to_Capacity-Building_in_Space_Law_and_Policy.pdf

Simma, B. (2012). Reciprocity. In R. Wolfrum (Ed.), *The Max Planck encyclopedia of public international law* (pp. 651–655). Oxford University Press.

Sloan, B. (1968). Implementation and enforcement of decisions of international organizations. *American Society of International Law Proceedings, 62*(First Session), 1–12.

Sloss, D. C. (2020). Domestic application of treaties. In D. B. Hollis (Ed.), *The Oxford guide to treaties*(pp. 355–382). Oxford University Press. https://doi.org/10.1093/law/9780198848349.001.0001

Stephan, P. B. (2017). Enforcement of international law. In F. Parisi (Ed.), *The Oxford handbook of law and economics: Volume 3: Public law and legal institutions*. Oxford University Press. https://doi.org/10.1093/oxfordhb/9780199684250.013.034.

UN. (2014). *Education curriculum on space law*. (UN Doc. ST/SPACE/64).

UN. (2015). *Paris agreement*. UNTS. (3156, 79).

United Nations (UN). (1997). *Kyoto protocol to the United Nations framework convention on climate change*. UNTS. (2303, 162).

UN Committee on the Peaceful Uses of Outer Space (COPUOS). (2023). *Education opportunities in space law: A directory*. (UN Doc. A/AC.105/C.2/2023/CRP.4).

UN General Assembly (UNGA). (1975). *Convention on registration of objects launched into outer space*. (UNGA Resolution 3235 (XXIX)). UNTS. (1023, No. 15020).

UNGA. (1998). *Rome statute of the international criminal court*. UNTS. (2187, 91).

UN Office for Outer Space Affairs (UNOOSA). (n.d.). *National space law*. www.unoosa.org/oosa/en/ourwork/spacelaw/nationalspacelaw/index.html

Vázquez, C. M. (1995). The four doctrines of self-executing treaties. *American Journal of International Law, 89*, 695–723.

Vidmar, S. (2002). Compulsory inter-state arbitration of territorial disputes. *Denver Journal of International Law and Policy, 31*(1), 87–112.

Waldock, C. H. M. (2003). Decline of the optional clause. In M. O'Connell (Ed.), *International dispute settlement* (pp. 279–322). Routledge. https://doi.org/10.4324/9781315092560

Whelan, A. (2023). *Reciprocity in public international law*. Cambridge University Press, p. 217. https://doi.org/10.1017/9781108980173

Young, M. A. (2023). Implementing international law: Capacity-building, coordination and control. *Cambridge International Law Journal, 12*(1), 4–23. https://doi.org/10.4337/cilj.2023.01.01

Zyberi, G. (2018). Enforcement of international humanitarian law. In G. Oberleitner (Ed.), *International human rights institutions, tribunals, and courts* (pp. 377–400). Springer. https://doi.org/10.1007/978-981-10-5206-4

Part IV

Conclusion

8 Conclusion

Global governance of space cybersecurity is indispensable for safeguarding the peaceful exploration of outer space, ensuring the security and sustainability of space activities, and guaranteeing cybersecurity, long-term human well-being, human survival, and development. This cannot be realised without appropriate international rules and institutions. However, this study reveals that the existing rules and the current status of institutional functioning cannot satisfy the needs of the global governance of space cybersecurity.

The existing international rules do not guarantee comprehensive space cybersecurity. The rules contributing towards combatting malicious cyber activities against space activities (MCASAs) are derived from various branches of international law, notably international space law and the emerging international rules on cybersecurity. A preliminary issue lies in determining the applicable law, as regulatory overlaps exist. It is important to determine the nature of MCASAs, that is, whether an MCASA constitutes a space activity to decide whether international space law shall apply, as this special law is most directly linked to space cybersecurity, particularly against the backdrop of the absence of international hard law for cyberspace. A two-step method focusing on appraising the weight of the 'space' factor in MCASAs would help.

Moreover, existing rules do not suffice to combat MCASAs, whether by imposing international obligations on States to maximally prevent the occurrence of MCASAs or by deterring potentially malicious actors by imposing criminal punishment on the actors and providing the victims with remedies. Other branches of international law, such as international environmental law, international human rights law, the law of armed conflicts, and international criminal law, may only apply to limited cases of MCASAs. Nonetheless, as they are not directly designed for space cybersecurity circumstances, in most cases, only the general principles of these branches could be applied to MCASA cases, and applying them would face interpretation difficulties. General international law could complement the special laws for combatting MCASAs, notably in terms of remedial and punitive rules; however, the complementary effects remain limited.

Therefore, regulatory gaps exist for combatting MCASAs, and space cybersecurity cannot be guaranteed. Several possible reasons exist for this discrepancy. The first is the ambiguous terminology of existing rules. Because no international

DOI: 10.4324/9781003561996-12

rules have been specifically elaborated for space cybersecurity, most existing rules applicable to MCASAs are principles or general rules that require further interpretation. This problem is exacerbated by controversial notions and terms contained in these principles. Therefore, the substantive international obligations of States in space cybersecurity are yet to be determined. The second reason is the absence of substantive rules specifically dedicated to space cybersecurity, without which States enjoy excessive freedom in interpreting the existing rules and applying them to space cybersecurity, leading to incoherence in their implementation. Although ambiguous, existing international law establishes the basic principles, rules, and norms for space cybersecurity, including the principles of maintaining international peace and security, environmental protection, due diligence, due regard, no harmful interference, protection of human rights, no threat or use of force, and the space-specific principle of State responsibility. They should be reified through a complete set of substantive international rules and norms countering MCASAs in hard law and soft law forms to prescribe specific international obligations for States, provide remedies to victims, and punish responsible subjects when MCASAs occur. This may have attenuated the impact of the first reason. Third, legislative lacunae exist under both remedial and punitive rules. Despite the two sets of attribution rules that exist for attributing MCASAs, there are cases that cannot be attributed to appropriate States. In addition, owing to the absence of an international treaty on cybercrime and the inadequacy of current international criminal law in handling the most devastating MCASA cases, the overall remedial and punitive effects of existing rules are limited.

As major actors in the global governance of space cybersecurity, institutions are important elements. Institutions are not isolated from the other elements. By implementing and enforcing the existing rules, they play a decisive role in the effectiveness of the entire global governance system. They help bridge the regulatory gaps as well. Institutions are law-framers; by implementing and enforcing existing rules, institutions demonstrate their understanding of the rules and help clarify their meanings. Thus, the two major functions of institutions in the global governance of space cybersecurity are to create new rules and norms and to implement and enforce the existing rules.

Because the space and cyber fields are more closely related to space cybersecurity compared to other fields, it is appropriate to endow the law-making institutions of these two fields with the task of initiating law-making activities. Considering the status quo of the law-making characteristics and processes in the two fields, space institutions are more suitable for taking the first steps. When the time is ripe, that is, when the decision-makers of other fields recognise the significance of space cybersecurity and the possible devastating consequences of MCASAs, the law-making institutions in these fields may be obligated to develop specific rules or norms to counter MCASAs. Regarding law-making in the space field, both top-down and bottom-up approaches have been adopted, reflecting the growing level of multistakeholderism. The top-down approach is applied by States through multi-lateral platforms to form the basic principles bearing on States or through State practice to form international customs. These principles and rules can take the form of both hard and soft laws; however, it is unlikely that they will be sufficiently substantive for application without further interpretation. The principles and rules, whether existing or to be made, could be complemented by rules formed through the bottom-up approach, which notably involves the participation of non-governmental organisations, the industry, experts, and other non-State actors (NSAs). Normally, these rules are incorporated into soft law instruments, such as guidelines and best practices. They help to clarify the implications of the principles. Existing rules and the new rules developed by States and NSAs form a complete regulatory framework to guarantee space cybersecurity.

Considering the myriad actors participating in the law-making process for space cybersecurity, and the fact that sectors other than the space sector may also be involved in this process, ensuring the coherence of future rules is indispensable. Therefore, intersectoral institutional interactions are necessary. Both horizontal and vertical interactions should be promoted. Horizontal interactions can be realised through parallel membership and institutional agreements and partnerships. Parallel membership is effective for coordinating the attitudes and performance of States, as the State participants in the formal institutions for law-making in the space and cyber fields, notably the relevant institutions of the United Nations (UN), significantly overlap. Nonetheless, parallel membership is not as effective for NSAs because the multistakeholder platforms of one field seldom involve NSAs from other fields. Thus, multistakeholder platforms must attract actors from other sectors to enhance intersectoral communication. Institutional agreements and partnerships can help harmonise the concerns and interests of different sectors. Vertical interaction among States and NSAs is relatively straightforward and spontaneous, considering the existence of multistakeholder platforms, which provide occasions for various participants in rulemaking to communicate and exchange ideas. In addition, States have left space for NSAs to develop non-binding norms, particularly technical norms, which may influence their understanding of existing principles and State practices in return.

Global governance of space cybersecurity cannot achieve its goals without the effective implementation and enforcement of the law, even if the law is perfectly designed. The institutions in charge of implementing international rules are essentially States, with subsidiary help from international organisations (IOs) and the industry. As States abide by varied international rules and may interpret them differently, a coherent implementation of international rules can barely be realised. IOs may encourage and induce States to implement international law, assist them in understanding the rules, overcoming the difficulties in implementation by providing financial and technical assistance, clarifying the content of international obligations, and engaging in dialogue with governments on implementation. Industry participates in the formulation of international technical standards. When international standards are adopted on a large scale, domestic standards are influenced such that the harmonisation of national standards is achieved to some extent. Despite the contribution of IOs and the industry in harmonising the implementation of international law by States, their impact is subsidised. States remain major implementers of international law and can unilaterally determine their perception of the rules and the measures to implement them. Thus, a more harmonised implementation of international rules cannot be realised without international coordination and cooperation, which is, unfortunately, not always possible.

States and international institutions, including those established by treaties and judicial bodies, have contributed to the enforcement of international law. States adopt self-help measures based on reciprocity, whereas international institutions play supervisory or supranational judicial roles. Self-help measures, primarily rewards and sanctions, can be ineffective under certain circumstances and are subject to the will of States. Considering the complexity of space cybersecurity issues, States tend to be prudent in adopting self-help measures, particularly sanctions. No international institutions have been specifically established to enforce the international rules relevant to space cybersecurity. Although in some related branches of international law, such as international environmental law and the law of armed conflict, international institutions have been established by treaties to ensure the enforcement of treaty provisions, the overall effect of these institutions in enforcing international rules for combatting MCASAs is minimal, considering that these branches can only apply to a small number of MCASAs, which may result in environmental pollution or violation of the law of armed conflict. The Security Council may also intervene when an MCASA constitutes a threat to the peace. Nonetheless, as a highly politicised institution with the veto right vested in the five permanent members, the Security Council can barely take any action. Dispute settlement is an important approach to ensure compliance. Despite the several methods of dispute settlement, judicial proceedings appear to be the most appropriate for disputes regarding space cybersecurity, as space cybersecurity is of a mixed nature, including technical, legal, and political. Nonetheless, judicial authorities, particularly the International Court of Justice (ICJ), which is the most promising in coping with space cybersecurity disputes, cannot enforce international law without the will of States, that is, it is upon the will of the States to submit a dispute to judicial authorities. The ICJ may suffer from lack of jurisdiction when handling some MCASA cases. Moreover, the implementation of ICJ judgements may be challenging at the domestic level. Promoting international law enforcement is challenging. This could benefit from empowering existing international institutions with supervisory functions and improving domestic judicial systems.

The regulatory and institutional aspects of the global governance of space cybersecurity are not isolated but closely connected. Institutions play a significant role in developing an optimal regulatory system, whereas international rules constitute the basis for institutions regulating space cybersecurity. This study demonstrates the existence of regulatory gaps and the difficulties in bridging these gaps and implementing and enforcing existing rules. Suggestions were made to resolve these problems. Two points must be highlighted when addressing these problems. First, it is important to balance the interests of the different stakeholders when developing new rules. States without space capabilities may prefer to impose stricter obligations on those conducting space activities to prevent the occurrence of MCASAs and their negative consequences, whereas States conducting space activities anticipate fewer legal restrictions on their activities. Moreover, as technological gaps exist among States, requiring them to bear international obligations to prevent all or most MCASAs would be unrealistic or too expensive for some States. States are responsible for their national activities in outer space and may require space operators to integrate cybersecurity measures into their space objects and activities. However, as cybersecurity measures imply higher costs, excessive requirements may negatively impact the national space industry. These factors should be considered when interpreting the current rules and developing new rules accordingly. In addition, with technological and industrial developments, the perceptions of the rules may change over time, leading to the modification of the existing rules or the formulation of new rules. Thus, despite the law-making approach proposed in this study, the actual path towards a harmonised understanding of current and new rules to combat MCASAs will not be easy.

Second, international coordination and cooperation constitute the underlying principle of international governance of space cybersecurity. As space systems become increasingly interconnected, space cybersecurity is and will continue to be a global concern. Deviating from multinational platforms and developing space cybersecurity-related rules and practices among like-minded States will not help counter this issue because the measures and standards adopted and implemented by a small group of States cannot curb the occurrence of MCASAs and their global effects. Thus, multinational platforms that imply a high degree of international coordination and cooperation, whether intergovernmental or multistakeholder, should still play an essential role in law-making. Given the fact that the will of States is decisive for international law implementation and enforcement and cannot be unified without international coordination and cooperation, harmonising the implementation and promoting the enforcement of international rules rely on international coordination and cooperation as well. Furthermore, international coordination and cooperation should be perceived in a broader manner to incorporate technological cooperation, particularly in cybersecurity technologies. The level of cybersecurity technology varies significantly among States. Even States with the capability to carry out space activities may fail to guarantee the cybersecurity of their space systems and activities owing to a lack of relevant technologies. This has also delayed the development process of international rules. Therefore, transferring cybersecurity technologies on the basis of international cooperation is indispensable.

Index

Note: References following "n" refer notes.

Kolibri 360 GmbH
Ferdinand-Jühlke-Straße 7
99095 Erfurt, Deutschland
produktsicherheit@kolibri360.de